R. S. Thomas

R. S. Thomas

Poetry and Theology

William V. Davis

BAYLOR UNIVERSITY PRESS

Scripture quotations are from the New Revised Standard Version Bible, copyright
1989, Division of Christian Education of the National Council of the Churches of
Christ in the United States of America. Used by permission. All rights reserved.

Cover Design: Donna Habersaat, dh design
Cover Image: Sir Kyffin Williams' Sun Over Gwnant @copyright Estate of Kyffin
Williams/Licenses by DACS 2007. Used by permission.

excerpts from Thomas's poetry were provided by the following:
—Gwydion Thomas: Originally published variously in *R.S. Thomas: Song at the
    Years' Turning* (London: Rupert Hart Davis, 1955); *Laboratories of the Spirit*
    (London: Macmillan, 1975); *Frequencies* (London: Macmillan, 1978); *The
    Bread of Truth* (London: Rupert Hart Davis, 1963), copyright ©Kunjana
    Thomas 2001.
—Bloodaxe Books: Originally published in *R.S. Thomas: Collected Later Poems
    1988–2000* and used by permission of Bloodaxe Books and Gwydion Thomas.
Further permissions are listed on p. 212.

Library of Congress Cataloging-in-Publication Data

Davis, William Virgil, 1940-
  R.S. Thomas : poetry and theology / William V. Davis.
      p. cm.
  Includes bibliographical references and index.
  ISBN 978-1-932792-49-2 (cloth/hardcover : alk. paper)
  1. Thomas, R. S. (Ronald Stuart), 1913-2000--Criticism and interpretation. 2.
Theology in literature. 3. Thomas, R. S. (Ronald Stuart), 1913-2000--Religion. 4.
Religious poetry, English--History and criticism. I. Title.

  PR6039.H618Z693 2007
  821'.914--dc22
                            2007014014

Printed in the United States of America on acid-free paper with a minimum of 30%
pcw recycled content.

For Carol

&

Bill

I have this that I must do

. . .

. . . go down into the green

Darkness to search for the door

To myself. . . .

. . .

. . . I must go down with the poor

Purse of my body and buy courage,

Paying for it with the coins of my breath.

—R. S. Thomas

Contents

Preface and Acknowledgments

This book will make a traveller of thee. . . .

—John Bunyan

Poets make pilgrimages. Consciously or unconsciously, they set out on jour-
neys. Some of them have goals in mind at the outset, but most do not—at
least not early on in the journey. The journey, the pilgrimage, is itself the path
of discovery. It leads where it leads, and the poet, if he or she is observant
and conscientious, will take note of the signs along the way and begin to
steer a course, begin to give the journey a direction, and the direction a goal.
For some, especially earlier writers, the journey was partially (or even fully)
defined by temperament or the times, or by both. This is especially the case
for poets who lived in distinctly history-haunted times or in places caught
in the grip of political or religious unrest or upheaval, or for poets whose
own lives were insistently directed by an abiding obsession in spite of place
or time. These poets often wrote long poems, filling up their lines and their
lives with their journey and their obsessions. Dante and Milton are classic
examples of such singular obsessions, and *The Divine Comedy* and *Paradise
Lost*, written in times when time and temperament were overtly joined, are
classic examples of such journeys or quests.

But for poets who by nature are lyric poets, who live outside the world—
in their words as it were—and who are at home primarily only in their own
lines and minds, such quests are less immediately obvious or visible, and they
are not necessarily thematic in nature or theological in theme, as Milton and

ix

Dante's were. Lyric poets often wander off the path, as it were, and they stop
to observe what they find or discover along the way. They are, in a real sense,
finding their ways, following their own directions, and often it is only after
the fact, late on, or indeed at the end of the journey, that they know where
they have been, are going, or have gone. Sometimes this means that near the
end of the journey they arbitrarily try to put everything into some order,
organize their own apparent disorder and try to make, or impose, a pattern
on it, or give it a definitive theme or focus.

Other poets combine the two kinds of pilgrimages—that is, even though
they have a lyric temperament and live in times when time and tempera-
ment are not seemingly inseparably intertwined, they maintain an overriding
theme and keep to a specific thesis throughout their lives and works. R. S.
Thomas is one of these kinds of poets, and the overriding theme of the lyrics
in his pilgrimage is the traditional theological quest that has sent people on
pilgrimages throughout the ages. As Thomas said in his autobiography, "Life
is a pilgrimage, and if we have not succeeded in coming a little nearer to the
truth, if we do not have a better comprehension of the nature of God before
reaching the end of the journey, why was it that we started on the journey at
all?" (*Autobiographies* 106)

And what then of critics? What then of *this* pilgrimage? This book does
not attempt to be comprehensive or conclusive, nor does it attempt to make
a systematic study of Thomas's long career. It does not attempt to consider
even all of Thomas's major poems. It is, rather, a series of studies of individual
poems and of themes and thematic sequences in R. S. Thomas's work.

I think of these individual chapters as motets, independent pieces brought
together by a common theme or specific focus and issuing from an abiding
interest in Thomas's life and work. This is, I think, the way that Thomas
himself must finally have thought of his poems—as isolated and independent
but related segments of a much larger project, one still in progress right up to
the end of his life.

The major theme that unified Thomas's work was the same theological
theme that unifies *The Divine Comedy* and *Paradise Lost,* although Thomas
had a lyric temperament rather than a narrative or epic one as Dante and
Milton had. Thomas, however, like Milton and Dante, was engaged in a
theological journey or pilgrimage, and, like them, he too sought to "justify
the ways of God to men" (*Paradise Lost* I:26) in the context of his own time
and place—twentieth-century Wales. These studies then attempt to trace and
track Thomas and his pilgrimages by following him (primarily through his
poetry, but taking into account his life and his other literary activities as well)
along the paths of the journeys he took to reach the goals of his poetic and his
theological quests, and to attempt to show how, in essence, Thomas's pilgrim-

age constitutes a twentieth-century theodicy, just as Dante's and Milton's did in their times.

In his introduction to *The Choice of Wordsworth's Verse* Thomas said: "[We] cannot fully grasp the significance of [Wordsworth's] greatest verse without considering the philosophy of life which helped to shape it." He then went on to describe what he took to be Wordsworth's "message for today" by suggesting that Wordsworth's poems "convey to us the thoughts and feelings of a literary genius living in a particular place at a particular time. . . . They speak of the peace that is to be found in solitude, the sublimity of earthly moments, the movement of the spirit of man" (14, 18). This description—to which I would append the words "and of God"—would apply, I think, to Thomas as well as to Wordsworth.

Therefore, rather than trying to be comprehensive or conclusive in these studies, I have followed Thomas where I have found him—in his obsessions and my own. In this sense this book is also my own pilgrimage, and it is very much a journey I have found and defined along the way. And the way *has* been long. A portion of one of these essays was originally written more than twenty years ago. Several are quite recent. Thomas—for both of our purposes, I would like to think—has continued to obsess me, leading me to and through some of his obsessive themes and theses. This means, inevitably, that these studies sometimes revisit themes and theses—sometimes even through the same poems—although I hope, in these cases, that I have found something new to say about the theme or the poem (or both) with each return I have made to it. And, rather than trying to edit these residual overlappings out, to keep the integrity of each of the essays intact I have left them essentially as they were originally written for delivery and/or published, each with its own thesis and sense of form, each contained and maintained within its own, as it were, "historical setting." (In some instances, I have added crucial new details and updated or added new information not available at the time of the original publication of the essay in question. I have also added cross references from essay to essay to facilitate ease of reference within these pages to themes and poems treated or discussed in more than one of these studies. In addition, I have had to take into account the differing formatting requirements of the essays as originally published and the quite different requirements demanded to make them fit into a consistent format for this book.) All references to Thomas's poems will be to his individual books—see the abbreviation key.

As will quickly be seen, the first several of these studies are general, overarching essays which attempt to establish a context and to suggest a continuum for Thomas's life and work by, first, tracing his "roots" in the theological crisis that began in nineteenth-century England and was most definitively evidenced (in a literary context) by Matthew Arnold, and by then placing Thomas within that historical context and its reverberations in late nineteenth- and early twentieth-century British and American poetry, and finally by providing an overview of Thomas's life and career in the context of his own poetry and of his conspicuous theological obsessions. The remaining studies have more specific foci as they attempt to deal specifically with some of the most important emphases in Thomas's work and life. The two final essays are insistently specific in focusing on Thomas's "obsession" with perhaps the two most important figures in his theological life and in his poetic career respectively, namely Søren Kierkegaard and Wallace Stevens.

The original "settings" of each of these studies need to be named, noted, and acknowledged. Most of these pieces were originally presented as lectures, and I am grateful for the invitations that led me to talk on Thomas. I am also grateful for the opportunity to publish these lectures subsequently as essays (usually with only very minor changes between the spoken and printed versions) and I want to acknowledge here, and to thank, the editors of the journals and books in which these pieces have appeared: all are used with permission. The details of the presentation and publication for each of the chapters of this book are as follows:

Chapter 1: Presented as a lecture at the Nineteenth Triennial Conference of the International Association of University Professors of English at the University of British Columbia (Canada). A portion of this chapter was also presented as a lecture at the South Central Conference on Christianity and Literature sponsored by Xavier University in New Orleans, Louisiana. Published as "'The Tide's Pendulum Truth': A Reading of the Poetry of Theological Crisis from Matthew Arnold to R. S. Thomas," *Christianity and Literature* (2006).

Chapter 2: Presented as a lecture at the University of Freiburg, Germany. Published as "R. S. Thomas," in *British Writers,* Supplement 12, ed. Jay Parini (New York: Charles Scribner's Sons, 2006). Reprinted by permission of the Thomson Gale Group.

Chapter 3: Presented as a lecture at the University of Wales at Bangor and at the University of Wales at Swansea as well as at the Northeast Regional Conference on Christianity and Literature at Farmingdale State University of New York. Published as "Evidence of Things Not Seen: R. S. Thomas's Agnostic Faith," *Welsh Writing in English: A Yearbook of Critical Essays* (2006–2007). A portion of this chapter was also published as "R. S. Thomas, *The Odyssey,* and Dereck Walcott: A Note on the Use of 'No One,'" *Notes on Contemporary Literature* (2005).

Chapter 4: Presented as a lecture at the South Central Conference on Christianity and Literature sponsored by Xavier University in New Orleans, Louisiana. Published as "R. S. Thomas: Poet-Priest of the Apocalyptic Mode" in the *South Central Review* (1987). Reprinted in William V. Davis, ed. *Miraculous Simplicity: Essays on R. S. Thomas* (1993).

Chapter 5: Presented as a lecture at the International Society for Phenomenology Conference on Aesthetics and the Fine Arts at Harvard University. Published as "The Presence of Absence: Mirrors and Mirror Imagery in the Poetry of R. S. Thomas," in *Passions of the Earth in Human Existence, Creativity, and Literature.* Analecta Husserliana: The Yearbook of Phenomenology Research 71, ed. Anna-Teresa Tymieniecka (Dordrecht, The Netherlands: Kluwer Academic Publishers, 2001). Reprinted in *Life—The Play of Life on the Stage of the World.* Analecta Husserliana: The Yearbook of Phenomenology Research 73, ed. Anna-Teresa Tymieniecka (Dordrecht, The Netherlands: Kluwer Academic Publishers, 2001). With kind permission of Springer Science and Business Media.

Chapter 6: Several versions of this chapter were presented as a lectures: one at the Conference of the International Association of University Professors of English in Copenhagen, Denmark; another at the Conference of the International Association of University Professors of English in Durham, England. Still another version of this chapter was presented at the International Conference on Literature and Theology at Oxford University, and also at a Conference on Literature and Christianity at Seattle University in Seattle, Washington. Published as " 'The Verbal Hunger': The Use and Significance of 'Gaps' in the Poetry of R. S. Thomas," in *The Page's Drift: R. S. Thomas at Eighty,* ed. M. Wynn Thomas (Bridgend, Wales: Seren Books, 1993).

Chapter 7: Presented as a lecture at the South Central Conference on Christianity and Literature in New Orleans, Louisiana. Published as " 'This Is What Art Could Do': An Exercise in Exegesis—R. S. Thomas's 'Souillac: Le Sacrifice d'Abraham,' " *Religion and the Arts* 4.3 (2000).

Chapter 8: Presented as a lecture at the International Conference on Contemporary British and Irish Poetry at Salzburg University, Salzburg, Austria. Published as " 'Going Forward to Meet the Machine': R. S. Thomas's Quarrel with Technology," in *Poetry Now: Contemporary British and Irish Poetry in the Making,* ed. Holger Klein, Sabine Coelsch-Foisner, and Wolfgang Görtschacher (Tübingen: Stauffenburg Verlag, 1999).

Chapter 9: Presented as a lecture at a conference sponsored by the Universities of Wales' Association for the Study of Welsh Writing in English at the Gregynog Conference Centre, Newtown, Wales. Published as " 'At the Foot of the Precipice of Water . . . Sea Shapes Coming to Celebration': R. S. Thomas and Kierkegaard," *Welsh Writing in English: A Yearbook of Critical Essays* (1998).

Chapter 10: A portion of this chapter was presented as a lecture at the Rothermere American Institute, Oxford, England. The essay was published, in several separate parts, as " 'An Abstraction Blooded': Wallace Stevens and R. S. Thomas on Blackbirds and Men," *The Wallace Stevens Journal* (1984) and as "Wallace Stevens and R. S. Thomas: Influence *sans* Anxiety," *The Wallace Stevens Journal* (2006).

In addition to the above, I would like to thank, first and foremost, R. S. Thomas himself for writing the poems that set me off, following him, on these pilgrimages, and for his kindness to me personally. I would also like to thank Gwydion Thomas for his kindness in granting me permission to quote from R. S. Thomas's poems and prose writings and for permitting me and my wife to visit the Thomas household at Sarn-y-Plas on the Llŷn peninsula.

Others who deserve special mention are Tony Brown, who generously made available to me the facilities of "The R. S. Thomas Study Centre" at the University of Wales at Bangor, and to M. Wynn Thomas, R. S. Thomas's literary executor of his unpublished work, who hosted my wife and me in Swansea and who permitted me to examine Thomas's uncollected and unpublished poems in manuscript. In addition, I want to thank the Baylor University Research Committee for a research grant that permitted me to travel to Wales to conduct some of my research. I would also like to thank the College of Arts and Sciences at Baylor University for a semester of research leave as well as several summer sabbaticals, each of which was crucial to the completion of some of the studies that make up this book. For her expert computer advise and assistance, I would like to thank Melinda Sanson.

Finally, I want to thank my wife and son, who lived through the work on many of these pages, and to whom this book is dedicated.

Abbreviations for R. S. Thomas's Books of Poetry

SF	*The Stones of the Field* (1946)
AL	*An Acre of Land* (1952)
M	*The Minister* (1953)
SYT	*Song at the Year's Turning* (1955)
PS	*Poetry for Supper* (1958)
T	*Tares* (1961)
BT	*The Bread of Truth* (1963)
P	*Pietá* (1966)
NHBF	*Not That He Brought Flowers* (1968)
H'm	*H'm* (1972)
YO	*Young and Old* (1972)
SP	*Selected Poems 1946–1968* (1973)
WW	*What is a Welshman?* (1974)
LS	*Laboratories of the Spirit* (1975)
WI	*The Way of It* (1977)
F	*Frequencies* (1978)
BHN	*Between Here and Now* (1981)
LP	*Later Poems 1972–1982* (1983)
D	*Destinations* (1985)
IT	*Ingrowing Thoughts* (1985)
EA	*Experimenting with an Amen* (1986)

WA   *Welsh Airs* (1987)
ERS   *The Echoes Return Slow* (1988)
C   *Counterpoint* (1990)
Frieze   *Frieze* (1992)
MHT   *Mass for Hard Times* (1992)
CP   *Collected Poems 1945–1990* (1993)
NTF   *No Truce with the Furies* (1995)
R   *Residues* (2002)
SPMC   *Selected Poems* (2004)
CLP   *Collected Later Poems 1988–2000* (2004)

1

Poetry in Theological Crisis

I

The decisive event which underlies the search for meaning and the despair of it in the 20th century is the loss of God in the 19th century.

— Paul Tillich

J. Hillis Miller has argued that Matthew Arnold's thought provides us with "one of the most important testimonies to the spiritual situation of the nineteenth century" and perhaps the quintessential transition to the twentieth. Miller concludes his argument by saying that "Arnold's last and most characteristic posture is that of the man who waits passively and in tranquil hope for the spark from heaven to fall. . . . He is . . . a survivor who has persisted unwillingly into a time when all he cares for is dead" (*Disappearance* 262). Elsewhere Miller comments, "In a time when the power of organized religion has weakened, people have turned, as Matthew Arnold said they would, to poetry as a stay and prop, even as a means of salvation" ("Literature and Religion" 34).

Because Arnold believed that "knowledge" comes primarily through literature—and most specifically through poetry—he argued that religion, which had traditionally informed men about themselves and their existences, would soon be overtaken, and then be replaced, by poetry. Arnold saw this beginning to happen in his own time, and he prophesied that "[t]he future of poetry is immense, because in poetry . . . our race . . . will find an ever surer and surer stay" since "the strongest part of our religion," "its unconscious poetry" (Arnold 9:161), provides us with our most certain guide.

Arnold's most succinct summary of his position occurs in his essay, "The Study of Poetry." He wrote:

> More and more mankind will discover that we have to turn to poetry to interpret life for us, to console us, to sustain us. Without poetry, our science will appear incomplete; and most of what now passes with us for religion and philosophy will be replaced by poetry. . . . [O]ur religion, . . . our philosophy, . . . what are they but the shadows and dreams and false shows of knowledge? The day will come when we shall wonder at ourselves for having trusted to them, for having taken them seriously; and the more we perceive their hollowness, the more we shall prize "the breath and finer spirit of knowledge" offered to us by poetry (Arnold 9: 161–62).

Arnold's prophetic testimony for the prestige of poetry and his prediction for its future privileged status could be supported through a detailed analysis of his writings, even though some of the most significant of these works, in Arnold's own estimation (such as the books he specifically devoted to religious issues and which he himself held in high regard), are rarely read or studied today, save by the most diligent of Arnold specialists.[1] To use Arnold's own words against him, if the religious essays were, to his mind, "the power of the moment," they are not now "the power of the man."[2]

T. S. Eliot is clear on the relationship between religion and culture in Arnold—and critical of it. He says:

> Arnold's prose writings fall into two parts; those on Culture and those on Religion; and the books about Christianity . . . are tediously negative. But they are negative in a peculiar fashion: their aim is to affirm that the emotions of Christianity can and must be preserved without the belief. From this proposition two different types of man can extract two different types of conclusion: (1) that Religion is Morals, (2) that Religion is Art. The effect of Arnold's religious campaign is to divorce Religion from thought. . . . The total effect of Arnold's philosophy is to set up Culture in the place of Religion, and to leave Religion to be laid waste by the anarchy of feeling. ("Arnold and Pater" 349, 351).[3]

But because it is, finally, as a poet that I want to place Arnold, and particularly so in terms of later poets and of the poetic progression that he initiated and put into practice, I intend to concentrate on him here primarily in terms of his poetry, and specifically in terms of his best known and one of his best poems, "Dover Beach." It is a poem which provides a paradigm of Arnold's personal theological dilemma as well as "a symbol of the Victorian dilemma"

(Cadbury 126) and, indeed, of the crisis in theological thought in the middle of the nineteenth century. If it is the case, as Miller contends, that "[f]rom DeQuincey through Arnold and Browning to Hopkins, Yeats, and Stevens there is a movement from the absence of God to the death of God as starting point and basis" (*Poets of Reality* 283), then it might be argued that, even if Arnold does not go as far back historically in this movement as DeQuincey, he comes almost as far forward in it thematically as Wallace Stevens—by way of Shelley, Francis Thompson, Clough, some of Browning, Tennyson, and the Rossettis, more of Swinburne, down through Hopkins, Hardy, Housman, Yeats—and as far forward as R. S. Thomas. One can believe that Arnold— and indeed most of these other poets—would support Stevens's statement that "[a]fter one has abandoned a belief in God, poetry is that essence which takes its place as life's redemption" (*Collected Poetry and Prose* 901).

Arnold has been called "the quintessential agnostic," or a "restless agnostic," and his "anguish" has been referred to as that of "a religious man without religion" (Shaw, "Agnostic Imagination" 119, 121). In this regard Arnold might be aligned with his contemporary, Henry Mansel, whose 1858 book, *The Limits of Religious Thought*, made a significant impact on the Victorian age and must have affected Arnold particularly. Mansel's hypotheses and his "agnostic theories" lead specifically to Herbert Spencer's "unknowable God" and to Arnold's "abstract re-definition of God as 'the Eternal, not ourselves'" (Shaw 125). Shaw sees Arnold, finally, as the "center of the new dark firmament of agnostic poetry," a man who, as "the victim of an *ultima solitude*," stands "isolated . . . by an utter personal, theological, and historical aloneness" (139). For Shaw, and for philosophers like Mansel, apropos of Arnold and the tradition in which I am attempting to place him, the "more closely [writers] approach the limits of the sayable, the more poetry may have to be used to define the indefinable or take the place of religion altogether" (Shaw, *Lucid Veil* 119).

II

Wandering between two worlds, one dead,
The other powerless to be born.

— Arnold, "Stanzas from the Grande Chartreuse"

Murray Krieger has argued:

> . . . [I]f we share Matthew Arnold's loss of faith, we can go either of two ways: we can view poetry as a human triumph made out of our darkness, as the creation of verbal meaning in a blank universe to serve as a visionary

substitute for a defunct religion; or we can . . . extend our faithlessness, the blankness of our universe, to our poetry. . . ("Literature vs. Écriture" 4).

Arnold maintained that "in truth, the word 'God' is used in most cases as . . . a term of poetry and eloquence, a term *thrown out*, so to speak, at a not fully grasped object of the speaker's consciousness, a *literary* term in short . . ." (Arnold 6: 171; italics in original). This passage occurs early in *Literature and Dogma*, the book in which Arnold details some of his most significant theological thinking. Arnold's argument, as he states it in brief, runs: "In the first place, we did not make ourselves. . . . So much is . . . incalculable, so much . . . belongs to *not ourselves*. . . . The *not ourselves*, which is in us and in the world around us, has almost everywhere, as far as we can see, struck the minds of men as they awoke to consciousness, and has inspired them with awe. . . . Our very word *God* is, perhaps, a reminiscence of these times . . ." (Arnold 6: 181–82).

Arnold continues:

> [T]he *not ourselves* which weighed upon the mind of Israel . . . was indubitably what lay at the bottom of that remarkable change which under Moses . . . befell the Hebrew people's mode of naming God. This was what they intended in that name. . . . The name they used was: *The Eternal*. . . . [A]nd therefore it was that Israel said, not indeed what our Bibles make him say, but this 'Hear O Israel! *The Eternal is our God, The Eternal alone*'. . . . [H]is words were but *thrown out* at the vast object of consciousness, which he could not fully grasp. . . . The language of the Bible, then, is literary, not scientific language; language *thrown out* at an object of consciousness not fully grasped. . . . God is simply *the stream of tendency by which all things seek to fulfill the law of their being*. . . . God or *Eternal* is here really, at bottom, nothing but a deeply moved way of saying 'the power that makes for *conduct* or *righteousness*' (see Arnold 6: 182, 187–89, 93).[4]

To move the argument forward into the twentieth century, toward R. S. Thomas, let me first turn briefly to Wallace Stevens, who is perhaps the key *poetic* intermediary or transitional figure between Matthew Arnold and R. S. Thomas. And just as Arnold influenced Stevens, Stevens (as well as Arnold) was a major influence on Thomas.

Stevens, like Arnold, attempted to "settle" his relationship with religion by "abstracting" himself and concentrating on religion as a "cultural force." He attempted to find a way whereby "he could use art to replace religion" by "putting into practice what he had internalized" through his reading of Arnold. As he wrote to his future wife, "I have become an intense Arnoldian" (see Richardson 269; cf. Stevens, *Letters* 133). But Stevens's early infatuation with Arnold, and with religion, did not last. As he reported late in his life,

"[I]t may be that I don't belong to that church anymore, or that I don't care for conversation with that particular set of gods; nor, perhaps, with any" (*Letters* 780).

In his *Adagia* Stevens remarks, "After one has abandoned a belief in god, poetry is that essence which takes its place as life's redemption" (*Collected Poetry and Prose* 901).[5] In his essay "Imagination as Value," Stevens says that "poetry does not address itself to beliefs." And yet, he adds, "the poet does not yield to the priest" because "poetic value is an intrinsic value." That is, poetic value is not, for Stevens, either "the value of knowledge" or "the value of faith" but, rather, "the value of the imagination." And, therefore, "if the imagination is the faculty by which we import the unreal into what is real, its value is the value of the way of thinking by which we project the idea of God into the idea of man" (*Collected Poetry and Prose* 731, 734, 735–36).

Perhaps Stevens's most insistent poem in terms of this tradition and the theological progression that I am trying to outline here is "Sunday Morning" (*Collected Poetry and Prose* 53–56), which Miller describes as Stevens's "most eloquent description of the moment when the gods dissolve" (*Poets of Reality* 222). "Sunday Morning" is Stevens's attempt to work out his own "theological" position at the beginning of his career. As he himself said, "The relation of art to life is of the first importance especially in a skeptical age since, in the absence of a belief in God, the mind turns to its own creations and examines them . . ." (*Opus Posthumous* 159—not included in *Collected Poetry and Prose*).

"Sunday Morning" begins with a woman alone on a Sunday morning, lounging in her peignoir, drinking coffee and eating oranges, while she "dreams a little" and begins to think of that "old catastrophe" in "silent Palestine / Dominion of the blood and sepulcher." In the second section of the poem, this woman raises the first of several theological questions:

> Why should she give her bounty to the dead?
> What is divinity if it can come
> Only in silent shadows and in dreams?

Her answer is that "Divinity must live within herself" (l. 23). And then she asserts that "Death is the mother of beauty" and "hence from her, / Alone, shall come fulfillment to our dreams / And our desires" (ll. 63–65). She then wonders about the Christian contention of a perfect Heaven in an afterlife and asks, "Is there no change of death in paradise? Does ripe fruit never fall?" (ll. 76–77). In short, she wants to know whether we can believe in what we have been told, since the facts of our existence and of our earthly knowledge seem to deny what Christianity asserts. Indeed, in a passage in one of his essays that might be thought of as a direct commentary on these lines, Stevens says, "What a ghastly situation it would be if the world of the dead was actually different from the world of the living" (*Collected Poetry and Prose* 689).

At the end of the poem the woman hears a "voice" crying out (as if from a wilderness?): " 'The tomb in Palestine / Is not the porch of spirits lingering' " (ll. 107–8). Her response to this voice (since we must assume that these are her thoughts, or her responses to the voice that has cried out to her) seems to be a nonsequitur. The poem ends ambiguously, with "casual flocks of pigeons" who "sink / Downward to darkness, on extended wings" (ll. 119–20).[6]

In *Opus Posthumous*, in what may be a comment on the final lines of "Sunday Morning" and, indeed, on the whole of the poem, Stevens suggests that the realization that there is nothing beyond the earth makes for a sense of satisfaction, or even relief. As he says generically in one of his "Adagia," "This happy creature—It is he that invented the Gods. It is he that put into their mouths the only words they have ever spoken!" (*Collected Poetry and Prose* 906). Even so, it is interesting that Stevens, here at the end of his "agnostic" poem, concludes with a secular image of a Christian symbol. The birds in flight at the end of the poem are nothing but "casual flocks" of pigeons (as opposed to the "awakened" swallows at the end of the fourth section of the poem) and even though they here make only "ambiguous undulations" as they sink "downward to darkness, on extended wings," they do so in the very pattern of a cross—a flying, feathered, living, cross.

III

I write poetry because it is part of my piety. . . .

—Wallace Stevens

If Stevens's position in "Sunday Morning" is a valid addendum to the conclusions reached by Arnold, then perhaps his formulation of the proper way of thinking about "poetic value" (or the value of poetry) provides a convenient vantage point from which to attempt to analyze the work of R. S. Thomas, the late Welsh poet and Anglican priest, who was so clearly indebted to Stevens and who has interested, intrigued, and confused so many (and especially so many Christian) readers in our own time. In "Homage to Wallace Stevens" Thomas said: "His poetry / was his church." And in defining his relationship to Stevens in the same poem, Thomas added: "I turn now / not to the Bible / but to Wallace Stevens" (CLP 266).[7]

The issue, in terms of Thomas's work, often seems to be characterized by a confusion between his "beliefs," which must be thought to be conventional or orthodox, given his priestly profession, and those poems in which he seems to be blatantly unorthodox, if not agnostic, or, indeed, essentially heretical.[8] The primary reason for the difficulty is that, often, Thomas's readers assume that a priest—even in his role as a poet—must maintain a consistent and orthodox set of beliefs which are similar to or even identical with the beliefs that are in evidence in his clerical role; that, properly (it would be argued), these two sets of "beliefs," that of the priest and that of the poet, should be similar—or even identical—in the person of the priest and in the personae of the poems. Thus, when the poems seem to contradict that system of received priestly "beliefs," readers do not know which way to turn—to the priest or to the poet. As difficult as it might be for some readers, and even though it might mean that they (especially those drawn to Thomas specifically because of what they assume, on the basis of his priestly vocation, his religious beliefs are) will be put off when they encounter what are, or appear to be, contradictions or difficulties, it seems necessary to accept Thomas, *as poet*, on poetry's terms exclusively—even when he deals with religious themes and, especially so, even when the poems seem to contradict the theological position espoused by the priest.

Thomas himself has explicitly addressed these issues in terms of "the relation of religion to poetry" and in terms of the poet/priest dichotomy by arguing that "it is within the scope of poetry to express or convey religious truth, and to do so in a more intense and memorable way than any other literary form is able to" do. "Religion," he says, "has to do . . . with vision, revelation, and these are best told of in poetry. . . . Jesus was a poet. . . . In another sense, he is God's metaphor. . . . [And] how shall we attempt to describe or express ultimate reality except through metaphor or symbol?" ("A Frame for Poetry" 169).

Thomas concedes that "the two professions of priest and poet are so divorced in the public eye as to be quite beyond the possibility of symbiosis" ("A Frame for Poetry" 169), but in addressing the issue specifically in terms of his own work as poet and priest, he says:

> A lot of people seem to be worried about how I combine my work as a poet and my work as a priest. This is something that never worried me at all. . . . [A]ny form of orthodoxy is just not part of a poet's province. . . . A poet must be able to claim . . . freedom to follow the vision of poetry, the imaginative vision of poetry. . . . And, in any case, *poetry is religion, religion is poetry*. The message of the New Testament is poetry. Christ was a poet, the New Testament is a metaphor, the Resurrection is a metaphor; and I feel perfectly within my rights in approaching my whole vocation as priest and as preacher as one who is to present poetry; and *when I preach poetry I am preaching Christianity*, and when one discusses Christianity one is discussing poetry in its imaginative aspects. The core of both are imagination as far as I'm concerned. . . . My work as poet has to deal with the presentation

of imaginative truth (see Ormond, "R. S. Thomas: Priest and Poet" 52–53; the italics are mine).[9]

Thomas later alluded to this statement (which he made in a TV interview), and added some additional—and perhaps even more controversial—comments:

> I'm obviously not orthodox, I don't know how many real poets have ever been orthodox. . . . I find it very difficult to be a kind of orthodox believer in Jesus as my saviour and that sort of thing, [sic] I'm more interested in the extraordinary nature of God. If there is God, if there is deity, then He, even as the old hymn says, He moves in a mysterious way and I'm fascinated by that mystery and I've tried to write out of that experience of God, the fantastic side of God, the quarrel between the conception of God as a person, as having a human side, and the conception of God as being so extraordinary. . . . So these are still things that occupy me, and every now and again, if you're lucky, you're able to make a poem out of this conception of God . . . so I suppose I'm trying to appeal to people to open their eyes and their minds to the extraordinary nature of God. You know I just can't sing the hymns and all the silly twaddle that there is. That, I think [i.e., the extraordinary nature of God], is something . . . worth pursuing. . . . [T]rue Christianity at its most profound is as good as you get. . . . I think I've been lucky in the period which I've lived through because obviously I would have been for the chop in earlier days. The Inquisition would have rooted me out; even in the 19th century I would probably have been had up by a Bishop and asked to change my views, or to keep them to myself etc. . . . I think that so much [sic] of our Christian beliefs . . . are an attempt to convey through language something which is unsayable. And this is partly where the trouble arises . . . there are aspects of language which are most successfully conveyed by metaphor and the risen Christ, [sic] the resurrection to me, as I said, is metaphor, it's an attempt to convey an experience of a kind of new life, an eruption of the deity into ordinary life, a lifting up of ordinary life into a higher level. . . . So those are the things that I'm interested in. . . . I can't rise to the great acts of faith of some of the saints and all that. I can't definitely say to you, oh definitely I believe I am going to live again, I am going to be raised: I am on a kind of neutral ground, [sic] I leave it to God. If I'm worth saving, if He is disposed to save me, I mean, you see, I'm using linguistic terms now, I only half believe in. We use these words, like "resurrection"—what does that really mean, what is going to be resurrected? . . . [If] He's going to resurrect people in His own time, He will resurrect them. Well, I can't really be dogmatic about that sort of thing (see "R. S. Thomas in Conversation" 97–99).[10]

What Thomas seems to be saying in these statements suggests both a connection with and a deviation from the Arnoldian position. If it is the case that, for both Thomas and Arnold, religion and poetry mix and intermingle, it is also the case that they describe this intermingling in somewhat different ways. Even though Arnold would no doubt agree with Thomas that "poetry is religion, religion is poetry," Arnold saw Christianity as falling within the sphere of influence dominated by literature, by being subsumed by literature, as he made clear in *Literature and Dogma* when he argued (as mentioned above) that "the word 'God' is used in most cases as . . . a term of poetry . . . a term *thrown out* . . . at a not fully grasped object of the speaker's consciousness, a *literary* term, in short." Thomas, on the other hand, seems to see poetry as the core or essence of his expression of Christianity. Thus, both Arnold and Thomas, each in his own way, conflates the disciplines of theology and literature so that the apparently inherent conflict between them disappears (or is diminished) and Christianity and poetry, at least in terms of the practice of these "professions" (in both senses of the term), come together metaphorically, finally, in such a way that religion, or Christianity, is almost fully enveloped by literature, or, more specifically, by poetry. As Thomas put it, "The message of the New Testament is poetry. Christ was a poet."

The issue, of course, is most conspicuous in terms of Thomas's poems which are most overtly focused on specific, or traditional, theological themes, or which make use of theological trappings or metaphors. A case in point is Thomas's poem "Tidal" (MHT 43), a poem literally and specifically indebted to Arnold's "Dover Beach."

Although there are things still to be said about "Dover Beach," especially from a theological perspective, this is not the place to go into an elaborate exegesis of the poem. Even so, particularly in relation to Thomas, one needs to remember Arnold's crucial third stanza:

> The Sea of Faith
> Was once, too, at the full, and round earth's shore
> Lay like the folds of a bright girdle furl'd.
> But now I only hear
> Its melancholy, long, withdrawing roar,
> Retreating, to the breath
> Of the night-wind, down the vast edges drear
> And naked shingles of the world.
>   (Tinker and Lowry 210–11)

Here, perhaps as vividly as anywhere, Arnold expresses the essence of what he believed mankind's "modern problems" were. In the "dialogue of the mind with itself," which was what Arnold (like Stevens and Thomas) felt poems were, he wanted to be certain that his readers could "hear . . . the doubts" and "witness the discouragement"[11] that he himself heard, was witnessing in his own day, and was personally "witnessing" to. Nowhere are these "doubts" and this "discouragement" more evident than in "Dover Beach." Both the sentiments Arnold expresses and the poem itself have echoed down the ages, through Stevens, to Thomas.

IV

Cold sea, cold sky:
. . .

The great problems
Remain, stubborn, unsolved.
Man leaves his footprints
Momentarily on a vast shore.

And the tide comes . . .

—R. S. Thomas, "Young and Old"

Thomas's "Tidal" (MHT 43) begins with the action of waves running "up the shore / and fall[ing] back," mimicking the speaker's action as he "run[s] / up the approaches of God / and fall[s] back." And thus Thomas's poem, unlike Arnold's, is indeed "tidal." There is ebb *and* flow in it.[12] Thomas then develops his metaphor in a rather intriguing (and Arnoldian) way as he describes how, with each "return," the "breakers" on this beach reach forth "a little further" to "gnaw away" at the "main land"—a mainland upon which he wishes to "land," a land which, metaphorically, is God.

They have done this thousands
of years, exposing little by little
the rock under the soil's face.

This passage is intriguing in several ways. The surface of the "soil's face" is gradually being worn away to expose the "rock" beneath it. Here Thomas seems to be alluding to the famous passage in Matthew 16:18 in which Jesus refers to the rock of faith and, punningly, to Peter as a "rock." Again, although this is not the place to attempt a detailed exegesis of this biblical text, it is worth noting that the passage reads: σὺ εἶ Πέτρος, καὶ ἐπὶ ταύτῃ τῇ πέτρᾳ οἰκοδομήσω μου τὴν ἐκκλησίαν (". . . you are Peter, and upon this rock I will build my church. . ."). Jesus is clearly punning on Πέτρος (Peter) and πέτρα (rock).[13] Therefore, the πέτρα here may well refer to Peter's confession of faith in verse 16 ("You are the Christ, the Son of the living God") and not to Peter the man, and Jesus may well mean that the rock upon which the church is to be built is the rock of faith and not the person of Peter. (Thomas would of course know this and, in his own exegesis of the passage, in his poem, he may be implying that the rock being "exposed" from "under the soil's face" is both the rock of Peter's confession and the rock of Peter's person—even if both are being, or have been, somewhat "eroded" by the "approaches" to God made by priests (and others) at prayer.

Thomas further elaborates on his metaphor by saying that his "assault" on God is like that of the waves on the land and rocks of the shoreline. (Note how the rhythm of Thomas's opening lines suggests the "tidal" rhythm of the waves, replete with a rushing forward and then a return or falling back: "The waves run up the shore / and fall back"). This shoreline—and, as Thomas's line break makes it, this shore line—is the boundary or borderline between these two quite different elements of water, land and rock, the place where they meet and intermittently touch, but it is also an area which itself remains essentially separated from each of these elements save for the friction of the somewhat fitful contact between them. Thus Thomas metaphorically compares his relationship to God to this kind of tidal rhythm and his description of this relationship parallels the words, and the rhythm, of the opening lines of his poem. It also suggests the fitful, fleeting contact between himself and God: just as the waves "run up the shore" and "fall back," so, Thomas says, "I run / up the approaches of God / and fall back" (ll. 3–5).[14]

Thomas then says that he "must imitate" the "breakers" in his "return to the assault." He must do this, if "not in their violence," at least, apparently, in his persistence. And this in spite of the fact that he knows that

> Dashing
> my prayers at him will achieve
> little other than the exposure
> of the rock under his surface.

Here again Thomas seems to be alluding to the passage in Matthew. If it is the case that "exposing" the "rock" under God's "surface" exposes—and the pun seems important—either the rock of the church's foundation, in the person of Peter, or the rock of Peter's confession of faith—or both—this would certainly seem to be an achievement larger than "little." Of course, Thomas may mean that the "dashing" of prayer on the rock of God's (sur)face may also expose (in the sense of to make known) the rock of faith, even though this definition of the word often carries a pejorative meaning.

Furthermore, Thomas here directly counterpoints "the rock under [God's] surface" with "the rock under the soil's face" (l. 9). The "soil's face" (cf. "soul's face?") and the surface he here attempts to "expose" (the word is used in terms of both referents, ll. 8, 14) makes the "gnawing" action of the waves on the shore parallel to the "breaking" of prayer on the rock of

God's "(sur)face." The suggestion is that prayers, sent forth like breakers, will not break or budge the substratum of "rock" under the external and super-ficial "surface" of the soil. The implication seems to be that prayers dashed at God—either hurriedly or hastily, and no matter whether thrust or hurled violently—are to little effect. Interestingly enough from a psychological point of view, they also seem to have had little effect on the supplicant. Even so, somewhat surprisingly, given what has already been said, Thomas says that his returns, in his prayers (as in his poems), his assaults on God's shores, must be "made / on [his] knees" (in the posture of devotion) and that even in the "despair" of his "ebb-tide" (in terms of the prayers' apparent futility), they may still "spring" upward and "brim" over and thereby surprise ("disarm" is Thomas's word) God. And, if this were to happen, it might then "arm," or morally fortify, man. These prayers then are attempts to "discover . . . depos-its of mercy" (l. 21) within the briefly exposed rock face and/or on or within the rock of God's face. One wonders if such "deposits of mercy" are real or imaginary? Are they deposits left behind by God for the prayers of believers to find, or are they only imaginary sediments or sentiments of "mercy" which believers, in prayer, have deposited on the face of the rock in the hope that God may "find" them—or, indeed, need to face them—when (or if) he looks or listens to the prayers?

Thus, if despair has been Thomas's ebb-tide, his hope is that in the "high tide" of prayer he will be able to find "fissures" in the face of the rock where faith can "take root and grow" (l. 22). And, therefore, in this poem, Thomas, like Arnold, acknowledges that although the "Sea of Faith" that was "once . . . at the full" is now at its ebb-tide, his despair is not as deep nor as strongly felt, not as definitive and pervasive, as Arnold's was.[15]

Although there is perhaps no other poem in Thomas's canon as explicitly indebted to Arnold as "Tidal" is, there are other poems that seem to suggest or to imply a comparison between these two poets so temperamentally alike. In "The Moon in Lleyn" (LS 30–31), for example, Thomas, using a similar setting and metaphor, describes himself

> on my knees in this stone
> church, that is full only
> of the silent congregation
> of shadows and the sea's
> sound. . . .

Here too he finds that "the tide laps," if not at God, "at the Bible" (ll. 12–13), so that it seems as if "Religion is over" (l. 18). But, even so, he hears "a voice sound[ing] / in my ear" (ll. 21–22) that seems to say "These very seas / are baptized" (ll. 23–24), that "people / are becoming pilgrims / again" (ll.

28–29). Thus, he realizes, "You must remain / kneeling" (ll. 31–32) and rec-
ognize that just as the moon moves through its phases and in and out of "the
earth's / cumbersome shadow, prayer, too, / has its phases" (ll. 33–35).[16]

Another poem by Thomas that ought to be mentioned is "There are
nights that are so still" (also known as "The Other").[17] "There are nights
that are so still" situates Thomas, as speaker, in an Arnoldian setting, and
in circumstances similar to those of the speaker in "Dover Beach"— "listen-
ing" to a "swell born somewhere" at sea "rising and falling, rising and falling
/ wave on wave" on a "long shore . . . that is without light." But, in contrast
to Arnold's speaker's sense of solitude and isolation—even though he is not
alone and Thomas is—for Thomas, "the thought comes / of that other being
who is awake too" and is perhaps also waiting and watching, anticipating
contact if not communication. And then Thomas, in a graphic "tidal" and
epistemological metaphor, imagines how "thought," transformed or trans-
posed as "prayer," can, or might, "break" on or over God—"not . . . for a few
hours, / but for days, years, for eternity." And then, even if there is still no
response, and no answer, at least there may be something which, if for no one
else save the speaker, might provide joy, love, light, certitude, peace, and help
for pain—the very things that Arnold's speaker feels he is deprived of. There
is, then, for Thomas, in place of ignorance, a kind of knowledge—even if he
does not know what, finally, it is, or how to interpret it fully.

But perhaps the most eloquent expression of the essence of Thomas's
variation on and possible refutation of Arnold's position occurs in his poem
"Sea-watching," a title which in itself (and with all the punning ramifications
in tack and on view) captures much of what Arnold, and Thomas, have been
about in each of these poems, and in their meditations in them.

"Sea-watching" (LS 64), a poem in which the lines themselves suggest the
tidal motions of the waves and in which the title is a pun on the visionary,
begins:

> Grey waters, vast
>   as an area of prayer
> that one enters. Daily
>   over a period of years
> I have let the eye rest on them.

This is an intriguing conflation of "grey waters" and "an area" (or an arena)
"of prayer." In the complicated final line of this passage, Thomas suggests
that, just as he has let his "eye" "rest" on the "grey waters," so too, in prayer,
he lets his "I" rest on God. (The buried echo of "him" in "them" may not be
heard by every reader, but Thomas clearly must have intended it to be.)

Thomas then asks—and answers:

> Was I waiting for something?
>   Nothing
> but that continuous waving
>   that is without meaning
> occurred.

Surely, the question is rhetorical. Even so, the response begins with the iso-
lated word "Nothing" set on a line by itself and placed directly beneath the
question mark of the previous line, as if to suggest itself as an answer to that
question: that the waiting for "something" resulted only in "Nothing," that
is, either that there was nothing there and that that was the only answer
to the question, or that there was nothing there to wait for. Or both. But
Thomas quickly adds a "but" at the beginning of the next line ("Nothing /
but") to indicate that the "continuous waving" of the waves (like the "waver-
ing" of the lines as they mimic the waves of the sea, and also perhaps like
Thomas's wavering faith) is not "without meaning." Indeed, the wavering, in
essence, *is* the meaning.

> Ah, but a rare bird is
> rare. It is when one is not looking,
> at times one is not there
>   that it comes.[18]

In his autobiographical writings Thomas describes his habit of watching
birds, how fall on the Llŷn peninsula during the migrations was a "good place
for seeing [birds] on their way south," and how he "came to see the similarly"
between bird-watching and prayer (see *Autobiographies* 100). The "rare bird"
that Thomas is watching for here in "Sea-watching"—and almost actually see-
ing, if only in his mind's eye—is obviously mixed together with his watching
and waiting for God. This is an interesting, confusing, and troubling passage
since it seems to say (or to suggest) that man may miss God either because he
"is not looking" for him carefully—both devotedly and devoutly—enough,
or that God comes only when man "is not there," is not prepared to see or to
receive him. Therefore, "You must wear your eyes out, / as others their knees"
(ll. 15–16). Then, speaking for himself, Thomas says, "*I* became the hermit /
of the rocks, habited with the wind / and the mist" (ll. 17–19; my italics).[19]

The end of "Sea-watching" seems to provide Thomas with his only
answer:

> There were days,
> so beautiful the emptiness
>   . . .
>   its absence
> was as its presence. . . .

And this absence of presence is

>   . . . not to be told
> any more, so single my mind
> after its long fast,
>   my watching from praying.

"[S]o beautiful the emptiness. . . ." This conclusion is reminiscent of Arnold, and even of Stevens, but it is not where Thomas ends. In another poem, "The Absence" (F 48), Thomas writes of a "great absence / that is like a presence," which "compels" him "to address it" even without any clear "hope / of a reply." And although God "is no more here / than before," still one can hope, even in the presence of the absence of any tangible "presence." Thomas acknowledges that his "equations fail," just "as [his] words do," and yet he asks, "What resource have I / other than the emptiness without him of my whole / being?" In short, Thomas would agree with the well known passage in Hebrews 11:1: "faith is the assurance of things hoped for, the conviction of things not seen." This hope, both a conviction and an assurance, is, finally, the essence of Thomas's faith. And, therefore, the "Sea of Faith" that had ebbed in Arnold, and largely disappeared in Stevens, in Thomas has begun to "flow" again—even if it has not yet returned to a high tide. As Thomas said at the end of his poem called "At the End" (NTF 42), he has "been made free / by the tide's pendulum truth / that the heart that is low now / will be at the full tomorrow."

2

Finding and Following R. S. Thomas

If every writer's life might in some ways be described as a pilgrimage, the adage holds especially true for the life and work of R. S. Thomas, the late Welsh poet-priest. Though his entire career can best be understood as a pilgrimage to, or toward, a sacred place, Thomas was a man of contradictions, and these contradictions quickly became evident both in his life and in his work. In spite of Thomas's protests—especially so with respect to his most controversial political and theological positions—the seeming inconsistencies between his professional life as an Anglican priest and his work as a poet (inconsistencies which he himself frequently, and often vehemently, denied) provide an intriguing sequence of developments through which his life and career can be described and evaluated. Indeed, it was out of the conflicts and contradictions of his life, which Thomas himself never flinched from describing and detailing, that much of his best, most memorable, and best remembered poetry grew.

But, more than in the conflicts and contradictions themselves, it is in the margins, at the edges, borders, or boundaries of his life, that the essence of Thomas's personal and poetic pilgrimages can best be seen and evaluated. These interstices in Thomas's life provide the thematic focus for much of his most important poetry, which, like his life, was itself obsessively focused on theological themes, issues, or concerns. In a very real sense then, Thomas lived a crisscrossed (and indeed a Christ-crossed) existence, and the most memorable moments in his life, as well as his most memorable and important poems, often occur at those points where things or themes cross or intersect. Yet these crossings and/or contradictions, these paradoxes, in his life or in his lines, were always more apparent to others than they were to Thomas, and while his readers were often confused or disturbed by them, Thomas never was, or never seemed to be.

Although Thomas was born in Cardiff and raised in a series of sizeable cities, he consciously and consistently chose to live in rural, out-of-the-way places, on the geographical margins of Wales, places literally not on most maps. Throughout his life Thomas remained a staunch supporter of Welsh nationalism, and he regularly railed against the English ("Scavenging among the remains / of our culture," as he wrote in "Reservoirs" [NHBF 26]) and the English language, contending that in large part the decay of the Welsh countryside and of Welsh culture and tradition was the direct result of the intrusions, incursions, and usurpations of the English into Wales. In Thomas's view, the English domination of the Welsh culture and countryside had a great deal to do with English's rapid supplanting of Welsh as the primary language of the people. He saw the dominance of the "alien" English language as a denigration which, ironically, Welsh apathy itself helped to forward, or at least did not sufficiently resist.[1]

Thomas also always lamented the fact that, as a Welshman, he had been taught English as his own first language. The fact that he wrote his poetry exclusively in English, arguing that one could only write poetry in his or her "native" language, remains perhaps the most conspicuous irony in Thomas's life. (He learned Welsh as an adult and finally did come to speak it as his primary language, writing most of his major prose works in Welsh. Late in his life, he spoke Welsh almost exclusively.) Yet Thomas wrote his poems in English, published them with English publishers, married first an English and then a Canadian wife, and sent his only son, Gwydion,[2] to an English boarding school.

Despite his professed pacifism, Thomas frequently followed the lead of other outspoken Welsh activists, such as the flamboyant Saunders Lewis (1893–1985). He took an active role in backing various causes, including the controversial Campaign for Nuclear Disarmament, and he even argued that in order to keep Wales for the Welsh he would support the use of force against British rule in Wales, and also against individual English citizens who, increasingly, were buying up homes and cottages throughout Wales. These intruders, Thomas argued, were not only taking over Welsh territory and thereby displacing native Welshmen, but they were overpopulating the land. To Thomas they were trespassers, and they ought to be kept out at all costs.

In terms of professional concerns, and specifically in terms of theological issues, Thomas likewise seemed to be bifurcated—although he himself consistently, and often vehemently, denied that there were any rifts in terms of the "orthodoxy" of his theological positions. Even so, it is difficult not to notice some of the obvious complications in Thomas's profession as pastor and cleric. Thomas was a priest of the Church in Wales, that is of the Anglican, the English, established (but minority) Church, within the "hostile territory" of a country filled, especially so in the Welsh-speaking rural provinces where Thomas served, with numerous rival, nonconformist churches and chapels. Thus, professionally, in his priestly role, Thomas was an outsider in Wales—in the very midst of those areas and arenas that he felt most at home in, personally and privately, as a Welshman.

Against the charge that in the working out of his dual professions of priest and poet the poetic position took precedence over the priestly, and, indeed, often seemed to cause him to waver or to veer dangerously close to an unorthodox or even an agnostic theological stance, Thomas responded in "A Frame for Poetry" (1966) by readily acknowledging that although "in the public eye" the two professions of poet and priest might well be "beyond the possibility of symbiosis," in his own view, any conflict between them, as he had worked them out in his own practice, did not concern him, for the simple reason that, as he later said in his BBC TV interview with John Ormond (52), "any form of orthodoxy is just not part of a poet's province." Furthermore, although Thomas acknowledged that "A lot of people seem to be worried about how I combine my work as a poet and my work as a priest," that that was "something that never worried [him] at all." He added, "A priest must be able to claim . . . freedom to follow the vision of poetry. . . . And, in any case, poetry is religion, religion is poetry." (For Thomas's full statement of his position, see chpater 1.) In short, both of his professions, as far as Thomas was concerned, dealt with "imaginative truth." And, therefore, the two professions of poet and priest were essentially one, or, when properly understood (or as least as Thomas understood them), they ought to be.[3]

Thus, in spite of all the complexities of his personal and professional life, Thomas was a man of wit and humor, well loved, even revered, by his friends and parishioners—even though his public persona was often wintry and aloof.

Life and Work

For some there is no future but the one that is safeguarded by a return to the past.

—The Echoes Return Slow

Thomas's poem "Biography" (EA 17–18) begins with the admonition that "life's trivia" should be committed "not to the page," but to "the waste-basket."

In "A Life" (EA 52) he calls himself one of "life's / conscientious objectors," and compares himself to a "Narcissus" who is "tortured / by the whisperers behind / the mirror." In his autobiography, *Neb* (which is Welsh for "no one" or "nobody"), Thomas, writing in the third person, provides a somewhat sketchy outline of his life, an account as remarkable for what it leaves out as for what it includes. Taking as his epigraph a line from the French poet Paul Claudel (*Et de ce néant indestructible qui est moi*; "this indestructible nothingness that is I") Thomas, immediately, but subtly, alludes both to his title, *Neb*, and to the paradox of his own existence (as well as all other existences) in terms rather specifically theological in import. In an uncollected poem, "Autobiography," Thomas calls himself, still unborn, "a nonentity with a destination." In his eccentric and unusual book, *The Echoes Return Slow* (which consists of parallel passages in prose and poetry printed on facing pages), Thomas provides further insight into some aspects of his biography, but in a "poetic" (i.e. "fictional") rather than in a factual format.

Even so, in spite of all his seeming protests and self-protective words, the basic facts of Thomas's life can be easily summarized. Ronald Stuart Thomas was born in Cardiff, the capital of Wales, on March 29, 1913, the only child of Margaret and Thomas Hubert Thomas (who was known as Huw). His mother, orphaned as a young girl, had grown up the ward of an Anglican priest—his father was an officer in the merchant navy. Thomas's father's work took the family from one port to another, although Liverpool was a frequent home stop. Because his father was often away at sea, Thomas was raised primarily by his mother, and she exerted a powerful influence over him, not only in his childhood, but in his young adulthood as well.

Finally, after much moving about, when Thomas was about five years old, his father found steady work on the ferries running between Caergybi (Holyhead) on the island of Anglesey in north Wales, and Dublin, Ireland. Holyhead, ("Holy Island" in Welsh), therefore, became the first permanent home for the family. Clearly, Thomas always felt that Anglesey and north Wales *was* home, and he would move back there again late in his life.

Often alone and sickly as a child (he was kept out of school for one year because of illness), but always under the anxious eye of his devout and dominating mother, Thomas then, and throughout his life, felt most at home in the out-of-doors, roaming alone over the hills and moors and, especially, loitering near the "true solitude" of the sea. Later he described the sea as having had a "certain magic" for him even as a child, so much so that he wanted his body to be "baptized" in it[4]—an interesting word choice, since he was early on, and not too subtly, steered by his mother to pursue a priestly profession. He did not object to or resist this direction, but dutifully began to prepare himself for the priesthood.

Thomas enrolled in the University College of North Wales at Bangor, where he read classics (Latin and Greek), graduating in 1935. He then went to St. Michael's College in Llandaff, near Cardiff, to study theology. Thomas admitted to being quite unhappy there, particularly because he was separated from his home in north Wales, from the rural environment he had grown to love, from the proximity of open land and, especially, from the stretches of sea and the migrating birds he so loved to watch.[5] After only one year at St. Michael's, having been ordained a deacon in 1936, and a priest of the Anglican Church in 1937, Thomas was happy to accept a call as curate in the small mining village of Chirk on the Welsh Marches, not far from the English border.

After serving in Chirk for four years Thomas took a curacy at Hanmer, even further east in Wales, in a small peninsula of land surrounded on three sides by England. It is somewhat ironic that Thomas thus began his career on the border of his beloved Wales, virtually marooned in English territory. Here Thomas met, courted, and married Mildred Eldridge, an English woman who was a teacher and painter. He and "Elsi" were married for more than fifty years, and as Thomas's reputation as a poet grew, so too did Elsi's reputation as an artist specializing in watercolors and in detailed drawings of nature, particularly birds and animals.

At about this time, his longing for the Wales of his childhood and youth growing ever stronger, Thomas began the long slow process of learning Welsh in an attempt to find through vocabulary, if not proximity, the "true Wales" of his imagination. Thereafter, Welsh was the language he would increasingly use in his personal life and in his prose writings—if not in his poetry, in which (much has he regretted it) he felt he was limited to his first "thin language" (*yr iaith fain*), English. After two years at Hanmer, in 1942 Thomas took an appointment as rector at Manafon, a small, isolated parish in Montgomeryshire, near Welshpool. Here Thomas was much more centrally located in the Wales he longed for. And he was much more at home. Here in Manafon Thomas began to write the poems that he would collect in his first books. And here too his only child, his son Gwydion, was born in 1945.

After twelve years at Manafon, Thomas was appointed vicar of Eglwys-fach in Cardinganshire, near Aberystwyth, a predominantly Welsh-speaking area. He was disappointed to find, however, that many of the inhabitants were English transplants to the area and that they were crowding out the Welsh natives and supplanting the Welsh language with their English. Even so, Thomas gave one sermon in Welsh every Sunday during his twelve years at Eglwys-fach.

In 1967 Thomas took his final priestly post, as vicar of St. Hywyn's Church in Aberdaron. Aberdaron was a tiny, primarily Welsh-speaking village at the very tip of the Llŷn peninsula in northwest Wales. And here, finally, Thomas felt fully secure, in what he considered "home" territory. Offshore lay Bardsey Island, famous as a place of pilgrimage since the Middle Ages, and on it was a well-known bird observatory where Thomas could easily indulge his obsession with bird-watching.

At Easter, 1978, having reached his sixty-fifth birthday, Thomas retired from the priesthood and moved a short distance from Aberdaron to a small stone cottage, already more than four hundred years old, that overlooked Porth Neigwl ("The Mouth of Hell") on the Plas-yn-Rhiw National Trust estate, a cottage made available to him and his wife by the Keating sisters, long time residents in the area who were well known for their philanthropic activities. Thomas was to live in this cottage until 1994. He spent much of his time in retirement watching birds, speaking out on causes that he felt were important—many of which he had been constrained from commenting on while he was in the ministry—and nursing his wife, who had had serious health problems for many years and was now also going blind. Elsi died in 1991. Left alone again, in 1994 Thomas moved back to the far north of Wales, where he had been most happy as a boy, and took up residence in the small, remote village of Llanfairynghornwy in northwest Anglesey. In 1996 he married a Canadian widow, Elizabeth Vernon (who was known as Betty). They moved to Pentrefelin, near Criccieth, not far from where the Llŷn peninsula joins the "mainland" of Wales and not far from the area that Thomas had always regarded as the most beautiful in Wales. There, on September 25, 2000, at the age of eighty-seven, Thomas died.

Thomas's first book of poetry was *The Stones of the Field* (1946). It was followed by more than twenty additional individual collections, through *No Truce with the Furies* (1995), the last collection of poems that Thomas saw into print. In addition to these individual collections of poetry, Thomas published several volumes of selected poems (*Song at the Year's Turning* in 1955, *Selected Poems 1946–1968* in 1973—a posthumous new edition of *Selected Poems* appeared in 2003), two collected volumes, *Collected Poems 1945–1990* (1990; the title is a misnomer since well over two hundred poems from the volumes listed and included in this collection were excluded from it), and the posthumous *Collected Later Poems 1988–2000* (2004), which includes *Residues* (2002), a selection of fifty-seven poems culled from the large number of poems in manuscript that Thomas left in the care of his literary executor and friend, M. Wynn Thomas. Thomas also edited half a dozen books, including *The Penguin Book of Religious Verse* (1963), and selections of poems by Edward Thomas (1964), George Herbert (1967), and William Wordsworth (1971). He also published numerous essays and reviews (many of them written and published initially—or only—in Welsh), and other occasional items.

Since Thomas kept such poor records and often published in small, short-lived journals of limited circulation, it seems certain that more poems (and possibly essays) will appear before his canon is fully and finally complete—a complete canon that is desperately needed. Still, at the moment, there are more than one thousand poems available in various places.

In the course of his long career Thomas received many awards and honors. Among the most notable are the Heinemann Award from the Royal Society of Literature (1955), the Queen's Gold Medal for Poetry (1964), four Welsh Arts Council Awards, the Cholmondeley Award (1978), the Cheltenham Prize (1993), the Horst Bienek Prize for Poetry from the Bavarian Academy of Fine Arts (1996), the Lannan Lifetime Achievement Award for Poetry (1996), and a nomination for the Nobel Prize for Literature (1996).

The Early Poetry

The young man was sent unprepared to expose his ignorance of life in a leafless pulpit.

—*The Echoes Return Slow*

Thomas's poetry, especially the poems in the first half of his career, can be best and most conveniently considered in terms of several biographical and thematic sequences. In some ways such a consideration follows the outline of Thomas's life as summarized above. His first three books, *The Stones of the Field* (1946), *An Acre of Land* (1952), and *The Minister* (1953) (conveniently collected in *Song at the Year's Turning: Poems 1942–1954* [1955]), contain poems focused on the Welsh landscape and the Welsh people, especially the farmers and laborers in the small rural villages and parishes where Thomas spent most of his life.

In some ways, Manafon was the quintessential place for Thomas, and it became the paradigmatic setting for much of his major early work. The poems written in Manafon are both place and people-oriented. They are also frequently concerned with nature (often dealt with in terms of Welsh history) and overlaid with philosophic or theological trappings. These early poems, perhaps not surprisingly, are also the most overtly formal poems Thomas was to write—although, in spite of appearances (especially late on), Thomas never abandoned his own kind of often quite subtle formality. Likewise, most of these early poems are short, a habit or practice Thomas kept throughout his life. (In his huge canon there are not many poems longer than a single page.)

Among the poems in his first books are several thematically important, indeed seminal, poems. These are the poems which first put Thomas on the poetic map and, for some readers (both Welsh and others), these early poems, with their Welsh characters and their obsessive Welsh settings, are what have kept Thomas on that map. Among them there are those poems, like "Welsh History" (AL 23), "Welsh Landscape" (AL 26), "The Welsh Hill Country" (AL 7), and "A Welshman to Any Tourist" (SYT 112), which focus specifically on Wales. In these, Thomas seems to be greeting his readers on behalf of his homeland. It is immediately evident though that his "invitation" to things and places Welsh is not without its warning. Although the sheep are "Arranged romantically" on the hillsides "in the usual manner" (AL 7), as if posed for a travel brochure, and even though there are the inevitable "Wind-bitten towers" (AL 26) scattered artistically around the Welsh hills, vestiges of ruined castles fabled by history and the tourist trade, these are the relics of a past peopled with "sham ghosts" (AL 26) and "bred on legends" (AL 23). The present truth is that Wales is home to "an impotent people" who, "Sick with inbreeding," continue to worry the "carcass of an old" and outmoded "song" (AL 26). From lines like these it is easy enough to see how some of Thomas's early poems disturbed some of his Welsh readers, and embarrassed others.

But other early poems, especially those which emphasized his pride of place, endeared Thomas to many readers and helped to establish his reputation at home and abroad. These poems are of several sorts. First, there were poems like "Cynddylan on a Tractor" (AL 16), an often anthologized poem. Cynddylan, on his tractor, with his "nerves of metal and his blood oil," is the paradigm of the new Welshman, here depicted as passing "proudly up the lane." But there are also more ominous hints of both future themes and past troubles in the poem, since Thomas here introduces, in his mention of "the machine" and the way it has mechanized man, a theme he will return to repeatedly throughout his career.[6] Even more importantly, Cynddylan would remind history-conscious Welsh readers of the tragic seventh-century Cynddylan, Prince of Powys, long lamented in a tenth-century Welsh saga, which Justin Wintle has called a "classic expression of *hiraeth.*"[7]

Two other paradigmatic kinds of poems first appear in these early collections. The first can perhaps best be represented by "In a Country Church" (SYT 114), which John Powell Ward calls "the nodal spiritual poem" in Thomas's early career.[8] Here, we find Thomas alone in an empty church, in his typical posture ("kneeling"), waiting for God's word to come to him. All the traditional trappings are in place; indeed, the place itself seems to be likened to a huge trap into which God might be lured and finally contained and constrained—as in the later, companion poem, "The Empty Church" (F35), in which Thomas makes this metaphor even more explicit by saying, "They laid this stone trap / for him," as if imagining that God would suddenly appear out of the darkness "like some huge moth" and be drawn to it. But, in spite of such hopes, prayers, or expectations, "no word came," and "the God" (as Thomas often refers to the deity) refuses to appear or to present himself, having already once before "burned himself / . . . in the human flame," as Thomas says in "The Empty Church." In "In a Country Church," then, and in other poems like it, Thomas, early on in his career, introduces what will become one of his most dominant and consistently mined themes.

But perhaps the most conspicuous poem in *The Stones of the Field*, a poem that likewise first introduces a theme that runs a long course through Thomas's career and canon, is the signature poem "A Peasant" (SF 14). One of the very first poems Thomas published, "A Peasant" opens with the introduction of his most recognizable protagonist: "Iago Prytherch his name." In his essay "Abercuawg," Thomas describes how "When I began writing I devised a character called Iago Prytherch—an amalgam of some farmers I used to see at work on the Montgomeryshire hillsides."[9] Prytherch quickly became, as Thomas himself said, "my symbol of the hill farmers."[10] In "A Peasant" (SF 14) Thomas describes Prytherch as

> Just an ordinary man of the bald Welsh hills,
> Who pens a few sheep in a gap of cloud.

His clothing "sour with years of sweat" and the hard labor of the fields, he sits "fixed" (just as Thomas fixes him here) before his fire at night, or "leans to gob" into the fire. His "half-witted grin" and his rare "spittled mirth" define the "frightening" "vacancy of his mind." Yet—as Thomas tells us in no uncertain terms—he "is your prototype." Prytherch, no doubt lonely, stands solitary and alone, "season by season" and year by year, against "siege of rain" and the "wind's attrition," as firm as an "impregnable fortress," not to be taken or "stormed even in death's confusion." This prototypical man, as Thomas himself suggests in "Abercuawg," developed, for many of his readers, "into a symbol of something greater." Even so, Thomas says, "I had to ask myself whether he was real at all."[11] Nonetheless, as Thomas insisted, Prytherch needs to be remembered and perhaps even revered for the simple reason that he *is*, that he exists, and that he will endure.

"A Peasant" ends:

> Remember him, then, for he, too, is a winner of wars,
> Enduring like a tree under the curious stars.

Thomas was to write more than twenty poems about Iago Prytherch, a character who can easily be (and has often been) seen, simultaneously, as his protagonist and antagonist, his personal persona, even as a kind of *alter ego*. Clearly, both Thomas and his early readers quickly took to Prytherch, and indeed even identified Thomas's work largely in terms of this character. Many readers were disappointed when Thomas turned away from Prytherch, and, with him, away from the other early poems in which rural folk and their interests and activities had figured so prominently.[12]

The Middle Years

The Cross always is avant-garde.

—*The Echoes Return Slow*

Thomas was now ready to turn, if often with a rather personal focus, toward more politically sensitive philosophical and theological themes. In his next several volumes, *Poetry for Supper* (1958), *Tares* (1961), *The Bread of Truth* (1963), *Pietà* (1966), and *Not That He Brought Flowers* (1968), Thomas's two most conspicuous concerns have to do with Welsh nationalism and with his growing concern for, and emphasis on, theological issues. In terms of the first of these emphases, as has already been suggested, Thomas took, or had begun to take, atypical, untraditional, and unconventional stances, and these often confused, annoyed, and even angered many of his readers—especially many of his Welsh readers, who had grown accustomed to, and were comfortable with, his more bucolic treatments of Wales and of Welsh characters like Iago Prytherch.

The incipient emphasis on more overt theological themes is perhaps so conspicuous and important, here in the middle of Thomas's career, because it represents what was to be the dominant focus of much of the major work yet to come. One of the earliest poems to emphasize this theological theme is "*Souillac: Le Sacrifice d'Abraham*" (BT 43), which is based on the Old Testament story of Abraham and Isaac. In focusing on this biblical father-son story and relationship, Thomas introduced the theme of family and family relationships, an important and (given Thomas's notorious obsession with privacy) somewhat surprising emphasis that appeared briefly during this period in his career.[13] But what is most suggestive about "*Souillac: Le Sacrifice d'Abraham*" is the way that Thomas associates theology with art and literature—beyond the fact that he is writing literature—by suggesting that "art" can "interpret" faith.[14] And, indeed, many of Thomas's most important poems do precisely that—interpret, or reinterpret, faith or theological doctrine.

Several other poems of this period signal additional concurrent themes: "Pietà" (P 14) introduces the symbol of the "untenanted" cross, an image that Thomas will return to in several other important poems; "Kierkegaard" (P 18–19) is the first of several crucial poems that concentrate on the Danish philosopher;[15] and "The Moor" (P 24), which mines the Wordsworthian theme of the relationship between God and nature, brings up what was to be another important and on-going issue for Thomas.

But, in the context of Thomas's primary focuses during this period, perhaps the two most significant poems are "In Church" (P 44) and "Llanrhaeadr ym Mochnant" (NHBF 21). Both are portraits of priests. Llanrhaeadr ym Mochnant is the name of the small village in central Wales where Bishop William Morgan (1545–1604) lived, and where he translated the Bible into Welsh, forcing, as Thomas said, the "unmanageable bone" of the Welsh language into "passages of serene prose," and thereby "expiating the sin / of his namesake"—by which Thomas meant Pelagius (ca. 400 AD), who argued that man initiated his own path toward salvation without the assistance of divine grace. Thomas himself has emphatically stated that he intended to conflate Morgan and Pelagius. His reasons for doing so are based on word play, since Pelagius's name is a Latinization of Morgan. And the reason that Thomas was so intrigued with Morgan (and remained so, as his later poem on Morgan, "R. I. P." [MHT 35–37] attests) is that, by translating the Bible into Welsh, Morgan was able to illustrate the importance of the Welsh language to Welshmen, to the English, and to the English government as well.[16] Obviously, Morgan is one of Thomas's heroes, and "Llanrhaeadr ym Mochnant" is a testament to the "heirloom" that Morgan left for all Welshmen.

If "Llanrhaeadr ym Mochnant" is an historical portrait of the priest in Wales, "In Church" (P 44) is Thomas's contemporary portrait of the priest. Indeed, it is essentially a self-portrait. The poem begins by focusing on the setting ("Often I try / to analyze the quality / Of its silences") and with some speculation as to how it might be that God would choose to hide from the priest ("Is this where God hides / From my searching?") in, of all places, the church—especially when the priest has waited, in hope and expectation, until "the few people have gone," for God to appear to him. But he finds that he waits in vain, and then he realizes that the church too, since it was built centuries before, has also been waiting in vain for God to appear ("It has waited like this / Since the stones grouped themselves about it"). But neither the enticing building nor the expectant priest at his prayers have been able to "animate" the divine to make its presence known. The only sound in the resounding silence of the vacant church is the sound of the priest's breath, "testing his faith / On emptiness," and "nailing his questions . . . One by one to an untenanted cross." And thus the priest, alone again, and, as always, lonely, finds not the presence he seeks, but only the voluble, indeed almost visible, presence of God's absence; he finds his questions unanswered and his faith tested by this ever-absent (but hauntingly present) presence of God.

If in "In a Country Church" (SYT 114) Thomas introduced the posture of obedience and obeisance as "kneeling," in the poem "Kneeling" (NHBF 32) he reintroduces this posture. "Kneeling" positions the poet-priest on his knees before an altar, "waiting for the God / To speak." Remembering St. Augustine's request ("Save me, God; but not yet"), Thomas says, "Prompt me, God; But not yet." Clearly, he wishes for God's word, not his own, even though he knows that God can and might well speak through him. He wishes and waits because he knows that the "meaning" that he is waiting for "is in the waiting." "Kneeling" thus both anticipates and provides a convenient transition to Thomas's major period, which begins with his enigmatically titled book, *H'm* (1972) and runs throughout most of the poems of the 1970s, including those in two of Thomas's most important books, *Laboratories of the Spirit* (1975) and *Frequencies* (1978).

This is a period which I have described as Thomas's "apocalyptic" period, calling it the climax of Thomas's entire career.[17] This period also, in some ways, most clearly represents and details Thomas's "dark night of the soul" (to use St. John of the Cross's well-known phrase). Certainly, this is the period in which Thomas most definitively felt the presence of God's absence, the *deus absconditus*. And this is clearly the single most important and the most productive decade in Thomas's career, a period filled with many powerful poems on his central theological theme. Indeed, in his autobiographical essay "No One" Thomas himself described this phase of his life as a period in which "he turned increasingly to the question of the soul, the nature and existence of God, and the problem of time in the universe." It was, he said, a time during which "he had reached the destination of his own personal pilgrimage."[18]

"Via Negativa" (H'm 16), a poem in which Thomas deals explicitly with this important apocalyptic theme, is therefore a conspicuous and an important poem. It begins: "Why no! I never thought other than / That God is the great absence / In our lives." God is here described as an "empty silence," a void—even though he "keeps" the gaps in our knowledge, even though we follow in his "footprints" and hear his disappearing "echoes" in our own voices, and even though we continue to try, and fail, to find him.[19]

"Emerging" is a key word in Thomas's vocabulary during this period, and it is therefore not surprising that Thomas titles two different poems with this single word title. The first poem called "Emerging" (LS 1), the opening poem in *Laboratories of the Spirit*, describes prayer as the "annihilation of difference" between God and man, the recognition of "myself in you, / of you in me." This annihilation of difference provides a way of "emerging / from the adolescence of nature / into the adult geometry / of the mind," and also a way of dealing with "the machine":

> My life is not what it was.
> Yours, too, accepts the presence of
> the machine?

This attention to the machine resurfaced in Thomas's poetry at about this time as a symbol for the increasingly mechanized society that he saw impinging on the life of the spirit, and this emphasis on the machine would continue to be conspicuous throughout much of the remainder of Thomas's career.[20]

The companion poem, "Emerging" (F 41), in *Frequencies*, begins with the poet, now living on the Llŷn peninsula, waiting for God on "some peninsula / of the spirit." But then there is the realization that God, beyond the "anthropomorphic" trappings he is so often clothed in, must be "put together / like a poem," that "what he conforms to / is art." This kind of description, if it is not something new for Thomas, is here newly evident in his poetry, and it adds a new complication to his theological musings, and to his meanings. The poem itself goes on "emerging" as it suggests that "no God" will bend down out of thin air to take the hand "extended to him." Rather, "it is matter is the scaffolding / of spirit," and God is simultaneously revealed and concealed by the "mind's tooling."

"The Gap" (F 7), the opening poem in *Frequencies*, is another seminal poem. In it Thomas describes the "verbal hunger" of man for God, and God's fear of man's entreaties or overtures toward him. The poem opens with God, seemingly startled, as he suddenly "awakens" to the "nightmare" of man's "nearness," as "Word by word / the tower of speech grew" upward toward him. God wishes to maintain the "gap" between himself and his creation, and he is terrified that that gap seems to be diminishing due to man's repeated appeals to him through incessant and unceasing petitions, prayers and entreaties:

> One word more and
> it would be on a level
> with him. . . .

God is afraid of this potential personal contact between himself and man, and he is, therefore, somewhat relieved to discover, when he "looked in the dictionary / they used," that there "was the blank still / by his name." And then "the darkness" "that is a god's blood swell[s]" and is then "let" as a "sign in the space / on the page." This a most enigmatic image—and poem—and it seems to satisfy two almost contradictory positions simultaneously. On the one hand, this "sign" might be read as a symbol of God's potential bridging of the gap between himself and man in Jesus; on the other hand, it might be read as an ongoing "sign" or symbol of the distance created and maintained by God between himself and man, a distance that he insists on maintaining, since he wishes to keep his "eternal / silence," and thus his "repose." As in so many of Thomas's poems, the reader here (as Thomas was to say in "Fishing" [F 11]) is left waiting for a "withheld answer to an insoluble / problem." If Thomas gives an answer to any of these "insoluble problems" it is an answer that throws the questions back on the speaker or seeker.

"Abercuawg" (F 26–27) is a poem based on the mysterious and enigmatic place first mentioned in a ninth-century *englyn* cycle of traditional Welsh poetry. Thomas appropriated his title (which he would use on several occasions in his poetry and in his prose, as has already been shown) from this *englyn* cycle to describe a similarly important, but mythic or imaginary place in his poem and in his own imagination. In his 1976 National Eisteddfod lecture,[21] also entitled "Abercuawg," Thomas asked, "Where is Abercuawg?" And even though he acknowledged that he "half feared" that it might not exist, he also said, "I see no meaning to my life if there is no such place as Abercuawg." And, he added, "For such a place I am ready to make sacrifices, maybe even to die." It is obvious that, for Thomas, Abercuawg is as important and necessary to believe in as God is—even if Abercuawg, like God, can never be fully or finally found, since both are "above time," and yet "ever on the verge of being."[22] Therefore, as he says at the end of his poem, Thomas is

> a seeker
> in time for that which is
> beyond time,

for that which is "always / about to be," and whose "duration is / of the mind" alone. In short, Thomas's quest, both in this poem and his essay, and in indeed in many of the poems of these books of his middle period, is ultimately more epistemological than it is ontological.

Frequencies includes several important poems. In "The Empty Church" (F 35), which is both a companion poem as well as a kind of complement to "In a Country Church" (SYT 114), and "In Church" (P 44), Thomas asks:

> Why, then, do I kneel still
> striking my prayers on a stone
> heart? Is it in hope one
> of them will ignite yet and throw
> on its illumined walls the shadow
> of someone greater than I can understand?

"Perhaps" (F 39) begins and ends in questions, and none of them are answered. Even "The Answer" (F 46) provides no answer. Likewise, "The Absence" (F 48) describes a "great absence / that is like a presence," but asserts that "he is no more here / than before."

In "Pilgrimages" (F 51–52), the last poem in *Frequencies,* Thomas describes the journey of his middle career as the pilgrimage it has been and asks, "Am I too late?" His final answer here is again only another question:

> Was the pilgrimage
> I made to come to my own
> self, to learn that in times
> like these and for one like me
> God will never be plain and
> out there, but dark rather and
> inexplicable, as though he were in here?

In many ways, then, Thomas's poetry during this time of self-questionings alternates between poems that are extremely bitter and biting (like "The Island" [H'm 20] and "H'm" [H'm 33] and others (like "The Coming" [H'm 35], and "Sea-watching" [LS 64]) that are moving and often beautiful descriptions of the power of a personal relationship between God and man—and between God and the man R. S. Thomas.

A Late Interlude

He was too insignificant for it to be a kind of dark night of the soul.

—The Echoes Return Slow

After this major decade filled with poems of self-questionings and self-questings, Thomas's career took a brief, but extremely important, ekphrastic turn. This almost seemed to be something like a necessary deep breath before he set out again on his pilgrimage and toward what he must have realized was the approaching end of his long journey, both literally and poetically. *Between Here and Now* (1981) and *Ingrowing Thoughts* (1985) contain fifty-four poems based on paintings (thirty-three "impressions" in *Between Here and Now* based on Germain Bazin's *Impressionist Paintings in the Louvre,* twenty-one poems in *Ingrowing Thoughts* focused on surrealist, Cubist, and twentieth-century expressionist paintings). In one obvious way this turn toward the graphic arts as a source of inspiration would seem to have been quite natural for Thomas, since his wife was a painter and their house was filled with art and books on art.[23]

But, of course, Thomas had always been a painterly poet, one who looked closely and carefully at things and rendered them precisely. Therefore, in looking at works of art—which are *meant* to be looked at and interpreted—it was almost inevitable that (following Horace's dictum *ut pictura poesis*) he should provide his own iconographical "impressions" of these "impressions."

As John Powell Ward points out, French Impressionism appeared at a time "when old certainties about essential and 'inner' reality were breaking" up. And it appeared almost in tandem with Edmund Husserl's philosophy known as phenomenology, a philosophy that could be defined as a "philosophy of appearances."[24]

After this brief respite, or even in the midst of it—in the thirty poems not based on paintings in *Between Here and Now* and in the forty plus "New Poems" published in *Later Poems 1972–1982* (1983), poems which appeared in *Between Here and Now* and *Ingrowing Thoughts*—Thomas quickly returned to his theological theme and to his obsessive pilgrimage. Indeed, the first of the non-ekphrastic poems in *Between Here and Now* is "Directions" (BHN 81), while the last is "Threshold"(BHN 110). It is as if Thomas was giving himself new "directions" and firming up a base from which to move forward again. In short, Thomas was off once more, and looking ahead, even if still balanced on the "edges" of "an abyss" (as he says in "Threshold," a poem which postulates a new point of departure for his continuing quest): "I emerge from the mind's / cave into the worse darkness / outside, where things pass and / the Lord is in none of them."

Among other important poems in *Between Here and Now*, "The Presence" (BHN 107) is memorable for its treatment of the relationship between prayer, Thomas's constant search for God, and the resounding silence that he continues to encounter in that search. "The Presence" begins, "I pray and incur / silence." This is a silence similar to "my own / silence," but nonetheless pregnant with possibility, with a prescient presence of presence. As he writes in one of two poems entitled "Suddenly" (LP 201), "I have no need / to despair" since everything "round me: weeds, stones, instruments, / the machine itself," are

> all
>> speaking to me in the vernacular
>> of the purposes of One who is.

Thomas's next two important books are *Experimenting with an Amen* (1986), in which he clearly turns back to his theological quest, and *The Echoes Return Slow* (1988), perhaps his most unique, and one of his most important books, a book in which Thomas returns to his own life as source and summarizes—in parallel passages of prose or prose poems and lined poems printed on facing pages—his entire life and work to date. The overt transition between these two books occurs in *The Echoes Return Slow*, where Thomas writes: "Concede // the Amens" (ERS 45). Having done so, he makes "the traveling," the quest or pilgrimage, itself "all." Or, as he says in another of the prose poems, "For some there is no future but the one that is safeguarded by a return to the past" (ERS 66). In another of the prose poems, he write that he is here attempting to commit "his silence to paper" (ERS 48). In doing so Thomas lets the silence itself speak.

The Echoes Return Slow begins abruptly—and memorably—with a description of Thomas's own birth: "Pain's climate" (ERS 2). This is reminiscent of the opening of Thomas's autobiographical essay, where he writes: "Pain, and a woman bearing it; the child, too. . . ."[25] In the companion poem in *The Echoes Return Slow*, as in *Neb*, Thomas says, "I have no name" (ERS 3). This book of "echoes," then, describes and details events and circumstances in Thomas's life, in antiphonal fashion, and in his usual guarded manner, more through metaphor than through actual literal detail. This guardedness is especially evident in Thomas's description of his close family ties, which, like the particulars of his own life, he never describes in any detailed way.[26] Indeed, *The Echoes Return Slow* is perhaps Thomas's most private book, as it is no doubt his most personal. Certainly it contains some of Thomas's strongest work—in prose and in poetry.

An excellent example of this powerful work is the brace of poems beginning "Minerva's bird, Athene noctua" (the prose poem) and "There are nights that are so still" (the poem in lines, ERS 78–79).[27] The prose poem contains a series or sequence of doubles, literal or implied, which work well within the prose poem itself but which also carry implications for the companion poem in lines. "Minerva's bird" is the owl "Athene noctua," the small night owl (but active during the day as well, "unlike its tawnier cousin," the barn owl) which sounds or calls its "lyrical . . . double note . . . under the stars in counterpoint to the fall of the waves." "Counterpoint" is a carefully chosen word, joining (as it contrasts) the two owls, their "double noted" songs during day and dark, and the stars and moon above the ocean waves. To all of these "doubled" details Thomas links the companion poem "There are nights that are so still" on the facing page—a perfect counterpoint (and counterpart) that both complements and contrasts the birds with their human listeners. In this lined poem the poet describes himself as a kind of "night owl," awake and awakened to the sounds of nature: "I can hear the small owl calling / far off, and a fox barking / miles away." It is then that

> I lie
> in the lean hours awake, listening
> to the swell born somewhere in the Atlantic
> rising and falling, rising and falling
> wave on wave on the long shore. . . .

This vigilance stirs a "companionless" recognition in the poet's mind—one typical of Thomas's constant quest for a relationship with "that other being"

who, he imagines, is also awake in the dark, who is also waiting for, even
anticipating, "companionship."

"There are nights that are so still"—which surely is one of Thomas's fin-
est and best-known poems (it is inscribed on a stone marker outside Thomas's
church in Aberdaron)—ends with these memorable lines:

> And the thought comes
> of that other being who is awake, too,
> letting our prayers break on him
> not like this for a few hours,
> but for days, years, for eternity.

The Final Decade

From a parsonage to a cottage.

—The Echoes Return Slow

During the 1990s, Thomas's final decade, he published three important
books: *Counterpoint* (1990), *Mass for Hard Times* (1992), and *No Truce with
the Furies* (1995). *Counterpoint*, like *The Echoes Return Slow*, is a unique book;
it might loosely be regarded as a book-length poem in four parts. The parts
are titled "B. C.," "Incarnation," "Crucifixion," and "A. D." Each part is
quite literally "counterpointed" with another, the means played off against
the extremes, and everything hung on a theological line, as Thomas's life-
long pilgrimage here takes its final turn toward home. The divisions and the
arrangement of the individual parts of the book and of the poems (all of
them, as in *The Echoes Return Slow*, untitled) force the issue of the figure of
Jesus into the forefront of human history. In this sense this book is easily
Thomas's most insistent theological text.

Counterpoint begins before history began, before man was man. The
opening line of the first poem reads, "This page should be left blank." The
poem then attempts to "imagine a brow puckered / before thought," and
"man rising / from on all fours" (C 8). The last poem in "B. C." describes
God staring "down into the empty / womb" (C 22) of the world. The two
central sections of the book conflate Christ's birth and his death on the cross
as if there was nothing between these two events. Nonetheless, in "A. D.,"
although there is the recognition of the modern ("the Middle Ages / are
over") and of the persuasive presence of modern science ("with radiation /
for candle, we make sacrifices / to the god of quasars / and pulsars"), there are
still all the old truths too, and the inevitable movement "from unfathomable
/ darkness into unfathomable light" (C 49, 40). The book ends, characteristi-

cally, with Thomas still face-to-face with an "illimitable" absence as the only presence, and with him asking, as he has always asked, "How can I / find God?" (C 58).

Mass for Hard Times is a difficult book and a diverse collection, but all of Thomas's central themes from his past collections are represented in it as he regirds himself "for the agon" (as he says in "The Reason" [MHT 27]) even as the universe[28] stretches, as God himself "stretches" "to embrace" the universe. The universe is hurriedly "drawing / away . . . at the speed of light" (as Thomas tells us in "Tell Us" [MHT 46]), and the "electron's confinement gives / birth to excess of speed" ("Could Be" [MHT 54]) in this world where, for many, God has become "an extinct concept" ("Eschatology" [MHT 48]).

This eclectic collection is dedicated to Thomas's late wife, and it includes one of his most moving and best-known poems (one of several memorable poems Thomas wrote for Elsi), "A Marriage" (MHT 74). "A Marriage" documents the couple's long marriage: "We met / under a shower / of bird-notes. / Fifty years passed." When death says "Come" to her:

> she,
> who in life
> had done everything
> with a bird's grace,
> opened her bill now
> for the shedding
> of one sigh no
> heavier than a feather.

Of the other poems in *Mass for Hard Times* that revisit recurring themes in Thomas's career, perhaps the most significant are the poems in which he focuses again on his beloved Wales ("Plas-yn-Rhiw" [MHT 30–31], "Pen Llŷn" [MHT 72], and "Afon Rhiw" [MHT 79]) and those that have to do with poetry *per se* or with language in general ("Question" [MHT 42] and "The Letter" [MHT 77]). But the most intriguing poems in this collection are those that deal with the world of nature and natural themes ("Moth" [MHT 65], "The Seasons" [MHT 67–69], and "Newts" [MHT 76]), literary themes ("Nativity" [MHT 21], "The Letter" [MHT 77], and "One Day" [MHT 19]), philosophical ("Markers" [MHT 47] and "I" [MHT 58]) and scientific themes ("The Word" [MHT 71], "Adam Tempted" [MHT 17], "Winter" [MHT 41], and the title poem, "Mass for Hard Times" [MHT 11–15]), or with Thomas's quintessential theological themes ("Preference" [MHT 32], "Aside" [MHT 34], "Tell Us" [MHT 46], "Bleak Liturgies" [MHT 59–63], "What Then?" [MHT 75], and "Migrants" [MHT 80]). There is even one poem, "Sonata in X" (MHT 81–85), which, in the image of "the spirit's /

adultery with the machine," contains an interesting mixture of science, technology, and theology. But, surprisingly enough, in a disconnected sequence of poems spaced intermittently throughout the book, Thomas here also turns (or somewhat adjusts) his obsessive Christian symbolism. The essence of this theological (re)visitation has to do with Thomas's configuration, or reconfiguration, of the symbol of the cross, a symbol that has been important to him throughout his career.

In the past Thomas had usually depicted the cross as an "untenanted" tree which, even though it was vacant, had a clear symbolic and historical presence. But here, in the first poem, the title poem of this late book, he asks, "how contemporary / is the Cross?" He then defines it as a "long-bow drawn / against love" (MHT 13). This is one of Thomas's typically elaborate images, and it is punningly accurate in several ways at once: the cross is simultaneously an "old-fashioned / weapon" (as he describes it in "Sure" [MHT 53], where the extended image—"its bow / is drawn unerringly / against the heart"—is almost identical to the image here in "Mass for Hard Times"), and it is something to bow down before. Thomas then complicates his metaphor by describing Christ on the cross as an "imperishable // scarecrow" ("The Word" [MHT 71]), and by comparing Christ's body on the cross to "lightning" ("Retired" [MHT 23]). And then, in "What Then?" (MHT 75), he asks,

> What boughs,
> then, will need to be crossed
> and what body crucified
> upon them for salvation
> to be won. . . ?

But then, as he complicates the image of the cross even further in a poem somewhat ironically entitled "Bleak Liturgies" (MHT 59–63), Thomas finally finds that, "as the day dawned," there will be those who will still find

> his body hanging upon the crossed tree
> of man, as though he were man, too. (MHT 63)

Clearly, Thomas will be among those at the foot of that cross—among those who find, in the mystery of Christ's incarnation and crucifixion, their ultimate hope and their most definitive identity.

In *Counterpoint* Thomas wrote, "On an evening like this / the furies have receded" (C 57). In a poem called "Question" (MHT 42) in *Mass for Hard Times*, Thomas asked, "what after-life is there / for the furies?" In *No Truce with the Furies*, his final book, Thomas addresses this question with a vengeance. Indeed, *No Truce with the Furies* itself addresses most of Thomas's familiar themes with a renewed vigor as it takes head on the reality of his situation in life (Thomas was in his eighties when the book was published). "Geriatric" (NTF 9), the opening poem, begins with a question:

> What god is proud
> > of this garden
> of dead flowers, this underwater
> > grotto of humanity. . . ?

It ends:

> > > I come away
> > comforting myself, as I can,
> > > that there is another
> > garden, all dew and fragrance,
> > > and that these are the brambles
> > about it we are caught in,
> > > a sacrifice prepared
> > by a torn god to a love fiercer
> > > than we can understand.

No Truce with the Furies ends with "Anybody's Alphabet" (NTF 88–92), in which Thomas, as an anonymous speaker (someone like "No one," perhaps?), catalogues in a playful alphabetically arranged sequence the themes his mind and his poems have played over during the course of his long life and career.

The title poem of *No Truce with the Furies*, "Reflections" (NTF 31), "reflects" on Thomas's lifework (his life and his work) as he focuses his gaze clear-sightedly and unblinkingly on the world and at himself here at the end of his life. "Reflections" begins: "The furies are at home / in the mirror. . . ." But Thomas warns us that we can "Never think to surprise them"; that there is, there can be, "no truce // with the furies." Certainly Thomas has never sought any truce with any of his furies, but he has never avoided any confrontation with any of them either.

The image of the raptor and of the owl figure prominently and powerfully in *No Truce with the Furies*, often in conjunction with one another. In "Raptor" (NTF 52) Thomas describes the deity in terms of a bird of prey. To those who "have made God small," Thomas responds by saying that he thinks "of him rather / as an enormous owl" who is "abroad in the shadows" and who brushes him "sometimes / with his wing." He is a creature who can fasten his talons either "in his great / adversary, or in some lesser / denizen . . . like you or me." Again, there is a buried pun in Thomas's metaphor here: if God is seen as a bird of prey, a "raptor," man is his victim, one who is at once enfolded or wrapped in his claws and at the same time willingly enraptured by being so captured and caught.

And so, for R. S. Thomas, there *is* no truce with his furies. And here, at
the end of his life, at the end of the long pilgrimage that that life has been,
Thomas includes a poem, entitled, appropriately enough, "At the End" (NTF
42). It begins:

> Few possessions: a chair,
> a table, a bed
> to say my prayers by,
> and, gathered from the shore,
> the bone-like, crossed sticks
> proving that nature
> acknowledges the Crucifixion.

"All night," Thomas says,

> I am at
> a window not too small
> to be frame to the stars
> that are no further off
> than the city lights
> I have rejected.

He knows that "the passers-by, who are not / pilgrims, stare" at him "through
the rain's / bars, seeing [him] as prisoner / of the one view"— even though he
now knows that he has

> been made free
> by the tide's pendulum truth
> that the heart that is low now
> will be at the full tomorrow.

Years before, in "The Combat" (LS 43), Thomas described his "wrestling"
with God in a passage reminiscent of the description of Jacob's wrestling with
God in the book of *Genesis*.[29] And now, he reports, as "night approaches,"
still "anonymous / you withdraw." There is, ever and always, "the failure of
language" to express the inexpressible. There is not even any way of know-
ing "why / on the innocent marches / of vocabulary you should choose / to
engage us," while, all the while, "belaboring us / with your silence." At the
end, then, all we know is that:

> We die, we die
> with the knowledge that your resistance
> is endless at the frontier of the great poem.

If God's resistance is endless, Thomas's quest and his pilgrimage is also
endless, and, here at the end of his long career, as he says in "Near and

Far"(NTF 46), he finds God still "vibrating" within him "with the resonance" of a blessing, "of an Amen." In the course of his long life R. S. Thomas has moved from pilgrim to prophet. His pilgrimage will long be retraced by faithful followers, and by readers still to come.

3

Agnostic Faith

Faith is *doubt*.

—Emily Dickinson

He who has not known the presence of God cannot feel His absence.

—Simone Weil

Proofs of the existence of God are . . . not needed, since his existence is in one sense obvious and in another of no religious interest. . . . The great difference between religion and metaphysics is that religion looks for God at the top of life and metaphysics at the bottom; a fact which explains why metaphysics has such difficulty in finding God, while religion has never lost him.

—George Santayana

I

Let us begin with a parable. . . . Once upon a time two explorers came upon a clearing in the jungle. In the clearing were growing many flowers and many weeds. One explorer says, "Some gardener must tend this plot." The other disagrees, "There is no gardener." So they pitch their tents and set a watch. No gardener is ever seen. "But perhaps he is an invisible gardener." So they set up a barbed-wire fence. They electrify it. They patrol with bloodhounds. (For they remember how H. G. Wells's *The Invisible Man* could be both smelt and touched though he could not be seen.) But no shrieks ever suggest that some intruder has received a shock. No movements of the wire ever betray an invisible climber. The blood-hounds never give cry. Yet still the Believer is not convinced. "But there is a gardener, invisible, intangible, insensible to electric shocks, a gardener who has no scent and makes no sound, a gardener who comes secretly to look after the garden which he loves." At last the Skeptic despairs, "But what remains of your original assertion? Just how does what you call an invisible, intangible, eternally elusive gardener differ from an imaginary gardener or even from no gardener at all?"[1]

In his essay "Imagination as Value" Wallace Stevens says that "poetry does not address itself to beliefs." He adds that "the poet does not yield to the priest," because "poetic value is an intrinsic value." That is, poetic value is not, for Stevens, "the value of knowledge" or "the value of faith," but rather "the value of the imagination." And, therefore, "if the imagination is the faculty by which we import the unreal into what is real, its value is the value of the way of thinking by which we project the idea of God into the idea of man" (see Stevens, *Collected Poetry and Prose* 731, 734, 735–36).

If Stevens is right, then perhaps such a formulation of these dichotomies and this way of thinking about poetic value (or the value of poetry) provides a convenient perspective from which to attempt to analyze the work of R. S. Thomas, the late Welsh poet and Anglican priest, who was so clearly indebted to Stevens[2] and who has interested, intrigued, and confused so many (and especially so many Christian) readers.

As already indicated above,[3] reaction to Thomas's work, often seems to be characterized by a confusion between his "beliefs," which must be thought to be conventional and/or orthodox, given his priestly profession, and those poems (and comments in some of his interviews) in which he seems to be bla-tantly unorthodox, if not agnostic—or, indeed, some would argue, essentially heretical, or even atheistic. The primary reason for this difficulty with respect to Thomas's position is that readers often assume that a priest—even in his role as a poet—must maintain a consistent and orthodox set of beliefs which are similar to or even identical with the beliefs that are in evidence in his cleri-cal role; that, apparently and appropriately, the two sets of beliefs, those of the priest and those of the poet, should be similar—or even identical—in the person of the priest and in the personae of his poems. Thus, when the poems seem to contradict the system of received priestly "beliefs," readers do not know which way to turn—to the priest or to the poet. As difficult as it might be for some readers, and even though it might mean that they (especially those drawn to Thomas specifically because of what they assume, on the basis of his priestly vocation, his religious beliefs are) will be put off when they encounter what are, or appear to be difficulties, it seems necessary to accept Thomas, as poet, on poetry's terms exclusively—even when he deals with religious themes and, even especially so, when the poems seem to contradict the theological position espoused by the priest.

Thomas himself explicitly addressed the issues raised by the poet/priest dichotomy, admitting that "the two professions of priest and poet are so divorced in the public eye as to be quite beyond the possibility of symbiosis" ("A Frame for Poetry" 169). As already mentioned, Thomas has addressed the problem specifically in terms of his own work as poet and priest:

> A lot of people seem to be worried about how I combine my work as a poet and my work as a priest. This is something that never worried me at all. . . . [A]ny form of orthodoxy is just not part of a poet's province. . . . A poet must be able to claim . . . freedom to follow the vision of poetry, the imaginative vision of poetry. . . . And, in any case, poetry is religion, religion is poetry. The message of the New Testament is poetry. Christ was a poet, the New Testament is a metaphor, the Resurrection is a metaphor; and I feel perfectly within my rights in approaching my whole vocation as priest and as preacher as one who is to present poetry; and when I preach poetry I am preaching Christianity, and when one discusses Christianity one is discussing poetry in its imaginative aspects. The core of both are imagination as far as I'm concerned. . . . My work as poet has to deal with the presentation of imaginative truth (Ormond, "Priest and Poet" 52–53).

Thomas subsequently alluded to the Ormond interview and added some additional—and additionally controversial—comments. Speaking in the third person in his autobiography, *Neb*, he wrote:

> But if he was unconventional in his attitude towards the services and practices of the Church, how was it with his theology? As already mentioned, people liked to ask him whether there was any tension between his two offices as priest and poet, and he would deny this through insisting on seeing Jesus as a poet. But what confused people was his use of the word 'metaphor'. So he didn't believe in it? But, of course, his point concerned the question of language. We do not have hard historical evidence for the resurrection of Christ. What we have are the words of the authors of the gospels and Saint Paul. They had a strange experience. They believed that the risen Christ had appeared to them. Accordingly, they sought to transmit their vision to future ages through the medium of words. If we have not had a vision of the risen Christ, we have to accept the verbal evidence of the Evangelists. But language is a symbol, a description of something in terms of something else. And, for R. S., that was the meaning of metaphor too.[4]

More recently, he added: "I'm obviously not orthodox, I don't know how many real poets have ever been orthodox."[5]

The "presentation of imaginative truth" then, for Thomas at least, would seem to satisfy both of his professions, as poet and as priest. Even so, although Thomas frequently begins or ends a poem with a theological theme, he inevitably deals with that theme in a traditionally *poetic* way. And he usually comes to a poetic rather than to a theological conclusion or resolution of the theme. This is not to say that Thomas rarely comes to a theological conclusion (since he often does), but only to suggest that, when he has to make a choice, he usually chooses to be true to the poetics—it is, after all, a poem—and to trust that he will, thereby, also be true to the, or his, theology.[6] This, in part at least, no doubt accounts for some of the confusion concerning some of Thomas's specifically "religious" poems, since some readers want, or expect, the poems to come to theological rather than literary conclusions, and they become confused when they find that they do not. Curiously, and seemingly because of this confusion, these readers seem to lose faith, or they seem to lose faith in R. S. Thomas. But Thomas never gets caught up in such confusions. And he never loses his faith—or his faith in poetry to express his position.

The issue, of course, is most conspicuous in terms of Thomas's poems which focus on religious themes, and it is particularly central to those poems which are most overtly focused on specific, or traditional, religious or theological themes, or which use, or make use of, overt theological or religious trappings or metaphors. In *The Penguin Book of Religious Verse*, Thomas specifically addresses the relationship of religion to poetry by "[r]oughly defining religion as embracing an experience of ultimate reality, and poetry as the imaginative presentation of such" (9). I take this to mean that, for Thomas, poetry is "the imaginative presentation" of "ultimate reality" and that this is what, he believes, religion "expresses." That is, through religion we are able to *experience* "ultimate reality," and through poetry (and only through poetry?) we are able to *present* (i.e., to make present or to represent) that experience. In short, Thomas is attempting to conflate the seemingly contradictory notions of "presentation" by punning on the terms present and represent. On the one hand, he seems to be suggesting that poetry is, or may be, the "imaginative" representation of the same kind of ultimate reality that religion presents or represents—that both might be considered as a gift or "present" from God to men. On the other hand, but simultaneously, he seems to be suggesting that the ultimate realities of religion can only be presented imaginatively through poetry—or, as he says, that this is at least "roughly" the case. Thomas puts his position powerfully and perhaps less cryptically in his poem "The Prisoner":

'You believe,
then?'
          'The poems
are witness.' (LS 52–53)

II

In terms of Thomas's own body of poetry, no poems are more conspicuous with respect to the theological theme than those set in churches. I want to consider three of these poems here.[7]

Perhaps the classic example of this theme is to be found in one of Thomas's early poems, "In a Country Church" (SYT 114).

> To one kneeling down no word came,
> Only the wind's song, saddening the lips
> Of the grave saints, rigid in glass;
> Or the dry whisper of unseen wings,
> Bats not angels, in the high roof.
>
> Was he balked by silence? He kneeled long,
> And saw love in a dark crown
> Of thorns blazing, and a winter tree
> Golden with fruit of a man's body.[8]

This poem begins with the speaker—who seems clearly to be both priest and poet, even though he is made anonymous by Thomas's use of the impersonal pronoun "one"—kneeling alone in an empty country church. The poem thus sets and describes the quintessential person, place, and posture at the center of an issue Thomas so often revisited, both "personally" and "impersonally," sometimes in the third person, as he does here, and sometimes in the first.[9] As in a later poem, "Navigation" (NTF 65), in which Thomas explicitly puts himself into a similar setting and situation ("When I / kneel down in the obscurity / that is God"), his third person persona is praying—kneeling, seeking, waiting—for some "sign," some response from God.

But in *this* country church, we are told, "no word" came.[10] "No word" comes to the "one kneeling" down and "no word" comes from the "one" to whom (apparently) words have been addressed or directed. Instead of any divine response, instead of any word from any source, either to the implied prayer or, indeed, to the pray-er, there is "Only the wind's song"—a kind of cosmic speech perhaps, but certainly not a fully interpretable "word"—nothing like God's λόγος described at the outset of the Gospel According to St. John. And, furthermore, this windy song seems a sad one, one which certainly "saddens" the "lips / of the grave saints"—who seem to be able to hear the song as well. This notion is itself an interesting one, and this is, of course, one of Thomas's quintessentially witty lines. Is the "wind's song" the "sad" speech of the "grave" (the dead, the somber, the venerated) saints, or is this song, whatever it sings, something that will "sadden" such saints, who now lie "rigid in glass" (just as they must have been "rigid" in life and, perhaps, equally transparent as well as potentially "shatterable?"). This seems to be one option. The other is that this "wind's song" is itself "the dry whisper of unseen wings"—but these "unseen wings" (lest we are beginning to think too loftily) are only the wings of "Bats[,] not angels."

The second stanza begins with a question—"Was he balked by silence?" That is, was he stopped, turned abruptly away, checked, or thwarted either by the fact that he is unable to pray, or, if he has, by the absence of any response to his prayer—or by both? The speaker, after kneeling "long," and waiting, seems to get an answer to his question(s) and to his quandary, or at least he seems to receive some sort of response—even if it is only a kind of vision that is visited on him. What he "sees" is:

> . . . love in a dark crown
> Of thorns blazing, and a winter tree
> Golden with fruit of a man's body.

Several things are worth noting in this vision, this version of the crucifixion story. First, it is a wintry vision: a vision of a "winter" tree, dead or barren. And the "love" hung on this winter tree wears a "dark crown." Only after the turn of the line are we told that this dark crown is a crown "Of thorns" and that it is "blazing" in the *sun*light (and in the light emanating from the *Son*?) there on that tree, wintry light which nevertheless makes "Golden" both the tree and the "fruit of [the] man's body" hanging on it. The suggestion is that, just as the tree is made golden by the blazing of Christ's body, so too is this "barren" tree made "ripe" (brought to perfection, and thus golden) by the body of Christ crucified upon it. It is interesting that the priest or worshiper, kneeling, is compared in the second stanza to Christ "kneeling down" and praying in the garden of Gethsemane.[11] And in the silence that greets the priest's prayer he has a vision, or a prefiguration (just as Jesus himself must have had), of Christ's death on the cross and of his possible resurrection.

Finally, it should be noted that this vision is an atypical one for Thomas, who, when he refers to the cross, invariably finds it empty—as he does in "In Church," a poem which can clearly be read as a companion poem to "In a Country Church."

In "In Church" (P 44), Thomas writes (in the first person):

> Often I try
> To analyze the quality
> Of its silences. Is this where God hides
> From my searching? I have stopped to listen. . . .

Here, in a situation similar to the one in "In a Country Church," Thomas, alone, listens in silence to the silence—and tries to "analyze" it. Is it possible, he asks, that it is here, in church (of all places), that God has chosen to hide, in this hide-and-seek game, from his "searching"? Is it possible, for instance, that God hides from man's specific searching for him in churches either because he cannot be found there, or because he cannot be found there invariably, inevitably or exclusively—that, rather, he is only "visible" unbiddenly, outside of any particular place, and only within one's heart or mind? It does often seem to be the case that Thomas had an edifice complex and that he is suspicious of what he regards as inadequate or inappropriate attempts to "entice"[12] God to respond to man's call, as it were—even perhaps especially to those "calls" on or to God made "in church."

Thus, as he has here "stopped to listen" (just as the line itself stops, even though it is not end-stopped),[13] so he has also been stopped by the silence—even as the air has quickly "recomposed" itself for its own "vigil." This absence, an almost voluble emptiness, has been a constant presence "Since the stones grouped themselves" around the church. The church itself, an edifice built by men, cannot be "animated," (imbued with life or, indeed, with *anima*, soul), by man's prayers, as God animated, gave life to, man by giving him the "breath of life" (Gen 2:7). Indeed, all that comes forth to greet the one waiting here in this church are the "shadows" of an encroaching darkness, advancing to "take possession / Of," to blot out, "the light [that] held / For [only] an hour." Are we to assume that the hour during which the light held was the hour of a service recently ended? That the God who is now "hiding" *was* there then? That this God is primarily a public, not a private God—one who appears as if on cue or call for ceremonies but eludes all private searches and entreaties?

Whatever the case, the building reverts to its usual, vacant situation: the pews return to their "ease," the bats "resume / Their business." All is silent and still "In the darkness"—save for one sound, that of a man

> Breathing, testing his faith
> On emptiness, nailing his questions
> One by one to an untenanted cross.

This solitary man, in the silence of his empty church, tests "his faith" on that very "emptiness" and hammers, nails, "his questions" (like Martin Luther

his theses) "One by one to an untenanted"—an empty—cross. There are
two questions implied by this fascinating image. First, what are the ques-
tions? And then, why is the cross empty? The second issue is related to the
first, and it may be that the reason the questions are unanswered is because
answers, to be given, must be given, by *someone*—and since the cross here is
"untenanted," empty, there is no one there to hear the questions or to answer
them. Does this mean, then, that no answers are possible? Does it suggest
that the questions are (or were), therefore, inappropriate or irrelevant? Or
does the fact that these "questions" are being nailed "One by one"—posted,
fixed methodically, even permanently, to this untenanted cross—suggest that,
even unanswered, the "questions" are nevertheless still relevant, appropriate,
and important? Indeed, does it suggest that the very fact that the questions
are unanswered make them *all the more* relevant, appropriate, and important?
And are the questions themselves, therefore, *more* important than any answers
ever could be? And is it the *answers* then that are finally irrelevant? All of these
issues, these questions and their potential answers, are, I would argue, what
Thomas wants to raise, or suggest, to show, in this poem. What he seems to
be saying is that we need to ask, and that we need to stop and listen—even if
we receive no answers, even if we hear nothing save the silence echoing in an
empty edifice, or in our own minds.

Even so, the image of the untenanted cross is perhaps more complex, and
more enigmatic, than it at first might seem. On the simplest level, Thomas
seems to be referring to the traditional Protestant cross found in churches
and distinguishing it from the Roman Catholic crucifix. A "tenant" is one
who uses or occupies a place or property owned by another. If we think of
the cross, symbol both of the crucifixion and the resurrection simultaneously,
certainly Jesus, as the Christ, is an appropriate tenant for this symbol, as the
Roman Catholic crucifix affirms by so depicting him there. If, on the other
hand, the cross is empty, untenanted, as it is in the Protestant tradition, this
is not to deny the fact of the crucifixion, but to affirm the truth of the resur-
rection. The symbol, as symbols do, stands for a truth beyond what it suggests
or symbolizes; it is a less literal, but equally valid, representation of the truth
it signifies or symbolizes.[14]

But there seems to be even more to the image. Thomas seems to be sug-
gesting that it is not that the symbol is untenable, but that the very fact that
the cross is untenanted makes the case *even more tenable*: that Jesus, as Christ,
even in his absence—indeed, perhaps *because* of, and by, his absence—sym-
bolizes and thus affirms his continuing presence; that, during the crucifixion,
he literally occupies the place and property of that other member of the Trin-
ity; and that the symbolic power of *that* presence remains (and is perhaps
even increased) by the symbol itself—which is a continuing evocation of his

presence, even in the presence of his visible absence! That is: the presence of Jesus's absence on the untenanted cross symbolizes the abiding *presence of Christ's presence*, as tenant, for God. That, as is always the case in a literary context, the symbol, the metaphor, the metonymy, is more powerful than the literal referent. And, therefore, the presence of the absence explicitly, symbolically, signifies the presence of presence—and it does so in a more powerful way that any literal "presence" would or ever could do.

"In Church," then, provides us with a direct prelude to "The Empty Church" (F 35). This poem opens with the image of an empty church described as a "trap" for a moth-like God:

> They laid this stone trap
> for him, enticing him with candles,
> as though he would come like some huge moth
> out of the darkness to beat there.

Thomas has said,

> One of the advantages and the challenges of living in a country parish as a priest is the silence and the loneliness, and one has spent quite a lot of time in small churches on one's knees, seeking for God, trying to establish contact and being rewarded by silence, and a feeling of absence, because it is we who are in him rather than he who is in any of our buildings or traps (see Harries, 69).[15]

Such a trap is not likely to work. "He will not come any more // to our lure," Thomas tells us, because "he had burned himself / before in the human flame." Although he had "escaped," it was with his "reason / torn." Again, this is an intriguing image. The clear suggestion is that God, become man— "enticed" through prayer or supplication, and acceding to man's pleas—had been "burnt" by the experience of incarnation, and that he had "escaped" (in body) but with his "reason / torn" by this seemingly harrowing experience. On the one hand, this suggests that, although the reason for the reason having been torn is not fully clear, it is clear that God (who might have been thought to know everything well in advance—including whatever reason there might be for everything that was to be) had been taken by surprise by what had happened to Jesus, and that he had, indeed, been burned by this experience—the experiment of the incarnation. On the other hand, and in part due to one of Thomas's signature line breaks, the word "reason" elides into the notion of consciousness to suggest that God's reason, his capacity for rational thought, had been "torn," disrupted, or (even) pulled to pieces—so much so that there is now no longer any possibility that he might fall for such a "trap" or be enticed into such a temptation. As the end of the stanza puts it explicitly, "He will not come any more." This is an unqualified assertion, and the clear implication is that there will be nothing that would, or could, change it, that there would or could be no possible reason for God to send another savior. Even so, one could argue that one incarnation ought to have been enough! It seems apparent that it was for God—"He will not come any more." The buried question seems to be: should not once have been enough for man as well?

This, then, is the setting and the thematic situation of the first stanza of the poem. In answer, or in response to his own comments, Thomas asks two questions:

> Why, then, do I kneel still
> striking my prayers on a stone
> heart? Is it in hope one
> of them will ignite yet and throw
> on its illumined walls the shadow
> of someone greater than I can understand?[16]

In short, why should we want God back? Why should we want him to return? And why, therefore, Thomas asks, "do I kneel still?" This phrase mixes two meanings rather neatly: why do I continue to kneel ("kneel still"), and why do I kneel "still," that is, locked in silent prayer and expectation? Why do I pray if my prayers fall only on a "stone," an obdurate and unrepentant, heart?[17] For what reason and to what end? If God will not hear—indeed, if God is not *here* in this "empty church," where he might come and be *heard* clearly—where is he, and what is the purpose of prayer?

The second question, a rhetorical one, suggests an answer to the first. It begins, "Is it in hope. . . ?" (In this question we hear both the question and the implied answer, "It *is* in hope.") But is it hope beyond hope? Hope in spite of all the odds against it? Hope that prayer, striking a stone heart, might ignite a flame which, if it will not bring God back or cause him to return, "like some huge moth," will at least "throw / on its illumined walls the shadow / of someone greater than I can understand"?

This question raises a host of additional questions. What is the referent for "its"? Does "the shadow"(especially in its context as the shadow "of someone greater than I can understand," with its hint at the ontological debate that goes as far back as Anselm and as far forward as contemporary philosophy) imply or demand a presence beyond itself? How can one "understand" "someone greater than I can understand"—someone, or something (since the shadow is still undefined), that appears, or may appear, only as an absence, a "shadow," an unembodied body or being? Indeed, how can one even "hope" for something like this understanding? If it is the case that the plea of this prayer is a petition to God not for his presence, not for his return in some sort of new incarnation, but finally and fully for what indeed is the only thing that can be asked—that God assert himself in the speaker's heart, imprint himself on "its" walls, illuminating them with even the "shadow" of a faith in the reality of a source beyond it, no matter how vague or incomprehensible it might be, no matter how much it might elude the head, the intellect, and the rational understanding, still it would be there, if not as a present reality, at least as a real presence, both mysterious and meaningful simultaneously.[18]

III

"Questions" (LP 193),[19] appropriately enough, seems to take up these same issues, these same questions. The poem itself is a dialogue. It asks a series of seventeen questions and purports to provide "answers" to some of them—or at least a "message" in response to them—but, more than any answer or message, it essentially raises additional questions, questions which are followed by a series of nonsequiturs that are hardly "answers." Indeed, after the first question, "You are prepared?," the only "answer" is a kind of stage direction: "Silence." And then we are told that "Silence *is* the message" (my italics). And then that the message is that we must "Wait." One speaker (since it seems there are indeed two persons present, making this a true dialogue) asks, "Are you sure?" And then this speaker, who is given no answer, wonders aloud about the possibility of an "echo" or of an "echo of an echo." The response again is another stage direction kind of statement ("Sound"), without any further stipulation as to anything particular or definitive—simply, it seems, sound for sound's sake alone. (How can sound alone "echo" or "echo" its own "echo?") There then follows another question, apparently an attempt to comprehend or to understand something of the mystery of this mysterious situation: "Was it always there / with us failing / to hear it?" Was what always there, one wonders—sound, silence, or only a silent, soundless echo?

Here, at almost the center of "Questions," and of his "questionings," Thomas begins to fracture his lines, introducing a stanza-like section filled with additional questions and ending with another directive:

> What was the shell doing
> on the shore? An ear endlessly
> drinking?
> What? Sound? Silence?
> Which came first?
> Listen.

The "listen" at the end of this sequence serves two purposes. First, it creates an expectant pause and gives a direction. We seem to be being told to stop and listen. But, simultaneously, this "listen" is a prelude to what is to come. This (empty?) shell on the shore may well be "endlessly / drinking" in sound, or silence, and wondering which came first—simply waiting, simply "listening," perhaps only to its own echoing silence.

Then the poem turns directions again—and ends with another non-sequitur. This final section of the poem, which uses the word "listen" as a transition, begins with what at first appears to be a narrative, or even a parable, one that promises to explain what has gone before and then to answer the questions that have been asked: "Listen. / I'll tell you a story. . . ." The whole poem has seemed to be a "story" or a drama, and so this section, which, as we can see in looking at the poem on the page, is the conclusion, promises to be conclusive. Of course, it is not. Instead of providing an answer or answers, the teller telling us "the story" tells us that it is a story told to him "by the teller / of stories." That is, it is a fiction. Thus, at best, the "story" will be applicable not in a literal but only in a literary way. But, even so, the teller, instead of telling the story, asks, wonderingly, "Where did he hear it?" And then he adds another series of questions, all of which relate to the storyteller and are about him, not the story he has told—the story we have been waiting to hear, the story that might provide an "answer."

> Where did he hear it?
> By listening? To silence? To sound?
> To an echo? To an echo
> of an echo?

What *is* the story? Who is the teller of the story? Why has this teller told this story to the teller of the poem? Why has the teller of the poem said that he plans to tell it to us? Why doesn't he? What are we to make of all of this? What are we to do with this information? There are no answers to any of these questions save for the command of the final line—if even it is an answer. We are told, finally, to "Wait." This one word line is centered on the page and centered at the end of the poem. The last four lines funnel down to this final word, to a point, as it were, pointing us, and pointing out what we have been told to do, what we *must* do. We must "wait."

Is this an answer? Is this a solution? Thomas is a poet of questions and of quests. He is a patient poet, given to the "interrogation of silence,"[20] but he is not a poet of answers. Indeed, as Thomas says in one of the poems in *The Echoes Return Slow* (ERS 81), "You have to imagine / a waiting that is not impatient / because it is timeless." Does such a "timeless" waiting accomplish anything? Are we willing to wait timelessly without hope or expectation? If so, the situation is not unlike the situation in Samuel Beckett's *Waiting for Godot* or, perhaps more to Thomas's point (since we know that Thomas read

Paul Tillich closely), it falls into the category of that kind of waiting that Til-lich describes in one of his sermons in *The Shaking of the Foundations*. The sermon itself is entitled "Waiting," and it is based on two biblical passages: "I wait for the Lord, my soul waits, and in his word I hope" (Ps 130:5), and "Now hope that is seen is not hope. For who hopes for what is seen? But if we hope for what we do not see, we wait for it with patience" (Rom 8:24-25). Tillich says, "Both the Old and the New Testaments describe our existence in relation to God as one of waiting" (149), and he argues that the waiting was "decisive for the prophets and the apostles. . . . They did not possess God; they waited for Him" (150). Likewise, "we must wait for Him in the most absolute and radical way" (150–51). Indeed, "He is God for us just in so far as we do *not* possess Him. . . . We have God through *not* having Him" (151, italics in original). Even so, "although waiting is *not* having, it is also having. The fact that we wait for something shows that in some way we already pos-sess it" since

> that for which we wait is already effective within us. . . . But if we know that
> we do not know Him, and if we wait for Him . . . we then are grasped and
> known and possessed by Him. It is *then* that we are believers in our unbelief,
> and that we are accepted by Him in spite of our separation from Him (151,
> italics in original).

For Tillich, therefore, since the "condition of man's relation to God is first of all one of *not* having, *not* seeing, *not* knowing, and *not* grasping," waiting "means *not* having and having at the same time" (149, italics in original). And, Tillich adds, "A religion in which that is forgotten . . . replaces God by its own creation of an image of God." He acknowledges that "It is not easy to endure this not having God, this waiting for God" (149–59). Indeed, the one "who waits . . . is already grasped by that for which he waits . . ." (151). "Waiting is not despair. It is the acceptance of our not having, in the power of that which we already have." It is the "waiting for the breaking in of eternity" (152).[21]

IV

"Waiting" (F 32) is a crucial poem for Thomas and it seems to pick up where "Questions" left off. Like "Questions," it too is divided into three stanza-like sequences. It begins with a question: "Face to face?"[22] Here there seems to be less anonymity than in "Questions" and certainly there is the prospect of more immediate contact or confrontation. And here too the two "protago-nists" (with all the anguish and agony that this word implies) are clearly more definitively defined. And, immediately, with the first line break, the confron-tation begins:

> Face to face? Ah, no
> God. . . .

Thomas has quite carefully arranged these opening lines to prepare us—both thematically and structurally—for the debate or confrontation to follow. How are we to read this line break? As "Ah, no" we are not "face to face" with God? Or are we to take the "Ah" as an interjection or an exclamation, an almost inarticulately articulate ejaculation over the astounding and stunning recognition—evoking both awe and bewilderment at once—that there is "no God?"[23] We are immediately told that "language falsifies" whatever the relationship is, and given inappropriate, if possible, proximities—"Nor side by side, / nor near you, nor anywhere / in time and space."[24]

The second section of the poem takes an historical turn, summarizing the relationship between God and men over the ages and coming down specifically to Thomas himself. If it is the case that God's name has "vouched" for him through the ages and is "ubiquitous / in its explanations," then the waxing and waning of man's response to and conflict with God throughout history makes perfectly good sense. When the "earth bore" and men "reaped" they were pleased and happy and they looked to God as a provider of both material and spiritual blessings. On the other hand, when the "wind / changed" and when death visited, "it was you / they spat at."

The third section of the poem is personal and particular. It begins, "Young / I pronounced you." This is a rather curious phrase and an extremely formal one, since a pronouncement is an official or ceremonial declaration, often uttered or recited without much personal commitment, a rather empty discourse. Even so, the next lines insist that "Older / I still do" pronounce you, even if it is "seldomer / now." And then Thomas alludes again to one of his favorite Kierkegaardian metaphors to describe himself as "leaning far out / over an immense depth" and

> letting
> your name go and waiting,
> somewhere between faith and doubt,
> for the echoes of its arrival.[25]

This is a fascinating passage. The "echoes" here harken back to the "echoes" in "Questions," but they are rather different echoes. Echoes, after all, are only "repeated" sounds, or words returned to their source or to the speaker who has spoken them. In this sense they "bring back" nothing new, and certainly nothing different from what was originally said, spoken or sent out. The argument then seems to run: once the "pronounced" word (presumably "God," or the words of a prayer) actually reaches God, it will be rebounded back to the man who has spoken it, and that, then, when this echo returns it will "prove" (or at least imply) that it has reached its (or some) sounding board or destination and been turned back or returned. This is a most curious argument. The metaphor suggests that a word or words, thrown like a ball at a backboard, rebound to the player as they would in a game or simple exercise. But, even if this were the case, what would be bounced back, what would return, would only be what was sent, not a response but simply the echo of the words originally sent out or spoken in the first place. In essence then this activity would be nothing but a solipsistic exercise.[26] And this is why the speaker waits, "somewhere between faith and doubt," anticipating the returning "arrival" of his own words in "echo." What might Thomas mean? The answer, I take it, is in the title of the poem, "Waiting," and should be understood in light of the terms that Tillich has suggested. All one can do is wait.

It is not necessarily a very hopeful situation—and yet, for Thomas, it somehow seems to be. As Thomas says in his autobiography: "Who ever heard Him speak? We have to live virtually the whole of our lives in the presence of an invisible and mute God. But that was never a bar to anyone seeking to come into contact with Him. That is what prayer is" (*Autobiographies* 104).[27]

<h1 style="text-align:center">V</h1>

"The Shadow," a poem that remained unpublished until after Thomas's death (see SPMC 326–27), is a very interesting poem in many respects. It alludes to much that is important to Thomas throughout his career, and to much that I have tried to describe and detail here. The title itself is significant, since shadows figure in, and fall across, so many of Thomas's poems.[28] Indeed, he seems to be as obsessed with shadows as he is with mirrors (and they often seem to serve the same purposes). In his poem "Pre-Cambrian" (F 23) Thomas, thinking "of the centuries / six million of them," notices his shadow "sunning itself" on the rock where he walks, and he "remembers the lava" which formed that rock, just as (he imagines) the rock itself remembers it.[29] In *The Echoes Return Slow*, seeing his shadow again on these same pre-Cambrian rocks, Thomas calls it "the locker without a key, where all men's questions are stored" (ERS 70). Later in *The Echoes Return Slow*, in another of the prose poems, we read:

> There is a rock on the headland mentioned by Dafydd Nanmor in a *cywydd*. But it was already immemorially old in his day, five hundred years ago. The mind spun, vertigo not at the cliff's edge, but from the abyss of time. In the strong sun and the sea wind sometimes his shadow seemed more substantial than himself. (ERS 86)

Finally, in his autobiography Thomas writes again about these ancient rocks on the coast of the Llŷn peninsula:

> For the inhabitants, the age of the area was to be seen in its religious connections with the Celtic period. And yet, gazing on the pre-Cambrian rocks in Braich y Pwll, R. S. realized that he was in contact with something that had been there for a thousand million years. His head would spin. A timescale such as this raised all kinds of questions and problems. On seeing his shadow fall on such ancient rocks, he had to question himself in a different context and ask the same old question as before, "Who am I?" and the answer now came more emphatically than ever before, "No-one."
>
> But a no-one with a crown of light about his head. He would remember a verse from Pindar: "Man is a dream about a shadow." ("No One," in Davies, *R. S. Thomas: Autobiographies* 78)[30]

And he adds:

> It is so easy to believe in God when you are on your knees with your eyes closed, just as it is easy to be a Christian far away from the clamour and the trials of the world of people. But the memory would come of him on his knees in the church porch as far back as Manafon. He was neither inside nor outside, but on the border between the two, a ready symbol of contemporary man. (*Autobiographies* 78)

"The Shadow" opens with the enigmatic image of a presence of an absence. This is precisely the kind of image that Thomas has often used, typically in an overtly theological context. Here, "this shadow / . . . projected by no substance," "fall[s] across our path" and "entices us / up and up the twin-sided helix only to abandon us." Thus, it is "one we wrestle with," just as Jacob wrestled with the angel in "Waiting."

Thomas calls this shadow "the original / anonymity," a phrase that hints both at God's unknown or unacknowledged name and to the pervasive absence of his presence, and, at the same time, it suggests the anonymity that Thomas often attributed to himself as a "no one." This "original / anonymity . . . leaves presents" (this is clearly another pun, suggesting both God's "presents," and the absence of his "presence," or the presence of his absence) which makes "casualties happen / in so fortuitous a manner / that there is nobody to blame."[31]

Thomas concludes "The Shadow" with these lines:

> There is an invitation
> we receive, standing outside
>
> the laboratory of the self,
> either to go in
> and have everything explained
>
> or take mystery by the hand
> and be led faltering towards the love
> that is at the centre of its withdrawing.

The "love / that is at the centre of its withdrawing." These are echoes that do indeed return slow. For Thomas, love (as well as faith and hope, as the famous trinity of 1 Corinthians 13 has it), is central to his understanding and to his belief. This well-known biblical passage, interestingly enough, picks up the phrase "face to face" dealt with above. The text reads, "For now we see through a glass darkly; but then face to face: now I know in part; but then shall I know even as also I am known. And now abideth faith, hope, charity, these three; but the greatest of these is charity" (1 Cor 13:12-13; this is the translation in the King James Version, which Thomas prized. The passage in the Revised Standard Version, which is the better known, translates the Greek word, αγάπη, more literally as "love" rather than "charity."). But faith and hope (and thus love) are also always on the verge of disappearing, of being removed or recalled, taken back, or taken away entirely. Therefore, since we stand "outside" of the "laboratory of the self" (which is also a "laboratory of the spirit," as the title of one of Thomas's books has it), we must make a choice: either we must "go in[to]" that laboratory and hope to have "everything explained"—as unlikely as that might be, given what we know of Thomas and what his poems tell us—or, more likely, we must take the "mystery by the hand" and be led forward falteringly toward love (and thus to faith and hope), to follow after all three, just as we must attempt to find and follow God, even, and in spite of that fact that he always seems to be "withdrawing."

And when this happens, when—in spite of all the odds against any sure success—we make the attempt to find and to follow God, then, instead of being "left alone / With no echoes to the amen / [we] dreamed of,"[32] we may discover that the "spirit" may well "revolve . . . on itself" and be "without shadow, and the mysteries to be removed."[33] This is the essence of R. S. Thomas's hope, and finally, of his faith.

4

Poet-Priest of the Apocalyptic Mode

R. S. Thomas was a visible figure in the landscape of twentieth-century poetry for some time, but, until recently, only a background figure. That he has moved to the foreground is the result of a major shift in his work which began with the publication of *Pietà* (1966), in which Thomas turned abruptly toward the apocalyptic.

If, as Thomas J. J. Altizer has said,

> . . . ours is an apocalyptic or eschatological time, a time of the end of what we have known as history, consciousness, and society, then the Christian theologian is called to a new task, a task of mediating what he has been given as apocalyptic faith and vision to a new eschatological time and destiny.[1]

A. M. Allchin considers the relationship "of the poet who is also a priest" as raising "the question of the relationship between poetry and the Christian faith in its most acute form," since "on the one side there is the free creative activity of the imagination ranging over the whole creation, on the other the bound service of a crucified God."[2]

R. S. Thomas, as poet and priest, is ideally suited for confronting the apocalyptic moment of recent history, and he has stressed the equal importance of both his professions in defining his position. Although he acknowledges, as mentioned above, that "the two professions of priest and poet are so divorced in the public eye as to be quite beyond the possibility of symbiosis,"[3] Thomas joins them by saying, "My work . . . has to deal with the presentation of imaginative truth.[4]

At least since the publication of *H'm* (1972), Thomas worked within an apocalyptic mode, and in *Frequencies* (1978) his use of that mode came to climax. I wish to consider here this book and the apocalpytic tradition in some detail.

In *Frequencies* Thomas confronted the apocalyptic theme head-on in a way fully in keeping with his poetic as well as his theological traditions. Indeed, in *Frequencies*, the dark night of the soul first announced in *H'm* and further developed in *Laboratories of the Spirit* (1975), is brought to fruition in a way which, for Thomas, must have seemed inevitable. Whereas many contemporary apocalyptic poets follow a path which seems to end in a kind of philosophical black hole, Thomas followed the more traditional mystic way which, although it is every bit as dark, holds out a ray of hope at the end. In this sense Thomas is best considered in terms of his literal contemporaries and in terms of their more "classic" tradition, rather than in comparison with the younger apocalyptic poets at work around him. He is best compared to poets of his own age, or to poets like William Butler Yeats, Wallace Stevens, Dylan Thomas, and John Berryman, or perhaps to his closest temperamental contemporary, Theodore Roethke.

Both Thomas and Roethke lived and wrote "near the abyss," as Roethke said.[5] And for both poets the business of poetry and the business of life was almost identical, and was ultimately defined in theological ways. Roethke's well-known statement, "I believe that to go forward as a spiritual man it is necessary first to go back,"[6] is clearly exemplified in his work,[7] and a similar path might well be charted through Thomas's work. It is enough to note here that both Thomas and Roethke, each no doubt influenced by Yeats, rather visibly followed the mystic tradition toward what Roethke described in his essay "On 'Identity'" as his central poetic concern, an "heightened consciousness" which forces a "break . . . from I to Otherwise, or maybe even to Thee."[8]

Thomas has said:

> The need for revelation at all suggests an ultimate reality beyond human attainment, the *mysterium tremendum et fascinans*. And here, surely, is the common ground between religion and poetry. But there is the question of the mystic. To him the *Deus absconditus* is immediate; to the poet he is mediated. The mystic fails to mediate God adequately in so far as he is not a poet. The poet . . . shows his spiritual concern and his spiritual nature through the medium of language, the supreme symbol. The presentation of religious experience in the most inspired language is poetry.[9]

Roethke might be made to speak for both poets when he says, "God for me still remains someone to be confronted, to be dueled with."[10] Such a confrontation requires the poet to deal with the presence of the absence of self in the context of an ontological and epistemological crisis which only the poetry of apocalypse can confront. Thus, for Thomas (as for Roethke), the dark night of the soul hints inevitably at the final union with the divine."[11] Indeed, it seems that only in such a context (and here Thomas and Roethke differ) can one account for the otherwise incredible poetry which Thomas produced in the middle of his career—poetry which, I think, has often been conspicuously misread or misunderstood because it has not been considered in terms of the apocalyptic mode.[12] In Thomas's apocalyptic poetry there comes a time, at the end of a dark night, when light begins to flicker if not fully flame. This usually occurs only at the end of a considerable period of doubt and questioning, often over a fairly long period of time. Because Thomas was prolific and because he lived and worked within a fully defined and active apocalyptic period, and because of his theological training and his pastoral responsibilities, the time frame for his initiation into and his movement through the traditional stages of this process was significantly reduced. Thus, as soon after *H'm* and *Laboratories of the Spirit* as *Frequencies*, we find Thomas already into the final stage of the process.

Frequencies opens with "The Gap" (F 7–8) a poem which immediately announces the rupture which has occurred between his earlier poems and those in this book. Clearly, there has been a "gap," a shift. This "gap," this "narrowness that we stare / over into the eternal / silence that is the repose of God," is described, interestingly enough, in terms of the word "word." Here Thomas neatly combines his literary and his theological theme through reference to the "word"—which is at once the *words* of his poetry and the Word (λόγος) of his theological tradition. Words are the only way the Word may be able to cross over the gap between God and man.

"The Gap" begins:

> God woke, but the nightmare
> did not recede. Word by word
> the tower of speech grew.
> He looked at it from the air
> he reclined on. One word more and
> it would be on a level
> with him; vocabulary
> would have triumphed. He
> measured the thin gap
> with his mind. No, no, no,
> wider than that! But the nearness
> persisted. How to live with
> the fact, that was the feat
> now. How to take his rest

> on the edge of a chasm a
> word could bridge.

What then? The poet, having established the necessity for the process and initiated the apocalyptic possibility, becomes the vehicle for its completion. Thus, in "Present" (F 9), the second poem in *Frequencies,* we find Thomas saying:

> I am at the switchboard
> of the exchanges of the people
> of all time, receiving their messages
> whether I will or no.

The poet, at the point of "exchange" between powers, between man and God, is like the prophet of an earlier age. Much of the difficulty, for poet and prophet, for priest as intermediary, has to do with the fact that, as Thomas says in "The Porch" (F 10):

> He was like
> anyone else, a man with ears
> and eyes, . . .

that:

> he was driven
> to his knees and for no reason
> he knew, . . .

that:

> He had no power to pray.
> His back turned on the interior
> he looked out on a universe
> that was without knowledge
> of him and kept his place
> there for an hour on that lean
> threshold, neither outside nor in.

Therefore, if "you want to know his name? / It is forgotten" (F 10). And because of all of this "we wait for the // withheld answer to an insoluble / problem . . . in the torn / light that is about us" while "the air / echoes to . . . inaudible screaming" ("Fishing" [F 11]). In such a world, "God breathes within the confines / of our definition of him" ("The White Tiger" [F 45]). This then is the place for poetry in the world, a place which only poetry, prophecy having been banished, can fill.

As we have seen, Thomas speaks of "the common ground between religion and poetry" and deals specifically with the problem of the *Deus abscon-ditus* in terms of the contrast between the mystic and the poet. Where "the mystic fails to mediate God adequately insofar as he is not a poet," the "poet . . . shows his spiritual concern and his spiritual nature through the medium of language, the supreme symbol." Again, Thomas here defines religion "as embracing an experience of ultimate reality, and poetry as the imaginative presentation of such" and asserts that "the presentation of religious experience in the most inspired language is poetry."[13]

It is this "significance / of an absence, the deprecation / of what was there, the failure / to prove anything that proved this point" ("Henry James" [F 20]) which becomes crucial to an understanding of Thomas's recent poetry. This "periphery I comprehend" ("Night Sky" [F 18]) is complicated, even at times confusing, but is important to an understanding of Thomas's work.

"Shadows" (F 25) is a significant poem.

> I close my eyes.
> The darkness implies your presence,
> the shadow of your steep mind
> on my world. I shiver in it.
> It is not your light that
> can blind us; it is the splendour
> of darkness.
>   And so I listen
> instead and hear the language
> of silence, the sentence
> without an end. Is it I, then,
> who am being addressed? A God's words
> are for their own sake; we hear
> at our peril. Many of us have gone
> mad in the mastering
> of your medium.
>   I will open
> my eyes on a world where the problems
> remain but our doctrines
> protect us. The shadow of the bent cross
> is warmer than yours. I see how the sinners
> of history run in and out
> at its dark doors and are not confounded.

Here, in the inevitable chairoscuro of the apocalyptic mode, Thomas uses the play of light and dark in a traditional manner, but he combines the shadow imagery at the end of the poem with the image of the "bent cross." The cross, the crucial Christian symbol, has been used in varying ways by Thomas over the years. This "tree / with its roots in the mind's dark / . . . the original fork / in existence" (LS 5) has become his obsessive symbol for the complexities and doubts which modern man faces. The word "cross" is a crucial word in Thomas's vocabulary as well, suggesting simultaneously the cross of Christ and a point of intersection or exchange from one state to another. Such rhetorical crisscrossing is typical of Thomas's work, both thematically and structurally, and it functions effectively both ways.

In *Frequencies* the image of the cross occurs again, significantly, and finally, in the poem "Epiphany" (F 50) where

> Far
>
> off from his cross in the wrong
> season he sits at table
> with us with on his head
> the fool's cap of our paper money.

Dyson raises the question as to what such imagery suggests when he asks: "Is there something *in* the Cross . . . which by its actual nature bypasses theology and, at the level of language and image, testifies to itself?" He then suggests what may well be Thomas's answer to such a question:

> . . . the image of evolved man, alone in a creation where God is dead, is held in exact silhouette against the other image of Christ on the Cross, when God is absent. If the Christian religion has this paradox at its heart, perhaps it is not irrelevant to modern doubt after all, but simply an anticipation of it by 2000 years.[14]

Thomas had been exploring such themes and theses throughout his career, but, in the 1970s, he became obsessed with them. "In Church" (P 44), from *Pietà*, and "The Empty Church" (F 35), here in *Frequencies,* read as companion poems and make for an interesting comparison in terms of their assumptions and in terms of Thomas's apocalyptic obsessions.

"In Church" attempts to "analyse" the quality of the silence after a service. The speaker, in the emptied church, has "stopped to listen" as the caught air "recomposes itself" for the vigil it has kept since the church was built around it. The prayers of the congregation have failed to animate it. Only the darkness is alive, with the blind bats and the man's breath, as he tests "his faith on emptiness," using his own air (his breath) to compose and recompose the prayers of his poem, "nailing his questions one by one to an untenanted cross."

In "The Empty Church" the church itself is a "stone trap" to which men have hoped to attract God "like some huge moth." But, having been burned once before, "He will not come any more to our lure." The church, as "stone trap," is to the world what the heart (also stone) is to man: both are traps to catch God. Man's prayers are like flint struck on his stone heart in the hope of creating a spark which will ignite—if only to create an illusion ("the shadow of someone greater than I can understand") on the empty wall of the church.

In both of these poems, as in so many of Thomas's poems, the emptiness becomes a sign or symbol for an original presence which it has displaced or replaced: hence the "untenanted cross"; the "empty church."[15]

"The Possession" (F 33) is an important transitional poem. The speaker, "a religious man," "looking around . . . with . . . worried eyes / at the emptiness," wants to believe. "There must be something," he says—even as he thinks there is "nobody there!" His "fused prayers" only allow him to reflect on the "infinite darkness between points of light" which he knows are only stars.

Thomas has always been drawn to images of reflection, and he uses these images in several ways simultaneously.[16] Reflection suggests contemplation, distortion, and meditation as well as the throwing back, shadow-like, as pictures or echoes, of images or sounds from mirrors or mirror-like surfaces. Perhaps something very much like Heidegger's notion of man's "throwness" is implied by Thomas's use of such images. Various meanings come to bear on lines like "All I have is a piece / of the universal mind that reflects / infinite darkness between points of light" (F 33). Indeed, as Calvin Bedient discovered, even in Thomas's early work, there is an "ambiguity of reflection" which is the "central and stubborn meaning" of his poetry.[17]

The poems which immediately follow "The Possession"—"Gone?" (F 34) and "The Empty Church" (F 35)—focus the transition which "The Possession" details, just as "Waiting" (F 32), the poem which immediately precedes "The Possession," implies it. In "Waiting" the speaker "leaning far out / over an immense depth," speaks God's name and then waits "somewhere between faith and doubt, / for the *echoes* of its arrival" (my italics).[18]

The next important poem, intriguingly enough, is called "Perhaps" (F 39). It begins:

> His intellect was the clear mirror
> he looked in and saw the machinery of God
> assemble itself? It was one that reflected
> the emptiness that was where God
> should have been. The mind's tools had
> no power convincingly to put him
> together. Looking in that mirror was a journey
> through hill mist where, the higher
> one ascends, the poorer the visibility
> becomes.

This:

> . . . could have led to despair
> but for the consciousness of a presence
> behind him, whose breath clouding
> that looking-glass proved that it was alive.
> To learn to distrust the distrust
> of feeling—this then was the next step
> for the seeker?

Here, the "clear mirror" of the intellect reflects on the "emptiness . . . where / God should have been," but it also discovers that man's mind is unable to make of these imaginary figments anything substantial, and that his "reflections"[19] become increasingly misty "the higher / one ascends." Curiously, the breath clouding the mirror "proved" the "consciousness" of "a presence" which is absent. This paradox is followed by a series of paradoxes, each detailing an absence which seems to imply a presence, or the presence of an absence: the "crossing / of a receding boundary which did not exist"; the yielding "to an unfelt pressure"; the "looking up / into invisible eyes." All of these images suggest the possibility, even the plausibility (note that the title is *not* a question, even though much of the poem is) of "the ubiquity of a vast concern" with which the poem ends. This is an important inching forward toward the realization of the apocalyptic moment in which *Frequencies* ends.

"Emerging" (F 41), a poem which draws some direct parallels between this book and *Laboratories of the Spirit* (the opening poem of *Laboratories* is also entitled "Emerging," see LS 1), begins a dialogue between the speaker and himself which will run to the end of the book. Indeed, this "pilgrimage," as "Pilgrimages" (F 51–52), the last poem in *Frequencies* would have it, is Thomas's parallel with and response to the age-old journey to a holy place. The difference is that his pilgrimage is not a physical journey but a metaphysical quest, and it arrives not at a site but at insight.

"Emerging" (F 41) reads:

> Well, I said, better to wait
> for him on some peninsula
> of the spirit. Surely for one
> with patience he will happen by
> once in a while. It was the heart
> spoke. The mind, sceptical as always
> of the anthropomorphisms
> of the fancy, knew he must be put together
> like a poem or a composition
> in music, that what he conforms to
> is art. A promontory is a bare

    place; no God leans down
    out of the air to take the hand
    extended to him. The generations have
    watched there
    in vain. We are beginning to see
    now it is matter is the scaffolding
    of spirit; that the poem emerges
    from morphemes and phonemes; that
    as form in sculpture is the prisoner
    of the hard rock, so in everyday life
    it is the plain facts and natural happenings
    that conceal God and reveal him to us
    little by little under the mind's tooling.

"[W]hat he conforms to / is art." ". . . [H]e must be put together / like a poem or a composition / in music. . . ."[20] This God, if he is there, if he was ever there, must be found by the mind moving and merging upon itself. Through such musings, through poetry and music, things unseen but sensed begin to emerge until, finally, "This great absence / that is like a presence" ("The Absence" [F 48]) presents itself for the mind's consideration. But even such possibilities, illusive and perhaps hallucinatory, are transitory, temporary structures, "scaffoldings" built to support and sustain something more stationary and permanent. This suggestion is in keeping with traditional apocalyptic notions, which always portend something more permanent—and imminent; something, as Thomas would have it, that is still "emerging." Such self-creation, "the mind's tooling," is a mental operation, a metaphorical / metaphysical maneuver for the sake of some kind of sanity in the midst of a world gone (and continuing to go) awry.[21]

As we look at the remaining poems in *Frequencies* it is difficult not to notice how much Thomas, poet and priest, must have wrestled with such notions. He has been able to deal with such matters, perhaps been forced to such answers, because he found himself living "in a contemporary / dwelling in country that / is being consumed"; because he is "A being with no / view but out upon the uncertainties / of the imperatives of science" ("Semi-Detached" [F 42]). And what he found and brought forward for view was something as elusive and rare as a white tiger, something that is "breathing / as you can imagine that / God breathes within the confines / of our definition of him" ("The White Tiger" [CP 358]). Here, like the rare bird in "Sea-Watching" (LS 64), "It is when one is not looking, / at times one is not there / that it comes," and thus "its absence / was as its presence." This presence of an absence is typical of poems in the apocalyptic mode, and it is Thomas's answer to the questions he has posed.

In short, if questions have been raised, answers are needed. Appropriately enough, "The Answer" (F 46) immediately follows. In it the poet asks, "Is there no way / other than thought of answering / its challenge?" The answer he makes to his question is the priest's answer, given in theological terms.

> There is an anticipation
> of it to the point of
> dying. There have been times
> when, after long on my knees
> in a cold chancel, a stone has rolled
> from my mind, and I have looked
> in and seen the old questions lie
> folded and in a place
> by themselves, like the piled
> graveclothes of love's risen body.

But if this is now—or ever was—an answer, it is not answer enough to sustain man, as the next poem, "The Film of God" (F 47), makes clear. Even though we now have cameras "sensitive to / an absence as to a presence," they seem to "see" nothing "and we are still waiting." In such circumstances, what must one do?

"The Absence" (F 48) is Thomas's answer.

> It is this great absence
> that is like a presence, that compels
> me to address it without hope
> of a reply. It is a room I enter
>
> from which someone has just
> gone, the vestibule for the arrival
> of one who has not yet come.
> I modernise the anachronism
>
> of my language, but he is no more here
> than before. Genes and molecules
> have no more power to call
> him up than the incense of the Hebrews
>
> at their altars. My equations fail
> as my words do. What resource have I
> other than the emptiness without him of my whole
> being, a vacuum he may not abhor?

"The Absence" is the climax of Thomas's poetry in the apocalyptic mode, and it has behind it the whole sequence of his thinking from *H'm* onward.

The central poem (and the thematic center) of *H'm* is "Via Negativa" (H'm 16), a poem in which God is defined as:

> . . . that great absence
> In our lives, the empty silence
> Within, the place where we go
> Seeking, not in hope to
> Arrive or find.

Again, the significance of the absence of God's presence, a typical apocalyptic obsession, haunts all of Thomas's poetry since *H'm*. For Thomas, this was "the common ground between religion and poetry."[22] It is this prescient presence of absence which Thomas, as poet, tries to "mediate." If God "keeps the interstices / In our knowledge," if God is only "the darkness / Between stars," still we can posit his presence *by* his absence. With such faith, "We put our hands in / His side hoping to find / It warm" ("Via Negativa" [H'm 16]). In such a situation, "new explorers" can "change our lives" because they can "interpret absence / as presence," as Thomas says in his poem called simply "They" (WI 28).

Thus, "The Absence" (F 48) begins with the conclusion to which Thomas's poetry of the apocalyptic mode has come, as "this great absence / that is like a presence . . . compels / me to address it." Into this room "from which someone has just / gone, the vestibule for the arrival / of one who has not yet come," the speaker enters in awe only to discover that "he is no more here / than before." Such a conclusion after so long a quest leaves the poet on the verge of ultimate despair as he acknowledges that even these words have failed to evoke anything but absence. All that is left to hope beyond hope for is that the emptiness that "his" absence makes in the "whole / being" of the poet may, paradoxically, elicit a "vacuum he may not abhor." This is a curious argument. Still, if one is in the habit of finding absences mysteriously filled with presences, it is possible to assume that a vacuum would be an open invitation to such a presence and that such a filling, were it to occur, would ultimately be as close as man could come to the fulfilling of his need for a presence beyond himself.

The apocalyptic moment having been defined in this inevitably paradoxical way, *Frequencies* draws quickly to a close. The three remaining poems each raise again what has become by now Thomas's constant theme, but they do something interesting and slightly different with it by forcing outward questions inward, into the mind's domain. "Balance" (F 49), which begins by briefly invoking Kierkegaard,[23] states "I have abandoned / my theories, the easier certainties / of belief," and concludes with two questions:

> Is there a place
> here for the spirit? Is there time
> on this brief platform for anything
> other than mind's failure to explain itself?

"Epiphany" (F 50), likewise, opens with a question: "Three kings?" The answer to the question of the manifestation of divine presence in the world is provided by the very Christ figure who "Far / off from his cross in the wrong / season . . . sits at table / with us with on his head / the fool's cap of our paper money." Thomas's pun on "fool's cap" is typical. On the one hand the dunce's cap which the savior wears is meant to remind us of our inability to see and understand anything beyond the immediate reality of our "paper money," symbol of a reality we never see but nonetheless believe in. On the other hand, the "fool's cap" may simply be a reference to a sheet of standard size writing paper, called fool's cap in Britain. This meaning may imply that Thomas is turning the irony another time, suggesting that the paper which holds the words of the epiphanic moment is used to make mockery of the moment.

"Pilgrimages" (F 51–52) is the final poem in *Frequencies*. It begins:

> There is an island there is no going
> to but in a small boat the way
> the saints went, travelling the gallery
> of the frightened faces of
> the long-drowned, munching the gravel
> of its beaches. So I have gone
> up the salt land to the building
> with the stone altar and the candles
> gone out, and kneeled and lifted
> my eyes to the furious gargoyle
> of the owl that is like a god
> gone small and resentful.

The pilgrim asks, "Am I too late?" Then he wonders, "Were they too late also, those / first pilgrims?" It is a question which echoes down the centuries, and it is the question which haunts Thomas's recent work, *his* pilgrimage, as he acknowledges here at the end of it: "It is I / who ask." "He is such a fast / God, always before us and / leaving as we arrive." "There is no time on this island, . . . the tide / has no clock" and "events / are dateless." Thomas acknowledges that his quest is not unique, but typical—however unique it is for him at the moment. He asks:

> Was the pilgrimage
> I made to come to my own
> self, to learn that in times

> like these and for one like me
> God will never be plain and
> out there, but dark rather and
> inexplicable, as though he were in here?

Thus, *Frequencies* ends—with an answer that is also a question. It is a question with which the poetry of apocalypse has always had to deal since answers are never, finally, fully available. The pilgrimage itself must be answer enough.

Frequencies ends, but the reverberations of this evocative book continue as the various accumulated meanings of the title work back and forth through the poems and through our readings of them. In "One Way," in *Between Here and Now* (BHN 95), Thomas speaks of "refining / my technique, signalling / to him on the frequencies / I commanded"—but without success. Perhaps his success was more definitive on the human level. But as he said in "Threshold," the final poem of *Between Here and Now* (BHN 110), "what balance is needed at / the edges of such an abyss."

Aptly enough, the last poem in Thomas's next book, *Later Poems 1972–1982*, was titled "Prayer" (LP 214). In it Thomas imagines his grave, "not too far from Baudelaire," and "not too far" from "the tree of science":

> somewhere within sight
> of the tree of poetry
> that is eternity wearing
> the green leaves of time.

In this Edenic metaphor for present existence, the "tree of poetry" becomes, for Thomas, equivalent to the tree of knowledge. And the fall into the present carries with it the prayer that, in an apocalyptic age, the poet-priest may be able to find salvation in the word, if not in the world.

What balance is needed on the edge of such an abyss.

5

Mirrors and Mirror Imagery

Life *may certainly not enter into philosophical discourse other than as* presence *to a reflection.*

—Emmanuel Levinas

He scratched on invisible
glass.

—R. S. Thomas

I

During his long career R. S. Thomas grew accustomed, and accustomed his readers, to seeing things in terms of mirrors and mirror images. Such images are, as he himself has acknowledged, one of his obsessions.[1] Even if such "reflections" are as old as poetry itself, Thomas has worked his own very modern and quite sophisticated variations on them, utilizing them as a way of defining his most insistent theme and as a means of elaborating his rather unique technique. He has thus brought forward into our day new ways of "looking" at this long poetic tradition, as well as having provided us with a fascinating way of looking at, of evaluating, his own considerable poetic output.

Of the many ways of reflecting on the mirrors and the omnipresent mirror images in Thomas's poetry, some are old, obvious, well known, and have frequently been used before. There is, for instance, what might be called his use of "human mirrors"—characters who are simply seen as emblems of the self. One such character, clearly the most obvious and probably the most important in Thomas's work, is Iago Prytherch, the Welsh peasant farmer Thomas has contemplated closely over the years, beginning with a series of powerful early poems about him. Indeed, in "A Peasant" (SF 14), Thomas described Prytherch as that "ordinary man of the bald Welsh hills," with his "frightening . . . vacancy" of mind, and called him "your prototype."

There are also many literal mirrors in Thomas's canon. Some of them are natural mirrors, such as pools of water, replete with their inevitably mythic or romantic trappings, which afford glimpses of *doppelgängers* or of Narcissus-like characters lurking within them. In the autobiographical poem "A Life" (EA 52), for instance, we find Thomas, "Visionary only / in his perception of an horizon / beyond the horizon," personally and poetically appearing as a Narcissus-like figure, "Saving his face / in verse," but nevertheless "tortured" (in a rather elaborately tortured metaphor) "by the whisperers behind / the mirror."[2]

And there are poems based on paintings, poems which reflect back and forth between poet and painter, as if one or the other (or both) were a mirror. "Gallery" (D 16) is an obvious example. In it Thomas tells us that "It is not [the paintings that] // are being looked at / but *we* by faces / which over the centuries // keep their repose" (my italics). Likewise, in "Similarities" (EA 24), we find "the face / that is life's trophy," staring from another "gallery," a face before which, "corrected by a resemblance," one becomes "silent." One of the most interesting of the portrait poems is "Self-Portrait" (LS 27). In it a mirror reflects an image quite surprisingly different from the one the spectator expected to find there—not at all "the portrait /   . . . posed for."[3]

But perhaps the most important and the most fascinating mirrors in Thomas's poetry are those in which, through the "reflections" that come from and through them, Thomas grapples with the relationship between God and the man "made in [God's] own image"—as if the metaphor itself were, or had become, a mirror. It is these mirrors and this mirror imagery, these "reflections," that I want to look at specifically in this chapter.

Absence—the presence of an absence, a *Deus absconditus*—haunted Thomas's mind and imagination throughout his career, but in the 1970s his insistence on the *presence* of this absence took on a double urgency—and a doubled ambiguity. The empty mirror, like "The Empty Church" (F 35) of one of his most famous poems, is seen or described as a trap tempting God to come into it, to make himself visible, and thus available, to man. But, we are told, God, having "burned himself / before in the human flame . . . will not come any more" to such a "lure." Even as man waits "upon / him as a mirror / . . . waits upon absence" (C 45)—even if one awaits or anticipates, looks forward to the possibility of some presence that might appear in, or out of, the mirror's "absence"—the absence, just as insistently as man anticipates its appearance, itself waits, holds itself back from appearing, from presenting itself as presence. Indeed, it is as if any such "presence" is as "illimitable / as its absence" (C 48). And thus the presence of this absence vanquishes any, or all, prospects of God's appearance, his presence. Therefore, the only hope for the "believer" is the prospect that he might be "ambushed in a mirror" (ERS 72), by the "concealed likeness" in his "looking-glass"—a likeness that is "always ahead [of him] in its [own] ambush." However, "with the refinement of the mirror," there occurs only "the refinement of [the] dilemma" (ERS 108).

From such a concealed position, where any suspected presence within the mirror is only "visible" as absence, the presence outside the mirror, the presence looking into it, lurking we might say within it, must be examined and evaluated. But this is to court Narcissism, egotism, or illusion—even, perhaps, all three. In such a situation one must imagine that *all* presences are their own mirrors or, as Thomas says in a poem entitled "Present" (F 9), they are "the mirror[s] / of a mirror, effortlessly repeating / [one's own] reflections."

II

These kinds of "reflections," then, became, in the second half of Thomas's career, his insistent thesis, his dominant theme. It is a theme that has significant, multifold, ramifications—poetically, philosophically, and theologically. And when we begin to think of these ramifications, to think them through, and to think *through* them, we rather quickly think of a philosopher like Emmanuel Levinas. Levinas, a student of both Edmund Husserl and Martin Heidegger, carried out the phenomenological agenda in his own rather uniquely complicated way, but in a way that might fruitfully serve to illuminate R. S. Thomas's central theological thesis in terms of his obsession with such mirrored reflections.[4]

Levinas sought to describe and to delineate an encounter with an "Other" that is both immediate and "present" at the same time that it is absent and transcendent. This, of course, caused him to court criticism from thinkers primarily obsessed with questions of ontology, and it also took him toward phenomenological limits. At the risk of drastically over-simplifying his complex thought, let me try briefly to summarize Levinas's description and analysis of "otherness" and of "the Other" in terms of the ways that I think his thought might fruitfully be associated with Thomas's poetry.

Going back to Husserl's *Cartesian Meditations* and *Phenomenological Psychology*[5] as primary sources, Levinas extracted for his own use Husserl's liberation of philosophy from the grip of "naturalist" epistemology through his reconsideration of the "phenomenon." However, Levinas criticized Husserl's solipsistic description of the Other as a reflection of the self, and he attempted to show that the "existence of transcendental Egos other than [one's] own in effect leaves no place for the Other *as* Other" (italics added).[6]

Furthermore, Levinas argued that there is "a relationship irreducible to adversity" in which "the Other [*Autre*], instead of alienating the uniqueness of the Same . . . only calls the Same from the depths of himself toward what is deeper than himself"—that is, "the Other" calls "'the Same' at and to the depths of himself."[7] Starting from this Other, then, Levinas (by way of Husserl) describes "transcendental subjectivity" as the "tearing [of] the I from its isolation in itself."[8] Therefore, the attempt to "reach the other," to attempt communication, can only be "realized" in terms of a "relationship with the Other that is cast in . . . language," even though the "other is maintained and confirmed in his heterogeneity as soon as one calls upon him."[9] But, Levinas asks, "What then can be this relationship with an absence radically withdrawn from disclosure and from dissimulation?" And he answers, "The other proceeds from the absolutely absent. His relationship with the absolutely absent from which he comes *does not indicate, does not reveal* this absent; and yet the absent has a meaning. . . ."[10] In short, the Other remains Other at the same time that it seems, simultaneously, to be part of the self, a self that Levinas calls "the Same."[11]

For Levinas, then, God, as "the Other," can be approached, but he can never be reached. God's "Otherness" is neither a presence nor an absence, but a "trace"—a trace that is "transcendent to the point of absence."[12] In short, "God is not the supreme Other, but rather the absent condition—or the incondition as Levinas frequently writes—of the encounter with the Other."[13] That is, "Levinas does not offer a personal God"; instead, "he depicts a trace or near-absence." And thus his "is no comfortable religion providing divine succour in need, or answers to questions beyond our competence." Indeed, for Levinas, "the question is more important than the answer, the search more urgent than the solution."[14]

For Levinas, philosophy, initially born of religion, becomes with it one of "two distinct moments" of a single spiritual process which he describes as "*the approach* of transcendence."[15] And perhaps then, finally, it is the case that discussions of such relationships, and attempts to understand them, can only be done (if they can be done or understood at all) in philosophy or theology—or in poetry.

III

The mirror melts and moulds itself and moves
And catches from nowhere brightly-burning breath.

. . .

And one trembles to be so understood and, at last,
To understand. . . .

—Wallace Stevens

And thus, with these considerations in mind, let us turn back to R. S. Thomas, who, in his own way, combines the disciplines of philosophy and theology as he considers such questions—or as he questions such answers. For Thomas, as for phenomenological philosophy and theology, the process is often enough a manipulation of metaphors and of the meanings of metaphors.

Mirrors and mirror imagery appear early on in Thomas's work. Usually, in the early work, this imagery is used in the rather obvious and automatic ways that I have already suggested and briefly described above. Perhaps the first crucial instance of Thomas's use of a mirror image occurs in his first book, *The Stones of the Field*, when he refers to an "unscrubbed" floor that "Is no mirror for the preening sun / at the cracked lattice" of the window (see "Ire" in SF 40). This is an interesting image in several senses, but it is perhaps most significant in that it is ultimately a double—and a negative—use of the mirror, an example of a mirror that fails in its primary purpose. The prospect of the illuminating light of the "preening" anthropomorphic sun, even though it shines through a "cracked lattice," is eliminated by the unscrubbed, dirty floor it shines in on. And thus this prospective mirror is made useless, blank or empty, a void, and voided. In short, it becomes a vehicle whose purpose is defeated by being deflected.[16]

But perhaps the first important poem in Thomas's canon to make overt use of the theological implications of mirror imagery is "Judgment Day" (T 20). "Judgment Day" is based on the reference in Genesis to man having been made in God's image. But Thomas conflates the biblical description of man's creation with man's final "judgment day" in terms of a dual, mirror-like, doubled "reflection" on the nature of God and man and on the reciprocal relationship between them. The poem begins in a self-reflective moment with a man seeing himself with clean eyes, with clarified vision:

> Yes, that's how I was,
> I know that face.

This man goes on to describe himself accurately and honestly in terms of "The knot of life" that he was tied to at the time of his creation. And then, suddenly, this man turns to God and prays to be taken into death, on this day of his judgment, as someone else, an other and new man, a man different from, and better than (he now sees) the one he has been. And in envisioning his new "birth" at the very moment of death—this rebirth into another (after)life—he envisions and describes it in terms of an amazing and complicated ontological mirror image, describing man's creation as God's breathing on a mirror, and man's death as God breathing again on that same mirror, erasing it, emptying it, voiding it in the same way that he first filled it. The basis for Thomas's metaphor is, of course, biblical. In Genesis God is described as having created the world through speech, breath—"And God said. . . ."[17] But Thomas here uniquely adds the complicating metaphor of the mirror, a metaphor which suggests rather startling theological ramifications, since the metaphor seems to suggest that God looked into a mirror, saw *himself*, and then decided to *make man in his own image.* He did so by breathing on the mirror. In terms of this trope, God, in creating man by *breathing* him in the mirror, by breathing into him the breath of life, simultaneously obliterates or replaces his own image. In its place he creates an "other"—an *other* that is initially an image in a mirror, an *other* that is similar to, but separate from himself, an *other* that he will name man.

But then, in the now of the poem, at the time of his final "Judgment Day," as he is about to be taken back by the God who created him, man, seeing himself as he is, or as he has become, consciously desires to be "blurred out," killed off, replaced, by God's *re*-doing of the original act of creation, by his breathing again on the mirror, by that second breath—a second creative, but simultaneously destructive act—destroying his own earlier creation. What Thomas suggests here is quite intriguing from a theological point of view—since when God breathes on the mirror this second time he blurs the first image, the image of man, out. But, when the mirror clears of God's second blown breath, the "original" image of God himself will (apparently) be restored to the mirror, will replace or take the place of the *displaced* image of man. Either that, or the mirror will become empty, will hold only the presence of absence. In one sense then, the man making this request on this "judgment day" is simply asking to be "breathed away" so that God, source of both breath and life, can be "reborn" or restored. In this way man can again become one with God. (This process, of course, both reverses the act of man's creation and reverses the sacrifice that God made for man by becoming man. But, at the same time, it shows that man has learned the lesson, that man has finally "found" the God hidden in the mirror—where before, when he looked into the mirror, he had only seen himself.) Even so, at the judgment day of "Judgment Day" (T 20) man seems not fully or entirely content with his own final request. And Thomas, in his typically complex way (and even though he acknowledges that these are rather "bleak reflections"), puts the man's final request in the form of a prayer: "Lord, breathe once more / On that . . . mirror, / Let me be lost / . . . for ever. . . . / Let me go back"

> . . . to undo
> The knot of life
> That was tied there.

IV

> *I would be the mirror*
> *of a mirror, effortlessly repeating*
> *my reflections.*
>
> —R. S. Thomas

There are many poems between "Judgment Day" and Thomas's most recent work that suggest the sequences and the consequences of such obsessions with mirrors and mirror imagery in terms of the turns of the development of his theological themes and theses. However, for our purposes here, a brief sampling of them will have to suffice.

Perhaps Thomas puts these "bleak reflections" most clearly in a poem entitled "Scenes" in *Laboratories of the Spirit* (LS 44), one of his first books to grapple meaningfully with his dominant theological theme. In "Scenes" (cf. seens) Thomas says:

> So in the huge night,
> awakening, I have re-interpreted
> the stars' signals and seen the reflection
> in an eternal mirror of the mystery
> terrifying enough to be named Love.

In another poem in *Laboratories of the Spirit*, one appropriately enough entitled "Probing" (LS 23–24), Thomas intriguingly combines a mirror-like image with an epistemological twist to suggest a phenomenological thesis, as he argues that "we never awaken / from the compulsiveness of the mind's / stare into the lenses' furious interiors." In the same book we encounter a "pure mirror / of water" to which "a face" comes, looks into it, and sees only absence, as if it were an empty mirror ("Gone" [LS 55]). In "Present" (F 9) Thomas, who "would be the mirror / of a mirror, effortlessly repeating / my reflections," speaks of "engaging" with philosophy and thus of being "at the switchboard / of the exchanges of the people / of all time." Then, bringing together many of these "reflections," catching up the imagery of "Judgment

Day," and looking forward to other poems and reflections still to come, in a poem enigmatically entitled "Perhaps" (F 39) Thomas raises a series of questions that he will spend much of the rest of his career trying to answer—or to ask further questions about.

> His intellect was the clear mirror
> he looked in and saw the machinery of God
> assemble itself? It was one that reflected
> the emptiness that was where God
> should have been. The mind's tools had
> no power convincingly to put him
> together. Looking in that mirror was a journey
> through hill mist where, the higher
> one ascends, the poorer the visibility
> becomes. It could have led to despair
> but for the consciousness of a presence
> behind him, whose breath clouding
> that looking-glass proved that it was alive.
> To learn to distrust the distrust
> of feeling — this then was the next step
> for the seeker? To suffer himself to be persuaded
> of intentions in being other than the crossing
> of a receding boundary which did not exist?
> To yield to an unfelt pressure that, irresistible
> in itself, had the character of everything
> but coercion? To believe, looking up
> into invisible eyes shielded against love's
> glare, in the ubiquity of a vast concern?

And thus, sitting "down by the still pool / in the wind, waiting for the unknown / visitant's quickening of its surface" ("Bequest" [EA 43]), after having "crawled out . . . / far as I dare on to a bough / of country that is suspended / between sky and sea," Thomas wonders if he can "console [him]self / with reflections?"—even as he acknowledges that "There are // times even the mirror / is misted as by one breathing / over my shoulder" ("Retirement" [EA 38]). Still, Thomas finds that even "With the refinement of the mirror" (ERS 108)—and in spite of the various games he plays with mirrors, the metaphors he makes "as though to take by surprise // the self that is my familiar" ("Looking Glass" [EA 40])—"there occur[s] only the refinement of [the] dilemma" that "life" must still be "brought round to confront" an "image in an oblique / glass" (ERS 109).

In *Counterpoint* (C 12) Thomas asks:

What is the virginity
of mirrors? Are they surfaces
of fathoms which mind
clouds when examining itself
too closely?

And then, in lines that point forward toward his fullest investigation of the theme of mirrors and mirror imagery, Thomas, "hungry for meaning / at life's pane" (an interesting pun), begins to believe that the face he sees disappearing, a face that blurs or that moves in and out of focus, is both God himself, glimpsed briefly, and also his own face, in life and in death, "a skull / brushed by a smile," and that these two "faces" are superimposed upon one another. This image of a "face, vague / but compelling" is, however, bleared "over as much with my shortness / of faith as of breath" (C 46)—as Thomas turns the image, adding an intriguing twist, an "infinite counterpoint / between mirror and mirror" (MHT 82)[18] on the "judgment day" referred to above.

No Truce with the Furies, Thomas's final book, a book which brings so many of his themes and theses to climax, likewise brings to climax his use of mirrors and mirror images and their metaphoric treatment in terms of his obsession with the Other in both philosophical and theological ways. There are several poems in *No Truce With The Furies* that we ought to look at.

The first of these is "Fathoms" (NTF 10). "Fathoms" is a brief autobiography. It begins with a natural mirror image—"Young I visited / this pool." And then, "In the middle years / visited it again." Then Thomas jumps forward to the present, and describes himself as if "on the margin / of eternity," at the point of contemplating his own "dissolution." Dissolution is a fascinating word in the context, and also in terms of the mirror metaphor the poem is built around. "Dissolution," related to both "dissoluble" and to "dissolve," is a word that clearly fits a context of watery pools in which things appear and disappear, into which, Narcissus-like, one peers and sees oneself or in which other presences and reflections can be seen, singly or simultaneously. Thomas, "on the margin / of eternity," facing *disill*usion and *dissol*ution, and fearing misapprehension, seeks to see and to find in the mirror of contemplation here beside this pool the "truth" of his life and of the human condition. He hopes, he says, to be able to "dredge up the truth." He describes his situation as "nothing but [a] self / looking up at the self / looking down."

In addition to the suggestion of a bifurcated self there also seems to be in these lines a second self, an Other, or another "self," that, as Thomas looks "up," looks "down" at him. As I have tried to show elsewhere, these doubled "selves" here in "Fathoms" may well have behind them (since Kierkegaard is invoked at the end of Thomas's poem) Kierkegaard's dual notions of "double

reflection," "inwardness," and "indirect communication."[19] But more impor-
tantly for our purposes, Thomas's "starings" here seem to suggest an "other"
who is not simply "self" but something or someone beyond the self—some-
thing or someone who is as intent on staring back at him as he, Thomas, is
on staring "up" at it.

In "S. K.," another poem in *No Truce with the Furies* (NTF 15–17),
Kierkegaard again provides Thomas with a way of reflecting on such ques-
tions.[20] With "truth" as his goal, as it was at the end of "Fathoms," Thomas
here again considers the question of the self in terms of a mirrored self-image
and also in terms of an "other" who may be either a mirror image of the self
as "Same," or a literal "other," or who may be the "Other" which is God—or
all three simultaneously.

"Imagining / from his emphasis on the self // that God is not other,"
Thomas, with Kierkegaard, discovers that "thought" is "brought to bay by a
truth / as inscrutable as its reflection." If such dazzlingly explosive thoughts
are "truths" as "inscrutable" as any "reflections" that can be made about
them, Thomas continues to contemplate and explore such thoughts and such
truths, and he comes to his conclusions in interestingly complex theological
statements—posed, as is typical of him, in a series of questions which often
describe the relationships between man and God in the context of overt mir-
ror images. First, following both Kierkegaard and his own sequence of specu-
lations in "Judgment Day" (T 20), in "S. K." Thomas raises the "heresy" of
seeing "the self / as God" (NTF 17), and then he immediately puts everything
into the context of prayer, in which, he says, there occurs an "exchange / of
places between [an] I and [a] thou" (NTF 17)[21] Then he asks whether such
an "emphasis / on the subjective" results only in "soliloquy" (NTF 17). The
final question, asked in the final lines of the poem, is an "answer" to these
questions—even as it poses another—and it is couched in a concluding mir-
ror image:

> Is prayer
> not a glass that beginning
> in obscurity . . .
> the longer we stare
> into the clearer becomes
> the reflection of a countenance
> in it other than our own?

Thomas here seems to suggest that prayer *is* a "glass," a mirror, and that that
glass, stared into long enough or looked at hard enough, may finally begin to
clear, and to suggest the possibility of a presence in it—a "countenance . . .
other than our own."

This "presence" is simultaneously present and absent. It is an "Other" that is both self and other; an "Other" that may well be God; an "Other" who, although not present, *is present as absence,* in the mirror of man's—or at least of R. S. Thomas's—mind.

6

Gaps in the Poetry of R. S. Thomas

Today, gaps speak as loudly as presences, and no story is complete without its absences.

—John W. Kronik[1]

R. S. Thomas, like all great poets, is a poet of obsessions. His obsessions (beyond the typical tics and tricks of language which are part of every poet's fingerprints on the page), his quintessential themes (as he turns them through his mind and through his characteristically spare lines, as he holds them fixed but freely lets them flow), have, we find in reading and rereading him, become, subtly and quite quickly, our own obsessions too, and, indeed, finally, our own possessions as much as they are his.

One reason that Thomas is so obsessed, and so possesses us, is that he has had, throughout his life and art, a singly dominant theme. This theme has come to climax twice: first, and most importantly for his literary work, in *Frequencies* (1978), and second, more in terms of Thomas's own personal life, in *The Echoes Return Slow* (1988). These books are two of his strongest individual collections, and taken together they contain some of his finest work, as well as much of what we need to know about him personally, as man and priest and poet.

The Echoes Return Slow is much the more personal of the two books and is, in some ways, the most unique of all of Thomas's books, both structurally and thematically. The prose-poem paragraphs which face the lined poems page by page provide a running commentary on Thomas's life (they need to be read along with his autobiographical *Neb*),[2] while the accompanying poems in lines are some of the most beautiful of all of Thomas's lyrics. (Is there any poem in his canon, for instance, more lovely than "There are nights that are so still," ERS 79?) *The Echoes Return Slow* may also be the most demanding of Thomas's books, from a critical point of view, since it requires a more thorough understanding of his biography than is yet available, or may ever be available.[3] The nuances in *The Echoes Return Slow*, as indeed the title itself suggests, will no doubt take years to be fully heard or unraveled.

Frequencies, on the other hand, both because it may be Thomas's single strongest volume of poetry per se and because it contains the clearest evidence of his continuing obsessions and of the dominating theme that runs throughout his work, is the book I want to concentrate on here.

However, before turning to the poems themselves, Thomas's title is worthy of some attention because of its significance for the theme of this book as well as for Thomas's work in toto.

No reader of Thomas can have failed to notice how often he uses a single word as title for one of his poems, or for one of his books. Four of his most important books (*Tares, Pietà, H'm,* and *Frequencies*) have one word titles, and so do hundreds of his individual poems (some of these title words being used more than once).[4]

Frequencies, like many of Thomas's single-word titles, is an immediately suggestive word, title, and title word. Thomas plays on all of its meanings. A simple mention of only the most obvious of these will serve to suggest the wide-ranging use Thomas makes of the word. As an adjective, "frequent" suggests the regular, the persistent, the habitual, the constant, an almost addictive association of things recurring in close association or at short intervals. As a verb, it means to busy oneself or familiarize oneself with, to visit or revisit often, to practice or habitually repeat, to celebrate or honor, to resort to (in terms of a person) or unto (in terms of a place). And if we add to these basic meanings of the word the newer nouns that have built up around the basic meanings, we can often find in Thomas's poems metaphors of his major themes. Perhaps the definitions alone will do to start the waves of metaphoric meaning so frequently at work in these poems to begin to mix in our minds:

> *frequency distribution*—"an arrangement of statistical data that exhibits the frequency of the occurrence of the values of a variable"

> *frequency modulation*—"modulation of the frequency of the carrier wave in accordance with speech or a signal"

> *frequency response*—"the ability of a device to handle the frequencies applied to it."[5]

All of these "meanings" reverberate through *Frequencies*—and through much of Thomas's work. To take only two examples from elsewhere, we might mention "Revision" (EA 22–23) and "One Way" (BHN 95). In "Revision" Thomas speaks of "the unseen / current between two points, coming / to song in the nerves." In "One Way" he speaks of "a frontier / I crossed whose passport / was human speech." He adds:

> God,
> I whispered, refining
> my technique, signalling
> to him on the frequencies
> I commanded.

And now, to use an archaic meaning of "frequent," let us look at *Frequencies,* R. S. Thomas's "song in the nerves," somewhat more systematically.

Thomas begins his book abruptly. The first poem, "The Gap" (F 7), suggests at once both the basic theme and the dominant metaphor which will run throughout the book, a theme and metaphor which run throughout much of Thomas's work.

"The Gap" begins, "God woke, but the nightmare / did not recede." These lines, here at the outset of both poem and book, indicate a shift from one state to another, from sleep to waking, from an unconscious to a conscious knowledge of reality. Even so, the transition, the gap between the physical states of sleep and waking and the epistemological states of conscious and unconscious knowledge, has not fully been bridged ("the nightmare / did not recede"). Perhaps more importantly, God's dream was a "nightmare," a nightmare which even in an awakened world will not now go away. Thus, this gap in consciousness has been bridged by God's "awakening," and by man's "awakening" to his waking, in both a literal and an epistemological sense. But, even so, the nightmare God dreamed remains, beyond this bridging of the gap.

And God's nightmare, of course, is man. Man has been trying to reach God with words, his "tower of speech." This phrase suggests a kind of human babel growing upwards like a tower toward God and seeping into his subconscious in sleep. And where are words more reminiscent of "towers" than in the columns of words which are poems? Are man's prayers poems? God, "reclining" on the air, as if in a fresco by Michelangelo, watches in horror as this tower of words rises toward him: "One word more and / it would be on a level / with him; vocabulary / would have triumphed." It is something to be feared, this metaphysical, indeed almost physical proximity, which man has with God through words:

> He
> measured the thin gap
> with his mind. No, no, no,
> wider than that!

God measures the gap between himself and man not with his hand, as we might expect (since this is clearly an anthropomorphic God, who sleeps and dreams), but with "his mind." God hopes that the gap is wider than he imagines, that man and his words are farther away than they seem to be. "But the nearness / persisted." God begins to wonder how he can continue to "live" with the "feat" of this "fact" of man's increasing closeness, how he can "take his rest / on the edge of a chasm a / word could bridge." God, clearly, is uncomfortable; his "repose" has been disturbed.

The second "stanza" of this broken column of words effectively suggests, visually and rhythmically, both the presence and the absence of this gap between God and man—and man's words, which, ironically, as they are written "down" in the columns of lines, continue to accumulate and thus push themselves "upward" toward him. There is no space, no gap, between lines 16 and 17, and yet the white space and the indentation of the line before the beginning of the new sentence suggest the presence of a traditional stanzaic "gap." This is a gap that is further indicated, if not "closed," rather neatly by the use of the word "bridge" at the end of line 16, the last word before the spatial "gap," and by the fact that the rhythm of the gapped lines 16–17:

> word would bridge.
> He leaned

is both maintained and simultaneously "broken" by the white space. We are told, apparently from God's point of view, that he "leaned / over" (and here the line itself leans over) to look into man's dictionary in an attempt to discover whether he had as yet been defined. He finds that "There was the blank still / by his name" (another gap), and he thinks, or seems to believe, that this blank is equivalent to "the territory / between them," a void which suggests the "verbal hunger" for a relationship through words, for meaning and identification. This relationship, God seems to see, is one that man wants to have with him—but which, apparently, he does not share in nor wish to have with man in return. Indeed, God cannot "rest" easy on the edge of such a "chasm / a [single?] word could bridge."

The final eleven and one half lines of the poem are one long complicated sentence in which "the darkness" (like the night in which one dreams? or in which things are shrouded in mystery?) "that is a god's blood" swells and is "let" (spilled, like ink?) to "make the sign in the space / on the page" (i.e., fill up a gap?). This ambiguous bloodily signed message, written "in all languages

/ and none," is a "grammarian's / torment," "the mystery / at the cell's core"
(like the mystery of life itself), and "the equation / that will not come out" (an
equation as in the association or identification of two related but not identical
entities which share in a single process). It is, finally,

> the narrowness that we stare
> over into the eternal
> silence that is the repose of God.

Here at the end of the poem (the line breaks working extremely effec-
tively) the point of view seems to shift to man's perspective, as he, in his own
version of a waking nightmare, also sees "the narrowness" of the gap between
himself and God. At the same time—perhaps even more terrifyingly—he
realizes that only "eternal / silence" greets his tower of words—these words,
this poem become prayer, in which he has attempted to reach God and to
meet him on his own terms. Here at the end of the poem, God, in "repose"
(with all the meanings of this word at work at once), seems to mock man's
feeble attempts at communication. If it was man's word which awakened God
from his nightmare sleep at the beginning of the poem, and even perhaps
briefly terrified him, here at the end of the poem the enigma of God's "eternal
/ silence" provides little hope beyond the torment of continuing the attempt
to reach him through more mere words.

But there is another suggestion which might be drawn from the enig-
matic final line. The "repose of God" implies sleep (literally, "repose" is "eter-
nal or heavenly rest"). If, at the end of the poem, God has gone back to sleep,
this would account for (even if it would not finally fully justify) the shifting
of the point of view, and it would also account for God's lack of response
to man's appeal, to his "tower of speech." It would also, perhaps, imply that
God's actions *are* his words, that, indeed, his only "action" *is* through words.
If this is the case, then God, like the poet, can only work through words.
Therefore, the "verbal hunger" would apply to God and man equally, recipro-
cally, and the only way in which man could meet God would be through his
words—just as the only way God can meet or has ever met man is through
his words. This poem, then, or at least the end of it, might be thought of as
an exegesis of the famous opening sentence of the Gospel According to John:
Ἐν ἀρχῇ ἦν ὁ λόγος, καὶ ὁ λόγος ἦν πρὸς τὸν θεόν, καὶ θεὸς ἦν ὁ λόγος
("In a beginning was the Word, and the Word was with God, and the Word
was God"). If God is Word, and can only be met through words, then, even
if he never responds, the gap between God and man can only be closed (if
indeed it ever can) through words sent back and forth through prayers and
poems. These words then would be, as the Greek text literally states it, "a
beginning."

Beyond this, and perhaps even more importantly for Thomas, every poem itself fills in a gap, both in knowledge and in experience. In so filling in a space where otherwise there would have been nothing, the poem becomes the means of voiding the void, of closing the gaps—both between God and man and between man and man. Thus, the poem communicates by its structure and by its statement, both by its being and by its saying. And furthermore, the poem itself fills up this gap between God and man, this void—even if, before it was written or spoken, the void had gone unnoticed. Thus, the poem satisfies the need as quickly as the need is noticed. And this may apply to both God and to man.

But, of course, one poem is not enough.[6] If the gap between God and man is ever to be bridged, it must be bridged, as we now know, by man alone—since the period of God's overt action, the sending of his son, is long since past. And so Thomas, again and again, presents us with one man, alone, lonely for and before God, calling across the gapped void between them, hoping beyond hope that, somehow, God will hear his "verbal hunger" and be moved—if not to respond, at least to listen. This is Thomas's constant theme, expressed and explored throughout his work, but insisted on in *Frequencies*.[7] Indeed, as Thomas said in an interview, "Granted that a certain kind of religion has made capital out of a God of the gaps, this does not mean that each closure of a gap is a kind of erosion of the reality of God."[8]

The second poem in *Frequencies,* "Present" (F 9), has an ironic, punning title. In a "present" which is both an immediate moment and a kind of gift, Thomas, "at the switchboard / of the exchanges of the people / of all time," continues to "engage with philosophy" and to present in poems the "gap" he has already discovered in "The Gap"—the presence of God's absence and aloofness.

"The Porch" (F 10) begins with questions and answers:

> Do you want to know his name?
> It is forgotten. Would you learn
> what he was like? He was like
> anyone else, a man with ears
> and eyes.

Here we see deity, "like / anyone else," on a "church porch on an evening / in winter," "driven / to his knees . . . for no reason / he knew." And, without the power to pray, He "kept his place / . . . on that lean / threshold" and "looked out on a universe / that was without knowledge / of him." This "lean threshold" which Thomas tells us is "neither outside nor in" is, of course, yet another "gap." Even God, leaning, almost lounging in the church's threshold, with "His back turned on the interior," seems simultaneously both stationary

and stopped in this gap—and thus stopping it up—even as he uses this tem-
porary (stopgap?) measure to attempt his failed communication with man.[9]

In short, the gap between man and God remains.

This litany continues throughout *Frequencies*. The fishermen in "Fish-
ing" (F 11) "wait for the // withheld answer to an insoluble / problem."
In "Henry James" (F 20) there is "the eloquence of the unsaid / thing, the
nobility of the deed / not performed," and "the significance / of an absence."
"Adjustments"(F 29–30) begins, "Never known as anything / but an absence,
I dare not name him / as God," and goes on to consider the "invisible struc-
tures / he builds," and to state that "There are no / laws . . . other than
the limits of / our understanding." In "The Possession" (F 33) the "religious
man," "looking around him with his worried eyes / at the emptiness," says,
"There must be something—but he has nothing to hold on to but "infinite
darkness between points of light." The protagonist of "The Film of God" (F
47), with his camera "as sensitive to / an absence as to a presence," wonders,
"What language / does the god speak?" Finally, in a poem intriguingly enti-
tled "Balance" (F 49), the poet wonders, "Is there time / on this brief platform
for anything / other than mind's failure to explain itself?"

But if this obsession with the gaps between man and God runs through-
out *Frequencies* in many subtle ways, it is treated in substantial detail in a
number of the most important poems in the second half of the book. And if
it is the case that Thomas, in this book, has forced furthest this crucial theme
and thesis of his life and work, then an analysis of these poems is essential to
any full understanding of him as a man and poet.

"Dialectic" (F 24), placed at almost the exact center of the book, has at
its center the thematic issue of the complete book: "the mind swinging / to
and fro over an abysm / of blankness." The title is immediately interesting.
A "dialectic," a discussion *via* dialogue between two parties, an intellectual
exchange or investigation of, historically (in Plato's dialogues for instance), the
eternal ideas, immediately suggests "gaps" and the crisscrossing of "frequen-
cies" back and forth over or between them. Man speaks, God listens (like "a
spider spinning its web"), but he does not answer except "as of old with the
infinity / I feed on." Thus, even though he "delights in" man's attention and
acknowledges that once "there were words" between them (even if "they could
not understand" them), now men must be left alone (in the lurch, with their
gapped knowledge?) and on their own with the "truth / . . . born with them,"
but with that truth to be shed, "sloughed off like some afterbirth of the spirit."
The poem "At It" (F 15) seems to suggest Thomas's threatening response to
this God: "I would have / things to say to this God / at the judgement." But,
he acknowledges, "there will be / no judgement" other than "that abstruse /
geometry that proceeds eternally / in the silence beyond right and wrong."

The "dialectic," then, is to take place in a shadowy world, as the poem, "Shadows" (F 25), makes clear:

> I close my eyes.
> The darkness implies your presence,
> the shadow of your steep mind
> on my world. I shiver in it.
> It is not your light that
> can blind us; it is the splendour
> of your darkness.

God's metaphysically mystical presence is only "visible" as a mental shadow, and as that, it is only an implied presence. This meeting, mind to mind, across the gaps of thought, creates a shiver of recognition so dark in "splendour" that it can "blind us." (This is a kind of mental groping in the dark, as Thomas has earlier suggested in his poem "Groping" [F 12].) Here, however, hearing the interior calling, the speaker begins the inward journey toward this (his) silent source of sound deep in the dark of the mind where (even there, strangely enough) "sometimes a strange light / shines. . . ." Such "journeys" are typical of the mystical tradition Thomas has always been attracted to and which he often follows in many of his most important and interesting poems, a tradition which perhaps first comes to climax at the end of his lovely poem "Sea-watching" (LS 64), where we read:

> There were days,
> so beautiful the emptiness
> it might have filled,
> 　　　　　　　its absence
> was as it presence; not to be told
> any more, so single my mind
> after its long fast,
> 　　　　　　　my watching from praying.

We need only mention Dionysius the Areopagite, Thomas's most obvious source in the substantial body of mystical literature, to see the immediate significance of this tradition for his work, here and elsewhere—but especially so here in the middle of his career. Dionysius describes the essence of the "negative way" in terms of the metaphor of light and darkness:

> Unto this Darkness which is beyond light we pray that we may come, and may attain unto vision through the loss of sight and knowledge, and that in ceasing thus to see or to know we may learn to know that which is beyond all perception and understanding. . . . [W]e strip off all qualities in order that we may attain a naked knowledge of that Unknowing which in all existent things is enwrapped by all objects of knowledge, and that we may

begin to see that super-essential Darkness which is hidden by all the light
that is in existent things.[10]

This is "the language / of silence" heard in "Shadows" (F 25) and the "sen-
tence / without an end" that runs throughout the reminder of *Frequencies.*

The next poem, "Abercuawg" (F 26–27), asserts that "An absence is how
we become surer / of what we want." And Thomas here describes himself as
"a seeker / in time for that which is / beyond time," for that which is "always
/ about to be; whose duration is / of the mind. . . ."[11]

It is perhaps now a time for "adjustments." Thomas's poem "Adjust-
ments" (F 29–30) begins:

> Never known as anything
> but an absence, I dare not name him
> as God.

Then he adds:

> We never catch
> him at work, but can only say,
> coming suddenly upon an amendment,
> that here he has been.

Yet, "Patiently with invisible structures / he builds"(F 29) across the gaps of
our comprehension, until, finally, "we are forced / into the game, reluctant /
contestants" ("The Game" [F 31]).

The next important poem in *Frequencies* is "Waiting" (F 32). Indeed, it
is almost as if Thomas himself has been waiting for "Waiting," as if he had
been expecting this meeting, here in the middle of these "frequencies." The
poem begins with the obvious question, which has been echoing through the
ages: "Face to face?" And the speaker immediately answers his own question,
"Ah, no / God; such language falsifies / the relation." Thomas knows that
God's name, "vouching for you, ubiquitous / in its explanations" and pres-
ent throughout time, needs only to be "pronounced" to echo back to man.
Therefore, he finds himself

> . . . leaning far out
> over an immense depth, letting
> your name go and waiting,
> somewhere between faith and doubt,
> for the echoes of its arrival.[12]

"Somewhere between faith and doubt." Such vacillation is an accurate
description of Thomas's position. It has, indeed, become a "possession," as
the next poem "The Possession" (F 33) asserts. Here, the speaker, "nothing /

religious," dreams his "fused prayers" and wakes to find the "reflection" (obviously both a physical and a metaphysical phenomenon and equally obviously another play on the word frequencies) of "infinite darkness between points of light." The main difference is that Thomas's "waiting" has here become noticeably more impatient.

"The Empty Church" (F 35), appropriately enough, follows "Gone?" (F 34). "The Empty Church" plays on another kind of echo, a shadow. The poem begins:

> They laid this stone trap
> for him, enticing him with candles,
> as though he would come like some huge moth
> out of the darkness to beat there.

"They." Who? In the second stanza the speaker invokes himself, "Why, then, do I kneel still. . . ?" His answer is only another question: "Is it in hope" that a "spark" of prayer, struck from his "stone / heart," will "ignite" and throw a "shadow" on the empty walls of the stone church? Thomas here hints, beyond his question, at another poem, "Passage" (LP 192), where we find the metaphor extended and further complicated as poem and church become conflated: "I stand now, tolling my name / in the poem's empty church." And, finally, one cannot help but think that Thomas's poems are, if not, like churches, "stone traps," perhaps they are verbal traps for such a "fast / God" (as Thomas calls him in "Pilgrimages," the last poem in *Frequencies,* [F 51-52]), "always before us and / leaving as we arrive."

But all is always tentative, as "Perhaps" (F 39), with its questions and answers (that seem to be further questions) indicates. "Perhaps" comes to its final question ("To believe . . . / . . . in the ubiquity of a vast concern?") through a series of questions and "answers" or "answers" which elicit further questions:

> His intellect was the clear mirror
> he looked in and saw the machinery of God
> assemble itself? It was one that reflected
> the emptiness that was where God
> should have been. The mind's tools had
> no power convincingly to put him
> together. Looking in that mirror was a journey
> through hill mist where, the higher
> one ascends, the poorer the visibility
> becomes. It could have led to despair
> but for the consciousness of a presence
> behind him, whose breath clouding
> that looking-glass proved that it was alive.

To learn to distrust the distrust
of feeling — this then was the next step
for the seeker?

Poems, for Thomas, seem always to end in questions—demanding more poems. Finally, however, something does seem to be emerging, as the poem "Emerging" (F 41) itself seems to suggest:

Well, I said, better to wait
for him on some peninsula
of the spirit. Surely for one
with patience he will happen by
once in a while. It was the heart
spoke. The mind, sceptical as always
of the anthropomorphisms
of the fancy, knew he must be put together
like a poem or a composition
in music, that what he conforms to
is art.

"He must be put together / like a poem. . . ." Only through "the mind's tool-ing," through words put down in poems, can man hope to discover God. God, as elusive as a rare bird or a white tiger, only "breathes within the con-fines / of our definition of him" ("The White Tiger" [F 45]). God, that is, only lives within our words about him (in poems) or in words directed toward him (in prayers). And then, as if the whole "tedious argument" of Thomas's book has led us "to an overwhelming question,"[13] here, late on, we come to a poem called "The Answer."

"The Answer" (F 46) begins with a twilight setting. Here is where "even the best / of minds must make its way." "And slowly the questions / occur . . . / They / yield, but only to re-form / as new problems." Sometimes, finally, "after long on my knees / in a cold chancel," Thomas tells us, "a stone has rolled / from my mind, and I have looked"

. . . and seen the old questions lie
folded and in a place
by themselves, like the piled
graveclothes of love's risen body.

This is a most intriguing "answer." First of all, we notice that the questions "lie." Does this mean that they are bad or inappropriate questions? That they are false, inaccurate, and intended to deceive? Whatever is the case, they are there still, "folded and in place" like the "graveclothes" on Easter morning. The questions are there and they remain. But the answer, any answer, is absent. And thus, although the title of the poem asserts that there *is* an "answer," the

poem itself ends with the absence of any definitive answer—indeed it ends
in yet another question. Right questions, in Thomas, and for Thomas, are
always more important than wrong answers. And, as he seems to be suggest-
ing here, the only possible answer is simply a sequence of correct questions.

"The Answer," with its lack of any answer, leads, appropriately enough,
to "The Absence" (F 48), where "this great absence / that is like a presence . . .
compels / me to address it"—even though, Thomas knows, there is no "hope
/ of a reply." Indeed, Thomas finds himself caught in a kind of metaphysical
gap:

> It is a room I enter
>
> from which someone has just
> gone, the vestibule for the arrival
> of one who has not yet come.

Acknowledging that "he is no more here / than before," that nothing, seem-
ingly, will call him forth—and that nothing ever has, neither "genes and mol-
ecules" nor "the incense of the Hebrews // at their altars"—Thomas comes
again to another question:

> What resource have I
> other than the emptiness without him of my whole
> being, a vacuum he may not abhor?

Unable to avoid the seeking, but coming again and again to a void (both
a physical and an epistemologically draining gap as large as an abyss), what
can one do save acknowledge the "emptiness" and hope against hope that
such a "vacuum" may not be "abhorred"? Is this definition by negation? Does
the presence of absence suggest or demand bounds to absence bordered by
presence? The poem seems to circle on itself, going back to its beginnings,
to assert that "this great absence," the essential essence of our first and final
knowledge, is, finally, only *"like* a presence" (my italics).

Such a state, teetering on the edge of gaps as large as these, and near such
deep abysses, demands the kind of intricate balance that perhaps only poems
and philosophy can have. The next poem, entitled, almost inevitably, "Bal-
ance" (F 49), invokes Kierkegaard, theological gap-leaper *par excellence* and
one of Thomas's frequent sources of reference.[14]

"Epiphany" (F 50), the penultimate poem of *Frequencies,* plays on the
meanings of ἐπιφάνεια, "manifestation," in several senses. The poem begins
with a question ("Three kings?").[15] But, rather typically, Thomas proceeds to
leap (fully in keeping with the kind of sudden manifestation appropriate to
epiphanies) back and forth across the gaps of ancient tradition and historical
precedent to present practice, then back again across time and the life-span

of a man, collapsing Christ's life from birth to death to rebirth and bringing it up to date, even if ironically, at the center of the poem. "The child / has become a man."

At the end of the poem the Christ, both child and man, out of place in space and time ("Far // off from his cross in the wrong / season"), comes to sit "at table / with us with on his head / the fool's cap of our paper money." This final image is rather elaborate. Christ, out of place in every sense in our day, has become a kind of fool, jester or dunce (even the traditional three flaps of the fool's cap mock the Trinity) who wears a cap of counterfeit (paper) money, not real gold as of old. And, finally, this "epiphany" is a watermark (another meaning of "foolscap") indelibly present, even if invisible, on the stamped writing paper (formerly called foolscap) that is typically used in Britain—the paper Thomas may have used to write this poem on. Thus, Christ is the indelible, invisible "gap" manifested only in his present absence.

The final poem of *Frequencies* is, appropriately enough, entitled "Pilgrimages" (F 51–52). The title is significant. After his epiphany, Thomas, journeying like others before him towards sacred places "the way / the saints went," comes to a "stone altar and the candles / gone out." Kneeling, lifting his eyes, he wonders, "Am I too late?" and "Were they too late also, those / first pilgrims?" How can one catch "such a fast / God, always before us and / leaving as we arrive"—this God of the gaps whose presence constantly eludes us, and who is known to us only as longing and absence?

The place of pilgrimage in this poem is an "island," a place surrounded by the sea. Literally, the island of the poem is Bardsey Island (*Ynys Enlli*), an island off the tip of the Llŷn peninsula across the strait from Aberdaron, where Thomas served his final years as a priest, from 1967 to 1978. (Following his retirement, he lived nearby, at Sarn-y-Plas, Rhiw, on the bay of Porth Neigwl, which he took delight in reporting was known as "the Mouth of Hell.")[16] In one of the prose poem meditations in *The Echoes Return Slow*, Thomas refers again to this place, defining both it and his purpose for being there:

> A bough of land between sea and sky with the clouds for apple-blossom, white by day, pink towards evening. This is where he had crawled out, far as he could go, repeating the pilgrimages of the saints. (ERS 68)[17]

But for Thomas, "repeating the pilgrimages of the saints," this "place" is truly a "peninsula / of the spirit" (F 41), more a metaphysical than a physical place: "There is no time on this island" and "the events / are dateless" (F 51). It is, therefore, a place, surrounded by "see," where an "I," through vision, "lands." It is where R. S. Thomas has come to.

His book and his quest end with a question:

                    Was the pilgrimage
          I made to come to my own
          self, to learn that in times
          like these and for one like me
          God will never be plain and
          out there, but dark rather and
          inexplicable, as though he were in here?

The answer is obvious, but it is beyond words.

7

Fathers and Sons

Generally people are of the opinion that what faith produces is not a work of art. . . .

—Kierkegaard, *Fear and Trembling*

. . . as form in sculpture is the prisoner of the hard rock. . . .

—R. S. Thomas, "Emerging"

For I have come to set a man against his father. . . .

—Matthew 10:35 (RSV)

Throughout his long career, R. S. Thomas was frequently, and perhaps not surprisingly, drawn to theological themes. Usually, however, Thomas took a philosophic approach to such themes or dealt with them indirectly, in general terms. Therefore, it is somewhat surprising to find him writing about a specific biblical text rather directly in his poem *"Souillac: Le Sacrifice d'Abraham"* (BT 43):

And he grasps him by the hair
With innocent savagery.
And the son's face is calm;
There is trust there.

And the beast looks on.

This is what art could do,
Interpreting faith
With serene chisel.
The resistant stone
Is quiet as our breath,
And is accepted.

Thomas's poem is, of course, based on the well-known story in Genesis 22:1-13, which is often referred to as "the testing of Abraham." The biblical text reads:

> After these things God tested Abraham, and said to him, "Abraham!" And he said, "Here am I." He said, "Take your son, your only son Isaac, whom you love, and go to the land of Moriah, and offer him there as a burnt offering upon one of the mountains of which I shall tell you." So Abraham rose early in the morning, saddled his ass, and took two of his young men with him, and his son Isaac; and he cut the wood for the burnt offering, and arose and went to the place of which God had told him. On the third day Abraham lifted up his eyes and saw the place afar off. Then Abraham said to his young men, "Stay here with the ass; I and the lad will go yonder and worship, and come again to you." And Abraham took the wood of the burnt offering, and laid it on Isaac his son; and he took in his hand the fire and the knife. So they went both of them together. And Isaac said to his father Abraham, "My father!" And he said, "Here am I, my son." He said, "Behold, the fire and the wood; but where is the lamb for a burnt offering?" Abraham said, "God will provide himself the lamb for a burnt offering, my son." So they went both of them together.
>
> When they came to the place of which God had told him, Abraham built an altar there, and laid the wood in order, and bound Isaac his son, and laid him on the altar, upon the wood. Then Abraham put forth his hand, and took the knife to slay his son. But the angel of the Lord called to him from heaven, and said, "Abraham, Abraham!" And he said, "Here am I." He said, "Do not lay your hand on the lad or do anything to him; for now I know that you fear God, seeing you have not withheld your son, your only son, from me." And Abraham lifted up his eyes and looked, and behold, behind him was a ram, caught in a thicket by his horns; and Abraham went and took the ram, and offered it up as a burnt offering instead of his son. (RSV)

In addition to the biblical text, I think it highly likely (since we know that Thomas read Kierkegaard widely and closely),[1] that Thomas knew Kierkegaard's lengthy analysis of the Abraham-Isaac story in his *Fear and Trembling*. Kierkegaard outlines the "argument" of a possible thesis with respect to the biblical story this way:

> I suppose that at first Abraham looked upon Isaac with all his fatherly love.
> . . . Then I think that Abraham has for an instant turned away from him,
> and when again he turned toward him he was unrecognizable to Isaac, his
> eyes were wild, his venerable locks had risen like the locks of furies above his
> head. He seized Isaac by the throat, he drew the knife, he said: "Thou didst
> believe it was for God's sake I would do this, thou art mistaken. . . . I want
> to murder thee; . . . despair thou foolish boy who didst imagine that I was
> thy father, I am thy murderer, and this is my desire." And Isaac fell upon
> his knees and cried to heaven, "Merciful God, have mercy upon me!" But
> then said Abraham softly to himself, "Thus it must be, for it is better after
> all that he believes I am a monster, that he curses me for being his father,
> rather than he should know it was God who imposed the temptation, for
> then he would lose his reason and perhaps curse God."[2]

And then Kierkegaard wonders: "But where indeed is there a poet in our age who has a presentiment of such collisions!"[3] It is not difficult to imagine Thomas reading this passage in Kierkegaard, being reminded of the biblical account, and turning to write his poem.

Thomas clearly counts on his reader's familiarity with the biblical text upon which he bases his poem. But, in addition to the possibility of the Kierkegaardian as well as the biblical text being behind Thomas's poem, Thomas bases it on an additional artistic source, another "commentary" on the biblical story, one that presents a somewhat different "interpretation" than that expressed in the Bible and in Kierkegaard's account. This is a twelfth-century piece of sculpture in the Abbey Church of Saint Marie in Souillac, France (see figure 1). It is, of course, this trumeau to which Thomas's French title explicitly refers. Although the sculptured column in Souillac clearly depicts the biblical story of Abraham and Isaac, it adds several elements, or details, to the story which supplement, supplant, or amend the biblical text, and which thereby suggest a somewhat different "interpretation" of the original biblical story. And, indeed, some of the passages in Thomas's poem make much more specific reference to the Souillac sculpture than they do to the biblical account.[4]

In terms of specific details, and especially in terms of differences between the biblical text and the Souillac sculpture, perhaps the most obvious point of divergence is the way the actual sacrifice is depicted. In the written text, the preparations for the sacrifice are described in terms of ancient sacrificial

Figure 1: Twelfth-century Sculpture from the Abbey Church of Saint Marie in Souillac, France. Used by permission of Jeff Howe.

tradition: Isaac is to be bound and placed on the altar, on a pallet of sticks or branches, in preparation for his being offered up as a "burnt offering" to God. Rather than showing Isaac lying bound on the altar, in the Souillac sculpture the figures of Abraham and Isaac are shown standing. Indeed, such a configuration of these figures is rather typical in artistic depictions of this story, since a standing or kneeling Isaac allows for richer visual possibilities than would be possible if Isaac were portrayed as bound upon a pallet or if he were shown supine on an altar.[5] Abraham's knife-held hand is raised high above Isaac's head, which is bent to one side. It would seem that Thomas's description of the "innocent savagery" in this scene, since it is so graphically depicted in the sculptured column, would seem to have been suggested more by the vivid portrayal of the figures there than by the description in the biblical text. Furthermore, Thomas's reference to Isaac's "trust" in his father—although such trust is clearly implied throughout the biblical story—is made much more evident in the sculpture, where Isaac seems almost to be smiling as he deferentially bends his head beneath Abraham's upraised knife. Another difference between the sculpture and Thomas's text is that in the biblical account the intervening angel calls to Abraham "from heaven" and speaks directly to him, telling him, "Do not lay your hand on the lad." In the sculpture, which must "speak" without the use of words, the sculptor shows the angel holding Abraham's upheld hand back as he is about to strike Isaac (see figure 2). Additionally, in the sculpture Isaac seems to lean almost complacently against his father's chest, his hand resting gently under Abraham's arm, almost as if he means to assist his father in carrying out his own sacrifice. This depiction of a seemingly naïve trust on Isaac's part—or is it meant to suggest his slowly growing comprehension, and even perhaps his accession to, or his own complicity in, his sacrifice?—while it is indeed implied in the biblical account, is made much more conspicuous in the sculpture. In short, although Thomas certainly has the biblical story well in mind, and expects his readers to remember it, he much more specifically draws the details in his poem from the Souillac sculpture.

Turning to the poem itself, the first thing that attracts a reader's attention is Thomas's title, "Le Sacrifice d'Abraham"—"The Sacrifice of Abraham." In terms of the biblical text, and even perhaps in terms of the Souillac sculpture, this title is somewhat surprising, perhaps even confusing, since literally it is Isaac who is to be "sacrificed," not Abraham. By shifting this reference in his title (as is indeed rather typical in the artistic depictions of the story, and also in many of the historical accounts), Thomas is able to suggest, and to stress, the dual notion of the "sacrifice" (which is only alluded to in the biblical story and in the Souillac sculpture)—namely, that by following God's command to sacrifice his son, Abraham himself is also making a "sacrifice" of and on his

Figure 2: Detail of Sculpture at Saint Marie in Souillac, France.
Used by permission of Jeff Howe.

own: that, indeed, Abraham's sacrifice is a sacrifice of self. That is, in obeying and in acting upon God's command to sacrifice Isaac, Abraham, in his acquiescence, is also "sacrificing" himself to God's command. And since God is traditionally thought of as a Father, Abraham is as a son to him. Abraham then, becomes the fulcrum in this sacrificial trinity. As the son of God the Father, and as the father of his son Isaac, Abraham, in carrying out God's command to sacrifice his son Isaac, is likewise sacrificing himself, as "son," to *his* father. In a very real sense then, as Thomas makes clear with his title, both the biblical story and his poem (but not the Souillac trumeau) focus most specifically on Abraham and his sacrifice, and not on the sacrifice of Isaac.

In addition, since this Old Testament text points forward to the New Testament message, it suggests an immediate comparison between Abraham's willingness to sacrifice his son Isaac and God's "sacrifice" of his son, Jesus. (The ultimate difference between these parallels, of course, has to do with the actual carrying out of God's "sacrifice" of his son, as opposed to the substitution of the sacrificial ram for Isaac in the Old Testament story.) Furthermore, the comparison between Isaac and Jesus seems to be clearly alluded to in the Old Testament text when Abraham says, "God will provide himself the lamb for a burnt offering, my son." This is a rather amazing comment and, interestingly enough—but not surprisingly—it renders Isaac mute for the rest of the story. What, we might ask, does Isaac understand from it? And what does Abraham really mean? The biblical text of this sentence (and it is indeed a "sentence" imposed on Abraham) seems to suggest both that God will provide a literal lamb (or ram) for Abraham to sacrifice in place of his son Isaac *and* that God "will provide himself"—as Christ—for sacrifice. In short, as it has been from the earliest times, the depiction of Abraham's sacrifice of Isaac can be—indeed must be—seen as a prefiguration of God's sacrifice of Christ at the time of the crucifixion. But if we read "offering" and "son" as if they were in apposition to one another, and not simply as an instance of direct address, the statement seems to suggest that Abraham, while clearly speaking directly to Isaac, is also, indirectly, telling him that he, Isaac, is to be "burnt" in "offering" as sacrifice. This would certainly be enough to make any son mute!

Meyer Schapiro has described and detailed the iconography of the Souillac trumeau both as an individual piece of artwork and in terms of its depiction, based on the Genesis text of the Abraham and Isaac story. Schapiro points out, for instance, that in numerous instances ranging from earliest times, pictures of Isaac "carrying the Faggots" were often paired with "Christ carrying the Cross," just as the sacrifice of Isaac was paired with "a picture of the Crucifixion," as has already been suggested.[6] Schapiro adds:

Yet it must be obvious that even without the concordant image, a picture of Abraham's Sacrifice could be seen as an antitype of the Crucifixion. Sometimes the context, the place of this Old Testament scene in a gospel manuscript or on a cross or altar, would be enough to turn the viewer's mind to Christ. Or this connection could be intimated in a more subtly allusive manner through a single detail: the position of the ram in the bush, suspended by its horns, or the rendering of the bush as a tall plant with two crossed branches, or the faggots on Isaac's shoulders in the form of a cross. . . . For Christians of the early period the Sacrifice of Isaac . . . was a promise of salvation through faith and also a model of obedience to God. [T]he presence of this detail shows that while theologians were occupied mainly with formal and final causes in explaining the great exemplary events in the Old Testament as prefigurements of the New, others, including artists, were interested as well in the immediate efficient cause of the miracle and applied their fantasy to supply the details of such causation, not provided in the biblical text. But in Souillac this speculative elaboration of the story has been carried much further.[7]

Schapiro further mentions that "One can interpret the series as a free conversion of the theme of Abraham and Isaac into a struggle between a young man and an old, perhaps son and father—a secular parody with a most serious sense"[8] (see figure 3).

In an earlier essay, Schapiro describes in greater detail what he calls the "inconsistencies" between the Souillac sculpture and the biblical text and stresses the "secular parody" depicted in the sculptured trumeau:

The artist's independence of the text is more far-reaching than appears from the detail of the angel and the ram. For the bush in which the ram was caught, an element crucial for Christian exegesis, . . . has been omitted, although the sculptor has taken pains to represent Isaac carrying the faggots and has shown this detail, not symbolically, across Isaac's shoulder or in the form of the beams of the cross, in analogy to Christ carrying the cross, but realistically, as a compact mass that a grotesque little Isaac, entangled in the twisted colonnettes framing the scene, holds before him like a torch. Instead of the familiar pairing of the Old Testament scene with the Crucifixion or with Christ carrying the Cross, there is carved on the other side of the trumeau the combat of an old man and a youth, in profane contrast to, or even parody of, the Sacrifice of Abraham in which the son submits to the father, as the latter to God.[9]

In yet another piece, his earliest essay devoted to the sculptures at Souillac, Schapiro suggests that, "Throughout his work the sculptor displays . . . an independent virtuosity of manipulation, beyond the needs of traditional, symbolic imagery." And he adds parenthetically "(In this he resembles the vernacular lyric poets of the time. . .)."[10] Furthermore, these various parallels

Figure 3. Sculture of wrestling figures at Saint Marie in Souillac, France. From Julius Baum, Romanesque Architecture in France *(London, 1928). Used by permission of Jeff Howe.*

between the sculptured column at Souillac and the biblical text upon which it is based are, as Schapiro points out, not unique to the Souillac trumeau, but are frequently duplicated in other artistic depictions of this story contemporary with the Abbey Church in Souillac. (One good parallel example can be found in the thirteenth-century Moralized Bible, in the Bodleian Library at Oxford.)

Turning back now to Thomas's "*Souillac: Le Sacrifice d'Abraham,*" we find several specifically literal and literary devices in the poem that Thomas seems to have drawn directly from the biblical text, his original written, i.e., literary source. The most conspicuous of these is the use of anaphora. Six of the sentences in the biblical text begin with an "And," and there are more than a score of instances in which "and" is used to stress continuity. Thomas uses the word "And" as the first word in four of the eleven lines of his poem, including the first, the last, and the central single-line second stanza. Indeed, the poem begins with the word *And*, as if to suggest, at the very outset of this poem based on this old and well-known biblical story, that something has preceded even what was there being told and is here being retold. Something had gone before, something is continuing, and it is something that was known before, before that first beginning, something that it is here beginning again in this new telling, this new retelling, of the story in Thomas's poem. Also, by using the anaphora of the word "and" to mark the turns of his poem—just as it marks the turns of the biblical story—Thomas is following the convention of anaphoric repetition so insistently used in his specific biblical source and, indeed, throughout the whole of the Bible, and he is thereby rather subtly suggesting that his poetic practice parallels the biblical precedent.

It is perhaps also worth noting several other uses of repetition in the biblical text: the phrase "Here am I" is repeated three times, and the sentence "So they went both of them together" is repeated word for word twice, as a kind of refrain. (It is also interesting that the phrase "Here am I" is spoken by Abraham in answer to three separate calls—the first from God, the second from Isaac, and the third from "the angel of the Lord." And, in each instance, these parallel passages make use of the same introductory phrase, "And he said.")

Both in the biblical text and in Thomas's poem, then, repetitions suggest continuity and they imply an ongoing sequence and tradition. This is a story that has been told and retold over and over; it is a story which Thomas's poem, like the Souillac sculpture before it, here retells. And thus this old story, even in its initial written telling in the Genesis account, is there only recounted again, in terms of its having already been "told" before. The *ands*, and the other repetitions, bring the story forward from the initial oral tradition—its original and quite literal "telling"—into the written text of the biblical account, *and then* into the depiction of the story in the sculpture at

Souillac, *and then* into Thomas's poem. This, obviously, is a story significant enough to be told over and over again. And so this old story "speaks" again here in Thomas's poem. And still it is as quiet, and yet as insistent, "as our breath," as Thomas's penultimate line asserts.

Thus, the first five lines of the poem set the stage for this old story, here retold. In the final six-line stanza Thomas provides his own interpretation of the biblical story and of the sculptured representation of the story in the Abbey Church at Souillac. Thomas begins by insisting on an artistic interpretation of the event: "This is what art could do." True to his most immediate source, Thomas refers explicitly to the Souillac sculpture, rather than the biblical text, when he describes the sculptor as "Interpreting faith / With serene chisel" (although, of course, words too can be "cutting" and, obviously, have also often been carved on stone). And even though his sources "resist" (as no doubt the stone resisted the medieval sculptor), Thomas is surely not unaware that his poem, like the "stone" and like the original biblical text, is "interpreting faith" through these words "chiseled" out on the white space of the page and finally left standing in Thomas's column-like poem—itself a configuration that very much resembles the trumeau of the Souillac sculpture to which it so literally and specifically refers. And Thomas's poem "speaks" as forcefully as the original biblical text, or as the Souillac sculpture. Like the stone carving, Thomas's "serenely" chiseled words are calm, august, and steady, and thus they satisfy at once all the meanings of the word "serene"—a word which might initially have seemed to be inappropriate in all of these contexts, but which has come finally to seem precisely the right word. This old story, retold in Thomas's poem, is as serene and tranquil, as new and as newly imagined, as it ever has been before—whether in the written text of the Genesis story or in the stony story on the column in Souillac.

And just as the "resistant stone" of the biblical text and the sculpture at Souillac have told their own stories, so Thomas's poem has told its story too. The words of his poem are indeed as "quiet as our breath." Poems are words made of breath—are breath itself—the life force forced into artistic forms. Poems, like sacred texts, and like stories told in stone, are made to stand both in and out of time, and for all time—beyond the time of the life of the teller who tells them or of the sculptor who carves them or of the poet who puts them into poems. They are artifacts, and like all artifacts (as works of art) they are as natural and inevitable as breath. And they have the permanent presence of final authority—like life itself does.

Then, finally, there is Thomas's final line. It is a most intriguing one: "And is accepted." Literally, this seems to say that the artifact, whether it is the sculpture at Souillac, or the biblical story upon which the Souillac sculpture is based, or R. S. Thomas's poem based on these two earlier sources, is "accepted." That is, it is willingly taken in or received, approved of, understood, and, finally, accepted—believed in. Surely, it is all of these things—and yet there seems to be even more meant in Thomas's final line. It seems that when we read "And is accepted" we cannot help but hear the *is* as *as*: "and *as* accepted." The sacrifice has come down to us. And it has become our own. And it too is accepted. This then is Thomas's final exegesis of the text of the biblical story—it *is as* accepted; it *is as* it is taken to heart. And when that has happened, it lives for us and in us—even as our breath allows us to live.

8

The Quarrel with Technology

I

If the labours of Men of Science should ever create any material
revolution, direct or indirect, in our condition, and in the
impressions which we habitually receive, the Poet will sleep then no
more than at present, but he will be ready to follow the steps of the
Man of Science, not only in those general indirect effects, but he will
be at his side, carrying sensation into the midst of the objects of the
Science itself. . . . If the time should ever come when what is now
called Science, thus familiarized to men, shall be ready to put on,
as it were, a form of flesh and blood, the Poet will lend his divine
spirit to aid the transfiguration, and will welcome the Being thus
produced, as dear and genuine inmate of the household of man.

—William Wordsworth

Throughout his long career as poet and as priest R. S. Thomas was nothing
if not controversial. Indeed, he seems regularly to have thrust himself forc-
ibly into the midst of controversies, to have taken up "causes"—and to have
thrived on them. Therefore, it is perhaps not surprising that what I want to
deal with in this chapter is one of Thomas's "quarrels." Even though Thom-
as's quarrel with technology—unlike his various environmental, nationalis-
tic, political, and theological quarrels—is one that has not received as much

notice as many of the others, it was as long-standing as any, and he pursued it more vehemently and at greater length than many of his other squabbles over the years.

Thomas's long attention to the complicity between science and technology is made immediately clear in an in-depth 1990 interview:

> Interviewer: *Could you say something about your reading in the sciences? . . . Would you say that science and religion are irreconcilable ways of knowing? If they are, is there any reason for preferring one as opposed to the other as a means of exploring reality?*
>
> Thomas: *To an austere scientist much of my imagery may be reprehensible, but as far as I have understood astronomy, relativity theory, and nuclear physics, I have found images in poetry, which I hope are not too muddle-headed. My joustings with scientists are probably with the lesser fry, because I imagine those of the first rank exercise a wonder at creation which is akin to religion.*
>
> .   .   .
>
> Interviewer: *You are sometimes described as anti-technology and there are certainly lines about "the machine" that seem to support this view.*
>
> Thomas: *It is of applied science as manifest[ed] in technology that I am suspicious. . . . So it is not pure science and religion that are irreconcilable. . . . If pure science is an approach to ultimate reality, it can differ from religion only in some of its methods. . . . But using the machine, as I have, as a symbol for a robotic takeover, it is hard not be antagonistic. It serves us, but at a price, and the Frankenstein specter is never far off, as science fiction's success shows. The main criticism is that the machine is de-humanizing. It also insulates man from natural processes. The reason I have tried to write poems containing scientific images and which show some knowledge of the nature of science, is because, owing to the enormous part science and technology play in our lives, a divorce would alienate people from it. . . . Science and technology are concerned with vital areas of man's concern, they are therefore taken seriously. So still is religion. The danger to poetry is that it should become a fringe activity. . . . [W]hat are we to make of a poetry that cannot embrace some scientific knowledge and that is incapable of using words which are daily on the lips of a growing section of the population?*
>
> .   .   .
>
> *We are becoming so conditioned by the scientific view of things that we are in danger of accepting as truth only an experiment that can be repeated; that is, of accepting as true only that which can be proved. Whereas the use of imagination should remind us that we are surrounded by mystery.*[1]

As John Barnie, one of Thomas's interviewers here, has, quite rightly, said elsewhere:

Thomas's attitude to science and technology is sometimes misrepresented as being negative, largely because of a misunderstanding in certain quarters of his use of the machine as symbol. He is not "against" developments in science and technology in themselves, but he is against their misuse in a civilization based on greed and self-love. Science could even be the source of a kind of kingdom of God on earth. . . . In fact Thomas is one of the few poets . . . to come to terms with the discoveries and terminology of science, and to incorporate them successfully in his poems. . . . [H]e has perceived that scientists at the frontiers of astronomy and particle physics are also finding themselves, with the mystic, at the frontiers of language and rational perception. . . . The physicist, the astronomer and the mystic are beginning to speak a mutually intelligible language again, and R. S. Thomas has synthesised this brilliantly in [his] poems. . . .[2]

II

[T]his thing we call the Machine . . . is no more or less than the principle of organic growth working irresistibly the Will of Life through the medium of Man.

—Frank Lloyd Wright

When we turn, then, to Thomas's "quarrel" with technology, we find that it is most often and most conspicuously treated in terms of his use—and his abuse—of what he usually refers to simply as "the machine." The genesis of Thomas's fascination with "the machine" can be traced to several initial, and literal, references in his early poems—poems in which the machine is no more than an obvious symbol of "progress." In "Welsh Summer" (LS 6), for instance, he describes the way in which the machine intrudes upon the "echoes" in the Welsh valleys, upon the "voices from vanished kingdoms" long lost in "their recesses / in time." Into this bucolic past the machine comes, and, indeed, takes over—devastating the landscape and destroying the ancient traditions. As Thomas says:

It is the machine wins;
the land suffers the formication
of its presence. Places that
would have preferred peace
have had their bowels opened.

And if the dead are dislodged and displaced, or rudely awakened in a mockery of the resurrection, they are only "resurrected / to mourn" man's and the land's losses to the machine. And if man has been dispossessed by

the machine, even God himself, in "God's Story" (the poem which imme-
diately follows "Welsh Summer" in *Laboratories of the Spirit* [LS 7]) has also
"felt the cold touch of the machine / . . . leading him // to a steel altar,"
where he seeks, apparently in vain, to find "himself among / the dumb cogs
and tireless camshafts." In short, the creator has created a man who has
invented a machine which now threatens to turn on both of them and to
control each of its creators.[3]

If Thomas's increased interest in "the machine" began to be clearly vis-
ible in the poetry of the late 1960s,[4] it became even more insistent in his
powerful poems of the 1970s. This growing consciousness of the presence
of the machine—and of the increasing power of the machine over every-
thing—coincides with Thomas's increasingly overt obsession with theological
themes. These two foci remain rather constant throughout the latter half of
his career, and they are frequently, as I hope to show, joined together—often
inseparably.

III

*I wish to take certain situations which have been discussed in
religious books, and have a religious aspect, but possess a close analogy
to other situations which belong to science, and in particular to the
new science of cybernetics, the science of communication and control,
whether in machines or in living organisms. I propose to use the
limited analogies of cybernetic situations to cast a little light on the
religious situations.*

—Norbert Wiener

When we turn to Thomas's poems that make explicit reference to his quarrel
with technology—keeping his comments on "the machine" in mind—we find
that there are several categories into which these poems can be divided. First,
as has already been suggested, there are those poems in which the machine
serves as nothing more than a rather straightforward symbol of the misuse of
power and of the devastation that man, through his use of the machine, has
visited upon the landscape and upon society in general.

Then there are those poems in which the machine is no more than a
way of describing the world itself writ large, "a self-regulating machine /
of blood and faeces," as Thomas calls it in "Rough" (LS 36). At other times he
describes the way the world, as machine, functions, and he details man's vari-
ous confrontations and quarrels with this machine-world. Perhaps the best
example of this view of "the machine"—of the machine at work in the world,

and of the machine working the world—could be found in several lines in *Counterpoint*, a book-length poem based on a Christian calendar of world history, where Thomas describes the machine as a kind of original mythological presence to be understood, made use of, and followed. As he says, "They will come to understand / our folk-tale was the machine" (C 56). And then he adds:

> We listened to it in the twilight
> of our reason, taking it as the hour
>
> in which truth dawned.

Then there are poems in which "the machine" seems to have a life, and a mind, and even a will of its own, to have its own full agenda and to take active (and often malevolent) action against man, to be in direct conflict with him, and to have imposed its own rules on all of men's struggles with one another. There is the suggestion, here and elsewhere (as there is in Thomas's versions of the creation story), that God and man are in league together in terms of their struggle with an anti-creative but equally powerful mechanical force at work against them. If initially God and man worked together "at the delivery of the machine // from time's side" ("Come Down" [MHT 39]), later on—the creature having turned against them—God and man will need to join together again as they go "forth to meet the Machine" (H'm 1).

The situation is perhaps most memorably described in *Counterpoint* (C 47):

> "The body is mine and the soul is mine"
> says the machine. "I am at the dark source
> where the good is indistinguishable
> from evil. I fill my tanks up
> and there is war. I empty them
> and there is not peace. I am the sound,
> not of the world breathing, but
> of the catch rather in the world's breath."

Finally, most interestingly and most importantly in terms of Thomas's dominant and dominating theme, there are those poems in which God, man, and the machine (in any or all of its mythic or symbolic manifestations) are described in terms of their overt conflicts with one another.[5]

Thomas's use of the way or ways in which God, man and machine interact is, clearly, complex, and he has treated these interactions more extensively than any of the other ways in which he has described or dealt with "the machine." I would, therefore, like to concentrate on the poems in which these interactions occur in somewhat greater detail, since it is in these poems and in terms of this conflict that Thomas most succinctly represents, and most definitively defines, not only his "quarrel" with technology but also man's "quarrel" with God, or—as Thomas more typically puts it—God's "quarrel" with man. (And this quarrel, of course, is the most insistent and most all-encompassing theme or thesis in Thomas's canon—the theme that runs throughout much of his major poetry.)[6]

The first poem in which these conflicts are made explicitly clear is entitled "Other" (H'm 36). It begins with God contemplating his creation, pleased with its perfection:

> It was perfect. . . .
>   . . .
>   Its waters
> Were as clear as his own eye. The grass
> Was his breath. The mystery
> Of the dark earth was what went on
> In himself.

Then, sensing the machine's imminent rebellion, even here early on, God begins to plan for the machine's destruction. But he discovers that things have already gotten out of hand, or gone too far. He sees the machine advancing, singing contentedly to itself, its "song . . . the web / They were caught in, men and women / Together." And when God, saddened by how far things have progressed, commands, "Enough, enough," the machine simply looks at him insolently and continues to advance.

In the first poem in *Laboratories of the Spirit*, significantly enough entitled "Emerging" (LS 1),[7] Thomas suggests that both man and God must accept what he here calls "the presence of the machine" in the world. "Emerging" opens with these lines:

> Not as in the old days I pray,
> God. My life is not what it was.
> Yours, too, accepts the presence of
> the machine?

Here Thomas seems to suggest, or to posit as possibility, that there may be some relationship between God and the machine—viewed through the medium of man. Later in the poem he seems to suggest this relationship even more specifically by implying that man's mind is a mathematically based machine when he uses the phrase "the adult geometry / of the mind." Therefore, in "Emerging" it *emerges*, or begins to dawn on man, that "There are [some] questions [that he is] the solution / to" and "others, whose echoes he must expand to contain" as he goes out into the "tall city / of glass" that is also "the laboratory of the spirit." In short, Thomas places man between God and machine as mediator or interpreter between that which man will make and that which has made him. This is the crux of the issue throughout the whole of Thomas's analysis of his "quarrel" with technology, as he describes it in terms of the inevitably complex relationship between man, God, and machine.

"The Hand" (LS 2), the poem that immediately follows "Emerging," is one of Thomas's most interesting, complex, and troubling poems. In it he describes God's creation of a hand.

> It was a hand. God looked at it
> and looked away. There was a coldness
> about his heart, as though the hand
> clasped it.

God, envisioning what the hand will do, immediately regrets having created it. "Tempted to undo the joints / of the fingers," God picks the hand up— i.e., takes the hand in his hand. The hand fights back—and it begins to make demands. It has plans. It questions and accuses God:

> "Tell
> me your name," it cried, "and I will write it
> in bright gold. Are there not deeds
> to be done, children to make, poems
> to be written?"

God, disturbed by such questions and by the "unnerving warmth" of the hand, begins to fight with it. It is as if he is engaged in a "long war with himself," Thomas tells us. And the hand presents God with a "question not / to be answered"—even though it is a question that has always been "forseen."

The poem ends in a stalemate. And God releases the hand (apparently rudely throwing it aside) without giving it his blessing. He sends it away, out into the world, as a "messanger to the mixed things" it will make, charging it in parting to "tell them I am." This is a curious parable indeed.

When Thomas turns to follow these suggestions up, or out, in terms of their most intriguing complexities, he begins with a description of the birth of "the machine" as a parody of the biblical description of the birth of Christ.

> "Come," life said
> leading me on a journey
> as long as that
> of the wise men to the cradle,
>
> where, in place of the child
> it had brought forth,
> there lay grinning the lubricated
> changeling of the machine.
>
> ("Bleak Liturgies" [MHT 59–63])

Having been born "grinning," this "changeling" quickly grows and begins to take control. The machines, "laughing / up what would have been sleeves / in the old days," say, "'We are at / your service'" ("Fuel" [EA 70])—although clearly they mean to make certain that we (both men and God) are at *their* service. And when men ask to be distanced from these machines, when they ask to be taken to "places that are far off" ("Fuel" [EA 70]) from them, the machines readily agree, and seem willing to comply—in the sense that their actions are described as an "alloy" between themselves and the men they seem to serve. Ultimately, however, they only seem to comply, imposing a price that makes them appear to be "allies" with men, even though, as they soon show, they are not. Indeed, when men look the machine "in the eye," they see how their own "image / gradually is demoted" ("The Seasons" [MHT 69]). Thus this "alloy," an admixture in which man, being the more malleable, is bound to be compromised, is clearly also an ally, inseparably fused with the machine. And, therefore, man's mind, and even his body, are under the control of the mindless machine that he has himself created.

But, even so, machine, man, and God are all part of a continuum, a progressive order moving backward and forward through its central constituent, man. And since both the God (as Thomas so often calls him) and the machine are silent, man is left to combine, order, mix and match everything; man is left, on his own, to attempt to understand the continuum and his own place in it. It all began, we are told, with God "pushing" "nodes and molecules / . . . against molecules / and nodes," writing "in invisible handwriting the instructions / the genes follow" ("At It" [F 15]).[8] That is, it all began with God creating man, making the man who will do his biding, the man who, in turn, will make the machine to do his biding. That machine will, perhaps inevitably, turn on man and become independent, become even critical of him, and establish an agenda of its own, one different from the one anticipated, prepared for, or programmed, just as man himself has often established his own agenda independently of what seems God's will for him. And, therefore, for all of their seeming independence, machine to man, and man to God, each must answer to the other in terms of the continuum they are all caught in, and caught up in. And each is bound by it—even if the continuum becomes a never-ending, circular cycle.

As Thomas asks in "Asking" (EA 51):

> Did I see religion,
> its hand in the machine's,
> trying to smile as the grip
> tightened?

And, later, more insistently, he wonders:

>   Is there a contraceptive
>   for the machine, that we may enjoy
>   intercourse with it without being overrun . . .
>
> as we
>
>   . . . go up
>   into the temple of ourselves
>   and give thanks that we are not
>   as the machine is. . .
>
> even though we know that
>
>   . . . it waits
>   for us outside, knowing that when
>   we emerge it is into the noise
>   of its hand beating on the breast's
>   iron. . . . (C 47)

Years before, God had asked, "[W]ho were these in the laboratories / Of the world?" And he had ". . . followed the mazes / Of their calculations, and returned / To his centre to await their coming for him," knowing full well that "It was not his first time to be crucified" ("Repeat" [H'm 26]).[9]

No answers are ever given—but, of course, none had been expected. Perhaps the best, the most, that can ever happen is that "the machine," this other "god" that man has created—has served and been served by—will finally acknowledge man as its maker. In short, as Thomas seems to suggest—and I think it is, finally, the crux of this whole history of his use of the metaphor of the machine—the machine is to man as man is to God. Therefore, if the machine acknowledges man's sovereignty, and if man recognizes God's sovereignty, then, and only then, will there be some hope for a peaceful accommodation between creature and creator—whether we think of the relationship as that between God and man or between man and machine. Only then will there be some hope for "salvation"—in terms of man's life on earth, in terms of his relationship with the machine, and in terms of his relationship with God.[10]

Thomas puts all of the dichotomies and seeming confusions of his long meditation on "the machine" together in the "Incarnation" section of *Counterpoint*, where he describes a crucifixion in which man, nailed to a cross, is taunted by the machine he has made—which, apparently, has put him on this cross. It is a passage with obvious and complex repercussions for the other, parallel, dichotomy of Christ on his cross—since the relationship between man and machine here precisely duplicates the relationship between man and God.

Thomas imagines "a voice" taunting man:

> "If you were so clever
> as to invent me, come down
> now so that I may believe." (C 24)

And then, stepping back from that cross (and perhaps from its parallel as well?) Thomas, asks:

> Was there a resurrection?
> Did the machine put its hand
> in man's side, acknowledging lordship? (C 25)

And then—most intriguingly—Thomas turns the metaphor again (in the way he has always intended, I think, for us to see it and to hear it) by shifting the players around on this cross, changing the scene while we watch. He takes man, crucified by his own creation, by the machine he has invented, down from this cross, and puts God in the guise of a man back up on his cross, with mortal man standing before it—before him—all over again. And, therefore, here at what seems like an end, there is the clear prospect of another new beginning—one in which God, man, and machine can work in the world together again. It is, Thomas says, the prospect of "Eden / [all] over again" (C 28).

IV

> *With science and technology so enormously influential, spawning as they do new words every day, and with the decay of traditional beliefs in God, soul, and the afterlife, surely what [we] should be waiting for is a poet who can deploy the new vocabulary and open up new avenues, or should I say airways for the spirit in the twenty-first century.*

> — R. S. Thomas

In such terms then, Thomas concludes his "quarrel" with technology.

Let me refer to two of his later poems to summarize his argument, and to conclude my own. In one of the untitled poems in the powerful book *The Echoes Return Slow*, Thomas says:

> I have waited for him
>   under the tree of science
> and he has not come; . . . . (ERS 89)

And then he adds:

> I have looked in
> through the windows of their glass
>   laboratories and seen them plotting
> the future, and have put a cross
>   there at the bottom
> of the working out of their problems. . . . (ERS 89)

Finally, in an as yet uncollected poem, significantly enough entitled "Journey,"[11] Thomas summarizes man's situation and looks forward to a future that is, literally, a re-vision of the past.

"Journey" ends:

> There came a day, when the one
> without name and whose signature
>
> is in cypher willed them to go back
> to their first home, destitute but wiser.
> They turned as to a familiar, seeing it
> for the first time, suspended in beauty,
> blue with cold, but waiting to be loved.

Thomas would seem, finally, to want to put everything back together again, to make the world work smoothly in the way it must have been originally intended to. He recognizes that this "journey" he is on, the same journey we are all on, is confusing, complex, and often incomprehensible; but he has also always seemed to have hope that, somehow, God, man, and machine might all strive together—and survive together—to make the world all that it could be, or that it ought to be. And, therefore, here at the end of his long life and literary career, we find R. S. Thomas still attempting to open up "new avenues," new "airways for the spirit," as he looks toward God, man, and the machine moving into "the twenty-first century."[12]

R. S. Thomas and Søren Kierkegaard

In Great Waters

You are there also
at the foot of the precipice
of water that was too steep
for the drowned: their breath broke
and they fell. You have made an altar
out of the deck of the lost
trawler whose spars
are your cross.

. . .

                    There is
a sacrament there more beauty
than terror whose ministrant
you are and the aisles are full
of the sea shapes coming to its celebration.

— R. S. Thomas

What is a poet? An unhappy being who in his heart harbors a deep
anguish, but whose lips are so fashioned that the moans and cries
which pass over them are transformed into ravishing music. His fate
is like that of the unfortunate victims whom the tyrant Phalaris

imprisoned in a brazen bull, and slowly tortured over a steady fire; their cries could not reach the tyrant's ears so as to strike terror into his heart; when they reached his ears they sounded like sweet music. And men crowd about the poet and say to him, "Sing for us soon again"—which is as much as to say, "May new sufferings torment your soul, but may your lips be fashioned as before; for the cries would only distress us, but the music, the music, is delightful."

— Søren Kierkegaard

I

In *Nature,* Ralph Waldo Emerson said, "The true philosopher and the true poet are one, and a beauty, which is truth, and a truth, which is beauty, is the aim of both."[1] And surely it is the case that R. S. Thomas was always interested in (even, one might say, obsessed by) the relationships, the interconnections, the overlappings, of philosophical notions and poetic "truths." In part, of course, this is because, for Thomas, philosophical ideas or notions (and especially those that impinge upon theological themes) *are* poetic truths—as is clearly indicated by his close linkages of poetry and philosophy and, even more specifically, by the insistent theological theme that runs through much of his poetry and prose.

As early as 1966, in "A Frame for Poetry," an essay specifically concerned with "the relation of religion to poetry," Thomas suggested that "it is within the scope of poetry to express or convey religious truth, and to do so in a more intense and memorable way than any other literary form is able to" do. "Religion," he said, "has to do first of all with vision, revelation, and these are best told of in poetry." And, he added, "the main reason for this surely is the poetic nature of the original message. . . . If the message is the man, then Jesus was a poet. . . . In another sense, he [that is, Jesus—and, by Thomas's metaphoric extension, the poet as well] is God's metaphor. . . ." And, furthermore, he asked, "how shall we attempt to describe or express ultimate reality except through metaphor or symbol?"[2]

In a 1972 BBC TV film, Thomas argued even more explicitly. He said: "[P]oetry is religion, religion is poetry. The message of the New Testament is poetry. Christ was a poet, the New Testament is a metaphor, the Resurrection is a metaphor. . . ." And, he added, "when I preach poetry I am preaching Christianity, and when one discusses Christianity one is discussing poetry."[3] Therefore, even though Thomas protests that he makes "no claim to being a philosopher,"[4] as a poet he has clearly been closely drawn to theological themes as they have been treated by philosophers.

It is not surprising, then, that Thomas was, early on, drawn to a philosopher like Kierkegaard, one of the most theologically obsessed of the major philosophers. And on the basis of the poems in *No Truce with the Furies* (1995), Kierkegaard remained until the end an important source and resource for Thomas's thinking and for his poetry. Thomas published half a dozen poems on or about Kierkegaard before *No Truce with the Furies*, and in it he added two more. I want to argue, therefore, that Thomas's obsession with Kierkegaard and with the significance Kierkegaard has, and has had, on his poetry and thought comes to climax in *No Truce with the Furies*. Before looking at these last poems on Kierkegaard, however, it will perhaps be useful to describe and to attempt to detail something of the significance Kierkegaard seems to have had for Thomas's thinking over the years, and to try to summarize Thomas's earlier relationship to Kierkegaard, both in his poems and beyond them.

Søren Kierkegaard (1813–1855), the Danish philosopher and theologian, is often considered to be both the founder of "Christian existentialism" and a revolutionary figure in terms of his impact on the history of Protestant theology. In arguing that all truth is subjective or "interior," Kierkegaard insisted on a man's need to make what he called a "leap of faith"—through which he might be able to escape the world and to enter into a personal relationship with God. Kierkegaard saw man's life as being filled with anxiety and despair, what he called a "sickness unto death." He believed that man's relationship with God was a private, usually agonizing, and often lonely experience, one in which man attempted to analyze his own solitude and to come to some sense of peace and accommodation with respect to his own finitude. And since God, for Kierkegaard, was not immanent in society but rather "wholly other," a being "absolutely different" from and fully separated from man, any and every attempt at a relationship between man and God was filled with "fear and trembling." Because of such sentiments, and in spite of the fact that he was trained in theology, Kierkegaard chose not to take a pastorate and to serve as a practicing cleric. Rather, he said, he preferred instead to serve as a "missionary." And he described his work, his mission, as an attempt to "reintroduce Christianity into Christendom," not in any general or universal way, but to men one by one as "particular individuals." As he wrote:

> The wish to be a rural pastor has always appealed to me and been at the back of my mind. It appealed to me both idyllically as a wish in contrast to a strenuous life and also religiously as a kind of penitence, to find the time and the quiet to grieve over that in which I personally may have offended. . . . [M]y personal guilt makes me capable of submitting to *everything*. . . . Then if I am a clergyman, the confusion will take on tragic dimensions inasmuch as I would have kept back something upon entering this profession.

My position as author is different. I contract no personal relationship to any person who can make claims upon my example or upon the antecedents in my life. . . . It certainly is true that it seems more humble to pull back and become a pastor, but if I do that, there can also be something vain and proud in proudly rejecting the more spectacular. On the other hand, from now on I must take being an author [as] my calling, my whole *habitus* was designed for this.[5]

One can only imagine what Thomas might have thought of this passage in terms of his own dual callings.

Thomas has reported that while he was still a curate he discovered Kierkegaard and began to read him. When asked if he read Kierkegaard "because it was new ground" or because Kierkegaard "confirmed" what he was thinking, Thomas answered:

It was new ground I think. I began collecting Kierkegaard almost when I was a curate. . . . It might just have been the name, you know, the strange name. I discovered one or two of his books in a bookshop. I bought them . . . and I just began to collect them and read them. And then, of course, he gradually came to the attention of the Twentieth Century. When we went to Birmingham I went to a bookshop and saw two volumes of *Either/Or* for sale and I snapped these up and I just built him up. I've got most of Kierkegaard now. I think Yeats and Kierkegaard are, you know. . . . [this final ellipsis is in the interview].[6]

In this same interview (in 1983), when asked if he still read Kierkegaard, Thomas answered, "I do, periodically, yes. . . . I think he's got a very subtle mind, and I think I've got a certain amount of stimulation out of reading some of his [work]. But I disagree with his thing [thinking?] about poetry, there's no room for poetry in his system and . . . I disagree with him there. I like him on the individual."[7] In addition, Thomas said, "You were talking about Kierkegaard. . . . I don't read his sermons and such. *Concluding Unscientific Postscript* is, I suppose—every few years it does one good to tackle it. . . ."[8] In terms of Thomas's reference here to Kierkegaard's *Concluding Unscientific Postscript* and in relation to his own pervasive use of Kierkegaard's metaphor of the "seventy thousand fathoms" (to be considered in detail below), it is perhaps pertinent to quote an important passage in the *Concluding Unscientific Postscript* that Thomas had surely taken to heart.

Kierkegaard writes:

The truth is precisely the venture which chooses an objective uncertainty with the passion of the infinite. . . . But the above definition of truth is an equivalent expression for faith. Without risk there is no faith. Faith is precisely the contradiction between the infinite passion of the individual's inwardness and the objective uncertainty. If I am capable of grasping God objectively, I do not believe, but precisely because I cannot do this I must believe. If I wish to preserve myself in faith I must constantly be intent upon holding fast the objective uncertainty, so as to remain out upon the deep, over seventy thousand fathoms of water, still preserving my faith.[9]

Of course, it is impossible to know precisely the depth of Thomas's grapplings with Kierkegaard. In response to the question "I wonder if you continue to read Kierkegaard and what he means to you these days?" Thomas, late in his life, responded, "I don't always understand, don't always agree, but his life is a theme, and his stress on the subjective, the nominative, very instructive."[10] In spite of the fact that Thomas himself remains somewhat vague about his relationship to Kierkegaard, the evidence of the poems, and Thomas's explicit references to Kierkegaard in his essay "The Creative Writer's Suicide" and elsewhere, attests to what has no doubt been Thomas's long-term in-depth meditation on Kierkegaard's thought and writings, and it would seem to be clear that Thomas has frequently used Kierkegaard to buttress his own thinking, or, even, to initiate it.

In "The Creative Writer's Suicide" Thomas discusses the "pressures" that a poet must bear by recalling Kierkegaard's definition of a poet as "one who suffers," and who only "opens his mouth" "in his anguish."[11] Thomas goes on to describe Kierkegaard's "three stages in the development of the personality," and he uses Kierkegaard as a springboard for the remainder of his essay. Although Thomas explicitly mentions Kierkegaard's *The Present Age* at the outset of his essay, the passage that he apparently has most specifically in mind occurs in another book by Kierkegaard, *Stages on Life's Way*. In a passage in *Stages on Life's Way* (and in similar passages elsewhere)[12] Kierkegaard writes:

> There are three existence-spheres: the aesthetic, the ethical, the religious. . . . The ethical sphere is only a transitional sphere, and hence its highest expression is repentance as a negative action. The aesthetic sphere is that of immediacy, the ethical is that of requirement . . . the religious sphere is that of fulfillment, . . . hence the religious contradiction: at the same time to lie upon seventy thousand fathoms of water and yet be joyful.[13]

Although this is a passage which clearly has burned itself into Thomas's mind and memory, and one which reverberates throughout his canon, it is interesting that he remembers it in slightly different terms from those Kierkegaard uses. In "The Creative Writer's Suicide" Thomas describes Kierkegaard's "three stages of development" as "the aesthetic, the moral, and the religious."[14]

Given Thomas's long-standing devotion to Kierkegaard and his conspicuous identification with Kierkegaard's life and his writings, it is somewhat surprising that most of Thomas's critics have not attempted to investigate the relationship between Thomas and Kierkegaard in any significant detail. And even though several critics have, as Wynn Thomas says, "nervously noted" a relationship between Thomas and Kierkegaard, they have done so only glancingly, choosing "perhaps wisely," according to Wynn Thomas, "to make little of it."[15] The purpose of this essay is to attempt to reverse this "traditional wisdom" and to make much of the relationship between R. S. Thomas and Søren Kierkegaard—especially in terms of Thomas's poems that are specifically related to Kierkegaard.

II

Before turning to *No Truce with the Furies*, where the Kierkegaardian influences are most specifically and most thoroughly detailed, it will be useful to look briefly at several of Thomas's earlier poems that refer to Kierkegaard or that make overt use of Kierkegaardian themes, theses, or allusions—both to see something of Thomas's on-going obsession with Kierkegaard's thought throughout his career and to see something of the preparation he made for the poems specifically related to Kierkegaard in *No Truce with the Furies*.

The first poem in Thomas's canon that makes mention of Kierkegaard occurs in *Pietà* (1966), a book that marked an abrupt shift in Thomas's work—a shift that turned him much more insistently toward philosophical and theological themes. This poem is specifically entitled "Kierkegaard" (P 18–19) and it is primarily a poetic retelling of the basic biographical facts of Kierkegaard's life. In his poem Thomas describes Kierkegaard as having been born to a "stern father" and into a "family that wore itself out / On its conscience." Kierkegaard was a boy, Thomas says, who found the "acres" of his imagination growing "unhindered"—although eventually his imagination was brought to "pause" by the "gesture" of a "warped / Crucifix." Living "with the deed's terrible lightning" of the crucifixion surrounding him, deprived of love and derided by the public press, Kierkegaard,

> . . . wounded, . . . crawled
> To the monastery of his chaste thought
> To offer up his crumpled amen.

If it is the case, as Moelwyn Merchant remarks, that in this poem "the progress of the imagery reads like a refashioning of the Passion narrative,"[16] it is also true that some of the events of Kierkegaard's early life mentioned by Thomas seem to be similar to Thomas's own life, and that these similarities may well have been one of the most obvious reasons that Thomas was drawn to Kierkegaard and to his writings in the first place. Both Thomas and

Kierkegaard were fascinated by doubles and by mirrors. Both had ambivalent relationships with their fathers, another fact which may initially have attracted Thomas to Kierkegaard. And both had ambivalent or distanced "relationships" with God as a "father-figure." Both Kierkegaard and Thomas often found themselves estranged from the society in which they lived, and this alienation or estrangement may well have contributed to a condition that made them feel separate and alone in terms of all of their relationships, whether with men or with God. In short, it is clear that both Kierkegaard and Thomas, early on, began experimenting with their own "crumpled amen[s]"(P 19), and it seems entirely plausible that Thomas was drawn to Kierkegaard because he saw in him a person with a background similar to his own and because he also saw him as someone sympathetic to his own thinking. Indeed, it might be argued that Thomas saw Kierkegaard, man and thinker, as a kind of mirror for his own life and thought.[17]

In "A Grave Unvisited" (NHBF 9), Thomas's next poem on Kierkegaard, he describes how, when he went to Denmark, he had "Deliberately not" visited Kierkegaard's grave in Copenhagen. Even so, from afar, Thomas does indeed "visit" Kierkegaard's grave imaginatively: "I imagine the size / Of his tombstone, the solid marble / Cracking his bones." And then Thomas wonders—had he made the literal visit—would Kierkegaard "have been / There to receive this toiling body's / Pilgrimage"?[18]

The second half of the poem begins with another question:

> What is it drives a people
> To the rejection of a great
> Spirit, and after to think it returns
> Reconciled to the shroud
> Prepared for it?

Then there is an overt reference to the Gospel According to St. Luke: "It is Luke's gospel / Warns us of the danger / Of scavenging among the dead / For the living" (see Luke 24:4-5). Of course, this is a reference to the statement made to the women who come to Jesus's tomb on Easter morning and are met by "two men . . . in dazzling apparel" who ask them, "'Why do you seek the living among the dead?'" The reference is, however, a rather curious one, fraught with various ambiguities both in terms of the biblical parallel and in terms of Thomas's associations with Kierkegaard. The play on "the living and the dead," the references to "the rejection of a great / Spirit," and to the reconciliation of "the shroud / Prepared for it," can each be interpreted in several intriguing ways. Nevertheless, Thomas's association of this passage with Kierkegaard forces the parallels between himself and Kierkegaard and also between both himself and Kierkegaard and Christ. Indeed, one wonders how far Thomas might have been tempted to extend these parallels—thereby extending his own relationship to Kierkegaard and to Christ? For instance, Thomas describes how he has gone "Up and down with him in his books." Is this a reference to Kierkegaard and his books, or is the reference to "him" a reference to Christ and to the books of the Bible which deal with him—or to both?

"Up and down with him in his books," and

> Hand and hand like a child
> With its father . . .

There are two curiosities in this passage: "Hand *and* hand," and "With *its* father,"—as opposed to "Hand *in* hand" and "With *his* father." The non-colloquial expression and the curiously anonymous adjective in place of a personal pronoun (which parallels the anonymous or impersonal way that Thomas often refers to God as "the God") both serve to "distance" their references, even as they insist upon the familiarity of the parallel that Thomas clearly intends to make between himself and Kierkegaard (and between both of them and God?). One wonders how, precisely, to read this passage. We know that both Kierkegaard and Thomas had distant relationships with their fathers—and distant relationships with God as a father-figure. Therefore, one wonders if Thomas is here putting himself in the position of a "child" with respect to Kierkegaard as suggogate father-figure, a father-figure who is a more understanding or a more "communicable" father than his own father was, or even than his Father God was?

There are several other interesting details in the poem. The first is the reference to the Danes' attempts to "anchor" Kierkegaard with "the heaviness of a nation's / Respectability." Surely, Thomas often worried about the weight of "anchors" in his own life, and was well aware of the parallels between himself in his society and Kierkegaard in his. Might not Thomas be thinking of "the heaviness of a nation's respectability" in relation to himself, as a Welshman in Wales? Just as the Danes attempted to force Kierkegaard to conform to their own views of "respectability," so some in Wales have attempted to pressure Thomas to conform in numerous ways as well. Furthermore, the metaphor is clearly an early allusion to the nautical imagery still to come, and to Thomas's use of Kierkegaard's frequently used reference to the "seventy thousand fathoms," a phrase that Thomas borrows from Kierkegaard and uses almost as obsessively in his later poems on Kierkegaard and elsewhere as Kierkegaard uses it regularly throughout his own canon.

One reason that Thomas was no doubt so attracted to Kierkegaard was because of the example he set in so strongly and so successfully resisting attempts to control, tame, or "anchor" him. Indeed, Thomas's long and ardent devotion to Saunders Lewis represents a Kierkegaardian example close to home, a point that has been made by M. Wynn Thomas—who has argued that, for Wales and for R. S. Thomas, Saunders Lewis represents a kind of father figure, a kind of Kierkegaardian hero, who chose "quite consciously to devote his accusatory life to the preservation of values which have been jettisoned by the community in its unseemly haste to catch up with what it takes to be progress," and who has therefore frequently been regarded as an enemy of "the public." Wynn Thomas sees in R. S. Thomas's description of Kierkegaard's rejection by his own "fellow-countrymen" a parallel between Thomas himself, Saunders Lewis, and Kierkegaard. He says, "For 'people' [in "A Grave Unvisited"—"What is it drives a people"] . . . read 'the Welsh public'; and for Kierkegaard read Saunders Lewis—or R. S. Thomas."[19]

"Synopsis" (F 44), "Balance" (F 49), and "I" (MHT 58) each mention Kierkegaard explicitly, if only in passing. "Balance" begins:

> No piracy, but there is a plank
> to walk over seventy thousand fathoms,
> as Kierkegaard would say . . .

Here (and in "Synopsis") Thomas directly mentions one of Kierkegaard's most frequently used metaphors, that of the "seventy thousand fathoms." Kierkegaard uses this metaphor to describe being "out in the sea of thought, out in '70,000 fathoms deep,'"[20] to suggest the depth of danger in terms of man's relationship with God. Kierkegaard continues to use this figure of speech regularly throughout his writings. He asks, for instance, "'How many men have any idea at all how strenuous life becomes in an actual relationship to God?" And he then describes the "daily fear and trembling, every day, every moment of the day, . . . because every spiritual existence is out in the depths of '70,000 fathoms.'"[21] Elsewhere, Kierkegaard says that "intellectual existence . . . for the religious man is not easy, [because] the believer lies constantly out upon the deep and with seventy thousand fathoms of water under him"; indeed, "up to the last minute he lies above a depth of seventy thousand fathoms."[22] And Kierkegaard describes the "religious contradiction" that exists in an individual who "at the same time [that he lies] upon seventy thousand fathoms of water [can] yet be joyful."[23] By this he means that man must "venture far out in [his] reliance upon God"[24] even though such a "venture" is often dangerous.

If "Balance," as Tony Brown suggests, is equivalent to "Kierkegaard's fear-filled universe," a world where "authentic existence is derived only from faith born of constant and strenuous spiritual struggle with doubt in a world where nothing is certain,"[25] Thomas is also working out his own version of Kierkegaard's trope of the seventy thousand fathoms here—but it is clear that

Thomas has by now fully internalized Kierkegaard's metaphor and made it very much his own as well. The reference to "piracy" in the first line of "Balance" suggests a world in which one makes one's living by the theft of someone else's goods, a world in which someone steals or appropriates something from another and keeps it for his own. But Thomas says that there has been "no piracy" in this instance. No one or no thing has been seized, captured, or stolen away. Still, and in spite of the fact that there has been "no piracy," Thomas feels as if he is in some sort of jeopardy—"there is a plank / to walk," "far out / from the land," over the "seventy thousand fathoms." This danger, however, seems to be a threat more to his mind than it is to his body. But it is also a threat to the "easier certainties / of belief." There are "no handrails to / grasp" and below, in the deep waters, there "is the haggard gallery / of the dead, those who in their day / walked here and fell." These, apparently, fell without being forced or pushed out on any plank; they fell because of a failure of mind. And, meanwhile, all around, above and below, there is the "chaos" of the anonymous and inimical "galaxies' / violence" and the "meaningless wastage / of force." Still, mysteriously, as if out of nowhere, there appears a "blond hero" who "leaps" "over my head" into the chaos. Is this blond hero Kierkegaard the Dane?—or the blond Christ of Sallman's famous portrait? Is this "leap" Kierkegaard's leap of faith? Thomas's only answer is his two final questions:

> Is there a place
> here for the spirit? Is there time
> on this brief platform for anything
> other than mind's failure to explain itself?

"Here." Where? "Mind's failure to explain itself?" As is so often the case, Thomas, like Kierkegaard, raises questions which in turn raise additional questions. And Thomas's poems often risk the kind of precarious "balances" that such questions raise or imply, and they often leave these questions unanswered—perhaps because they are unanswerable.

III

With this Kierkegaardian context, and with these earlier poems in mind, I want to turn now to *No Truce with the Furies*, the book in which Thomas's Kierkegaardian influence comes to climax. The first "Kierkegaardian" poem in *No Truce with the Furies* is—perhaps it should not be a surprise—"Fathoms" (NTF 10).

Young I visited
this pool; asked my question,
passed on. In the middle years
visited it again. The question
had sunk down, hardly
a ripple. To be no longer
young, yet not to be old
is a calm without
equal. The water ticks on,
but time stands, fingerless.

Today, thirty years
later, on the margin
of eternity, dissolution,
nothing but the self
looking up at the self
looking down, with each
refusing to become
an object, so with the Dane's
help, from bottomless fathoms
I dredge up the truth.

The first stanza describes Thomas's youthful and then his middle-aged encounters with "this . . . bottomless" pool. His first visit was brief, casual, inconsequential: "I visited / . . . asked my question, / passed on." This youthful question (whatever it was) apparently hardly created a ripple on the surface of the pool, or on him. During a second visit, "in the middle years," Thomas finds that his "question" has now "sunk[en] down" below the surface, that it is now no longer even "a ripple." As he has matured the "question" has taken on "depth." It has merged with the depths of his consciousness, just as it has submerged into the depths of the pool.

In the second stanza Thomas seems to be clearly aware both of where he is and of what he is about. He is now "on the margin / of eternity," nearer death and "dissolution." The next several lines are intriguing and somewhat ambiguous. They explicitly say that he is split into a bifurcated "self," one half of which is "looking up" and the other half "looking down." But Thomas here also seems to suggest the presence of an additional "self." Instead of simply the bifurcated self contemplating its separate sides, there seems to be the clear suggestion of another "self" that is "looking down" on or at Thomas's "self" as it looks up. On the one hand, Thomas seems to be describing his own "starings" at himself, and on the other, his "starings" at God—or God's "staring" at him. Both stare silently. Both refuse "to become / an object" to or for the other. And from the "bottomless" depths (or heights) of these mute contemplations, with Kierkegaard's "help," Thomas dredges up "the truth." Is this "truth" a truth of man's condition, in terms of man alone, or is it the "truth" of man's condition in terms of his relationship with God? Or is it both? Again, any answer hangs on silence. Several things are significant, however. As he does here, Thomas frequently invokes the Narcissus myth, and he often displays an obsession with mirrors and mirror images, as I have tried to show above.[26] In this passage both of these associations are important. The doubled halves of the self (or the dual "selves") which Thomas describes as staring back and forth at one another in these lines seem to be indebted—especially so in terms of the addition of the Narcissus allusion—to Kierkegaard's dual notions of "double reflection" and "indirect communication."

"Indirect communication" (or "inwardness") and "double reflection" are related terms in Kierkegaard. Kierkegaard argued that "direct communication," which attempts to define truth by conveying "results," is inadequate when applied to ethical and religious truths because such "truths" can only be known subjectively. "Double reflection" is, however, "an instance of indirect communication requiring [the] artful suppression of the communicator, who as a 'subjective existing thinker' becomes aware . . . that the truth he has acquired 'interests' his existence. . . ."[27] Furthermore, both "double reflection" and "indirect communication" can be associated with Kierkegaard's frequent use of pseudonyms. For instance, the three "existence-spheres," or "life views," in *Stages on Life's Way* are represented by pseudonymous "characters" who purport to be the authors of some of Kierkegaard's earlier books. Kierkegaard's pseudonyms and, in turn, the additional characters that *they* invent, are a crucial part of Kierkegaard's dialectical method. And it might be argued that some of the ambiguity in Thomas's work comes about as a result of the essentially "pseudonymous" character of some of the speakers in his poems. This tactic, then, is a device, used both by Kierkegaard and by Thomas, to distance things, to communicate "indirectly" certain things that may be too personal or private for a more direct telling, to find by "indirections" "directions out."[28]

In "Fathoms" Thomas seeks, "with the Dane's help," to find an answer to his question and to understand his condition or circumstances—to, as he says, "dredge up the truth." The implication is that, by the end of the poem, "with the Dane's help," Thomas *has* been able to "dredge up the truth" from these "bottomless fathoms." But this is all still rather vague since the reader is never fully enlightened or informed as to what "the truth" dredged up from the depths of these "fathoms" really is. Indeed, Thomas seems to suggest that his readers must attempt to *fathom* both the question and the answer or answers on their own, simply taking his testimony of *his own success*, with Kierkegaard's help, as an example of the possibility of their success. If the poem, finally, remains somewhat vague, it does seem to be clear that, for Thomas, the experience has met with success—through Kierkegaard's example.

"S. K." (NTF 15–17) is a much longer poem, and in many ways a more important and a much less cryptic one. In it Thomas summarizes and brings to climactic conclusion most of his earlier references to, and much of his earlier thinking on, Kierkegaard.[29]

"S. K." is divided into four distinct sections. The first section consists of seven stanzas in couplets in which Thomas compares Kierkegaard to Christ and, as the stanzaic structure suggests, links them inseparably together. The comparison begins at the very beginning of the poem:

> Like Christ we know little
> of him when he was young.

Thomas then focuses on Kierkegaard's birth, again explicitly linking Kierkegaard to Christ: "Peering into a Danish mist / we discover no manger // to which the wise brought their gifts, . . ."

The final three couplets in this first part of the poem subtly shift the focus from an overt comparison between Kierkegaard and Christ to a comparison between "S. K." and "R. S." Surely, Thomas's title immediately suggests a comparison between himself and Kierkegaard, since both men are frequently referred to by their initials. Indeed, it might be argued that Thomas is specifically calling attention to such a comparison by entitling his poem "S. K." (there are no further direct references to Kierkegaard, by name, in the poem itself). Still, after the cryptic or coded "naming" he uses in his title, Thomas manages to make Kierkegaard almost anonymous, just as Thomas made himself anonymous in his autobiography by calling himself "Neb," "No One." And, indeed, we are quickly told that "S. K." "learned / his anonymity from God himself"—just as "R. S." must have as well. Surely the two final couplets in this first section of the poem seem to apply more to "R. S." than they do to "S. K.," and they simultaneously seem to suggest, *via* a somewhat curious progression of references, a parallel between R. S. Thomas and God.

First we are told that "S. K."

> . . . learned
> his anonymity from God himself,

and then that, as a result of this, he leaves

> . . . his readers, as God
> leaves the reader in life's
>
> book to grope for the meaning
> that will be quicksilver in the hand.

There are several interesting suggestions in this passage. First there is the fact that Thomas tells us that Kierkegaard "learned / his anonymity from God himself." If God is "anonymous," and if Kierkegaard, who sets the example for Thomas, "learned his anonymity from God," then Kierkegaard leaves Thomas, as God has left Kierkegaard, to "grope" for the "meaning" of the "message" of this God—just as Thomas, in his turn, leaves his readers to grope for the meaning of the message he himself communicates, through this philosopher, concerning God. And whatever the message is, it will be like "quicksilver" once it is "in . . . hand." Thomas's anonymous God, so difficult to find or communicate with, so removed and so mysterious as to seem almost totally absent, is placed in parallel with the "anonymity" of Kierkegaard (who often communicated in his writings only through "anonymous" pseudonyms) and with Kierkegaard's equally anonymous God.

Then there is the word "quicksilver," a particularly interesting word in its own right, but especially so in this context. In addition to the significance of its component parts, quicksilver, mercury in its liquid form, is used in scientific experiments to determine subtle fluctuations in temperatures. The suggestion here seems to be that degrees of meaning are ultimately determined by conditions that depend not upon the instrument used to measure them but upon the "environment" surrounding the instrument or, indeed, upon the way that the meaning—or the instrument—is "read" and understood, or interpreted, by the "reader." This seems to suggest that, to any individual man, God's meaning in "life's book" depends upon the "temperature" of man's own mind. That is, the meaning of God's word, and of Kierkegaard's philosophy, and of Thomas's poems, varies according to the temperature or the temperament of the mind that receives it. Therefore, the meaning made of the message by the interpreter is not "objective," not inherent in or intrinsic to the words of the message themselves, but it subjectively resides within the interpreter alone. Thus these lines echo, "repeat," or "recollect," both forward and backward—in Kierkegaardian terms. They recollect, repeat, and "remember" any number of other lines in other poems throughout Thomas's canon, lines in which the reader, in his own life's book, must "grope for the meaning," just as Thomas does here, only to discover that, whatever he takes the meaning to be, whatever he makes it mean, it will often only be like "quicksilver in the hand." This notion is consistent with one of the most constant themes that runs through Thomas's (and Kierkegaard's) work, namely that God and the meaning of the Christian message in life's book cannot be fixed; that both God and the meaning of His message are constantly changing, and that no human "instrument" can measure either fully or finally.[30]

The second section of "S. K." consists of three quatrains indented from the hard left-hand margin established by the couplets of the first section.

This simple device seems to suggest that Kierkegaard's literal life—since that is what this section of the poem is concerned with—will be, or should be, "indented," set inside of or made parenthetical to, the mental life of his thought and work. Such a suggestion certainly applies to Kierkegaard in terms of the relationship between his literal life and the life of the mind, since Kierkegaard's "life" *was* essentially his mental life.

Beginning with the banal banter of lovers, "'Kiss me, kiss me not.' / 'I love you, I reject you'—," this section of the poem describes the "perilous game" of lovers, even though the mix of metaphysical reference and overt sexual suggestion would seem to be—but is not—as uncharacteristic of Thomas as it would be for Kierkegaard. This section concludes with an explicit reference to Kierkegaard's "gaiety in public," a gaiety that "was a shirt of nettles for him // at night." Thomas also makes specific mention here of Kierkegaard's lover, "Hapless Regine / with her moonlight hair," who was never to know that "no apparent / lunatic was ever more sane." Kierkegaard's long and complicated relationship with Regine (Regina) Olsen was, as his biographer Walter Lowrie says, "an amazing love-story."[31] But, as Thomas says, "The game was perilous / to them both." Surely, as Kierkegaard attested to in the scores of references that accumulate throughout his voluminous works with respect to "Her," "His gaiety in public," after his loss of Regina, "was a shirt of nettles for him" throughout the rest of his life.[32] (And yet, one wonders, had he not lost "Her," whether he would have written any or all of what so frequently seem pieces specifically composed as compensation for her loss.)

The third section of "S. K." consists of nine tercets or triplets, a triune verse form that suggests a linkage between Kierkegaard, God, and Thomas himself. This section begins, somewhat surprisingly, with the suggestion that Kierkegaard "was the first / of the Surrealists, picturing / our condition with the draughtsmanship // of a Dali." The reference to a "draughtsman" conjures up a particularly rich set of suggestions. On the most literal level, the word of course refers to a "draftsman," one who draws or paints. However, Thomas no doubt also has in mind several additional meanings of the term: the notion of "drafts" in terms of writing; the notion of a "draft" as part of the process of purposeful selection; the idea of a draft as a preliminary sketch or version, a plan for something not yet finished or completed. And, of course, Thomas also has an abiding interest in painting, and in the relationships between poetry and painting as art forms, as is most obviously indicated by his galleries of poems on paintings in *Between Here and Now* (1981) and in *Ingrowing Thoughts* (1985), and in painters and works of art in general.[33]

The next part of this third section of Thomas's poem (ll. 6–18) deals specifically and exclusively with Kierkegaard and his life and thought.

Kierkegaard's prose is described as "limpid" but with "a cerebral gloss / pro-
hibitive of transparence." This glossy surface luster that prohibits or inter-
feres with what it purports to present so glaringly is obviously an apt way for
Thomas to associate Dali with Kierkegaard, and both of them with himself.
These lines are clearly packed with significance, and Thomas seems to be
using the word "gloss" in terms of all of its meanings, from the simplest sense
of an explanation of meaning, to the notion of surface luster and/or an attrac-
tive appearance, to the possibility of masking the true nature of something in
the sense of "glossing it over." The possibilities extend even to the sense of a
"gloss" as a false or willfully misleading interpretation (as of a text), or to the
possibility of a brief explanation (as, for instance, in the margin or between
the lines of a text) of a difficult or obscure expression, or, indeed, to the idea
of a continuous commentary accompanying a text. These are all things that
paintings, poems, philosophy, and criticism often make use of or attempt
to accomplish. The passage, further, states that Kierkegaard's "laughter" was
"that // of an author out of the asylum / of his genius." "Asylum," perhaps
prepared for by the reference to Dali and the Surrealists, is an interesting
and ambiguous word in the context. An asylum is an inviolable place. It is
a place that provides shelter, security, refuge, and protection. It is, indeed,
a sanctuary—and certainly such a definition would be a "loaded" word for
both Kierkegaard and for Thomas. The asylum of "genius" and the "laughter"
that "an author" laughs from such a place may well be an accurate descrip-
tion (from both sides of the walls) of the lack of communication between
those inside and those outside such asylums—whether they be poets, paint-
ers, philosophers, or madmen. Asylums, places of shelter, refuge, and protec-
tion, sanctuaries intended to provide safety or to insure immunity, may also
imprison—imprison even their own makers.[34]

Next we are told that Kierkegaard, "Imagining / from his emphasis on
the self // that God is not other,"[35] leads us to be "arrested"—seized, stopped,
captured—"by his shadow." The passage is complicated and, again, some-
what ambiguous. "That God is not other" suggests that God is similar to or
the same as "the self," an anthropomorphic deity made in man's image and
seen, known, or knowable both in or through the self and in or through other
selves in such a way that he is made visible *via* "his shadow"—not in the face
of the beloved, but in an afterglow "in which the face of the beloved // is as a
candle snuffed out," or

> in the darkness following
> on the mind's dazzling explosion.[36]

This seems to suggest that in the "shadow" of God's presence (a present absence,
as always, with Thomas) we are "arrested"—stopped, seized, captured—and

we see, through the "dazzling explosion" in our mind's eye, the "face of the beloved," which glimmers or glows momentarily like a candle extinguished or "snuffed out." This brief "lightning flash" made by the "mind's dazzling explosion" is followed by full dark.

The final lines of this third section of the poem (ll. 19–27) suggest a kind of Kierkegaardian "either/or," or, perhaps better, a "both/and." This section begins, "Either way there was terror." The remaining lines in the section are devoted, rather explicitly and specifically, to Kierkegaard:

> Backwards there was the moor
> in Jutland, where his father,
>
> from the Calvary of himself,
> had accused God.

Kierkegaard's father, Thomas says, had "accused God." Really, the statement ought to be more strongly put. Michael Kierkegaard had *cursed* God. And, thereby, as Thomas suggests, and as Kierkegaard would surely have agreed, Michael Kierkegaard "crucified" himself at a "Calvary" of his own making and—as Kierkegaard thought—"crucified" his son with him as well. This is obviously an interesting elaboration on, or extension of Thomas's (and Kierkegaard's) treatment of, the father/son relationship.[37] Kierkegaard was obsessed, and tormented, throughout his life by what he felt was his own continuing complicity in his father's guilt, and the constant presence of the father's sin visited on the son is a theme that recurs over and over again in his writings. Even more significant here, however, is Thomas's specific allusion to "Calvary," the place where Christ himself "accused God." Such "accusations," it would seem, may have different meanings, and yield drastically different results.

This section of the poem concludes:

> Forward
> there was one overtaken
>
> by his own speed, thought
> brought to bay by a truth
> as inscrutable as its reflection.[38]

This passage certainly applies to Kierkegaard, and it seems to apply to Thomas too. The "inscrutable" truth remains a mystery, in "reflection," to the end. It is thought cornered and crying out in the reflected presence of an inscrutable truth—like Calvary, like the life and work of Kierkegaard, or like the life and work of Thomas?

Such an inscrutable truth is the constant theme and thesis of all of
Kierkegaard's—and Thomas's—work. It appears again, conspicuously, in
"Reflections" (NTF 31), the title poem of *No Truce with the Furies*. "Reflec-
tions" begins, "The furies are at home / in the mirror." Mirrors, what they
reflect, and what they fail to reflect, like the sea and windows, have always
been of interest to Thomas; indeed, he has specifically linked mirrors with
windows and called them one of his "obsessions." He has said, "I became
obsessed with the mirror image, comparing the sea now to a window, now to
a looking glass."[39] It is not surprising, therefore, here in a poem itself entitled
"Reflections," the title poem of *No Truce with the Furies*, a book that "reflects"
his entire career, and one in which he is "reflecting back" on his long life, on
all of his work and his world—and perhaps, *via* Kierkegaard, also "reflecting
forward" to the identity he will have left behind him as man and poet—that
Thomas finds his "furies" "at home / in the mirror."

As Marie-Thérèse Castay has pointed out, the mirror as a key image
in Thomas's work is evident as early as *Tares* (1961)—in a poem entitled
prophetically enough (in terms of the present discussion) "Judgment Day"
(T 20)—in which "Thomas visualizes man's creation as God breathing on
a mirror" and man's "death as God breathing again" on the mirror, thereby
"blurring that first image" out.[40] Likewise, in a very intriguing image in *The
Echoes Return Slow*, Thomas describes "the face of the believer, ambushed in
a mirror."[41] And in *Counterpoint* (1990) Thomas imagines "God's mind" as
two mirrors echoing / one another," and he then describes mirrors as "surfaces
/ of fathoms which mind / clouds when examining itself / too closely."[42] But
perhaps most importantly, in "A Life" (EA 52)—a poem in which Thomas
speaks as personally and as openly as he ever has about himself—there is a
passage in which he joins the Narcissus image (and theme) to his obsession
with mirrors as he describes himself as:

> A Narcissus tortured
>   by the whisperers behind
>   the mirror.

With these earlier poems "echoing" behind it, here then, in "Reflections,"
like elsewhere in *No Truce with the Furies*, Thomas's "furies are at home / in
the mirror." (Lest we miss the double pun, Thomas tells us in the same line,
"it is their address." And, he adds, we should "Never think to surprise them,"
stating finally that "There is no truce // with the furies.") Thomas's "furies"
are, at once, states of frenzy, anger, and exaltation, as well as the avenging
deities of mythology who torment mortal men's minds, and/or any avenging
spirit in general, including anonymous, mirror-like, or self-imagined ones.

We might expect Thomas's "S. K." to end at this point, his "inscrutable" theme and the reflection on it come to conclusion—but there is a fourth, final, coda-like summary section. In this final single stanza of twenty lines Thomas concludes his argument. He concludes, likewise, not only the "argument" with Kierkegaard that has run throughout his work, but the definitive "argument" that has been the most obsessive theme of his long life and much of his major work, early and late.

This final section of "S. K." contains four sentences, three of them questions. It begins:

> How do we know his study
> was not the garden
> over again, where his mind
> was the serpent, insinuator
> of the heresy of the self
> as God?

These lines are typical of Thomas, filled with his fully packed words and his inevitable ambiguity. Kierkegaard's "study," like Thomas's, has always been an exploration of the mind as subtle serpent in the garden, as "insinuator" / of the heresy of the self/ as God," the mind in mirror-like confrontation with itself, and with God. And for Thomas such confrontations usually take place in prayer. In the next sentence Thomas defines what he calls the "difficulty / with prayer." It is the "exchange / of places between I and thou, / with silence as the answer / to an imagined request." Such an "exchange / of places" suggests Thomas's typically reciprocal relationship between God and man, but, just as typically, the relationship is put into the context of an "imagined" relationship and in terms of an "imagined request."

The two final sentences are also questions.[43] Thomas first asks:

> Is this the price genius
> must pay, that from an emphasis
> on the subjective only
> soliloquy remains?

Then, more fully, and more confusingly, he asks:

> Is prayer
> not a glass that, beginning
> in obscurity as his books
> do, the longer we stare
> into the clearer becomes
> the reflection on a countenance
> in it other than our own?[44]

This final question goes back to the end of the third section and to that "inscrutable . . . reflection" that brought truth to bay. And it brings to climax (if not to full or final resolution or conclusion) Thomas's Kierkegaardian "reflections" in *No Truce with the Furies*. Related to the earlier Narcissus imagery, and with the suggestion of the dual expectations and terrors inherent in solipsism, and of the notion of endless reflection as well as self-imprisonment—with beyond it little or no hope—this section seems to suggest that prayer *is* a "glass," and that that glass, stared into long enough, may finally begin to clear and suggest the possibility of a presence in it—a "countenance" (and perhaps even a presence that can be "counted" on) "other than our own."

Thus, in this glass, this mirror which mirrors mind more than anything else, this Kierkegaardian mirror into which he has so often looked and through which he has found sanction and approval, and within which he has seen, even if darkly, a "countenance" "other than [his] own," R. S. Thomas has come, "with the Dane's help," to stand above "bottomless fathoms" and attempted to "dredge up the truth."

10

R. S. Thomas and Wallace Stevens

I

Our religion is the poetry in which we believe. . . . Poetry raised to
its highest power is then identical with religion grasped in its inmost
truth; at their point of union both reach their utmost purity and
beneficence, for then poetry loses its frivolity and ceases to demoralize,
while religion surrenders its illusions and ceases to deceive.

—George Santayana

In his "Letter about Mallarmé," Valéry writes:

From my first glance at his work it became . . . a subject for wonderment.
. . . He played . . . a great part in my inner history without knowing it; he
changed so many of my values merely by existing; his simple *act of pres-*
ence assured me of so many things, confirmed me in so many things, and,
even more, has been an inner law forbidding me so many things, that I can
hardly distinguish what he was from what he was to me.

He adds:

No word comes easier or oftener to the critic's pen than the word *influence,*
and no vaguer notion can be found among all the vague notions that com-
pose the phantom armory of aesthetics. Yet there is nothing in the critical

field that should be of greater philosophical interest or prove more rewarding to analysis than the progressive modification of one mind by the work of another. . . . Opposites are born from opposites."[1]

Valéry makes clear here that by "influence" he does not mean "imitation"—even if the earlier "work acquires a singular value in the other [writer's] mind." Indeed, he argues:

> We say that an author is *original* when we cannot trace the hidden transformations that others underwent in his mind; we mean to say that the dependence of *what he does* on *what others have done* is excessively complex and irregular. . . . It is when a book or an author's collected work acts on someone not with all its qualities, but with one or a few of them, that influence assumes its most remarkable values. The development of a single quality of one person by the full talent of another seldom fails to produce results marked by an *extreme originality*.[2]

Almost as if he is following up on Valéry's suggestion, Harold Bloom, in his studies of the history of poetic theory and practice, *The Anxiety of Influence* and *A Map of Misreading,* defines and documents what he calls "the anxiety of influence" as it has affected poets and poetry during the past several centuries by charting the influence of "strong, authentic poets" on one another. Bloom argues that such an influence "always proceeds by a misreading of the prior poet, an act of creative correction that is actually and necessarily a misinterpretation" of the one poet by the other. This influence and its attendant anxiety has, according to Bloom, been evident throughout "the main tradition of Western poetry since the Renaissance," and it constitutes a "history of anxiety and self-saving caricature, of distortion, of perverse, wilful [*sic*] revisionism without which modern poetry . . . could not exist."[3]

Speaking of any two particular poets, Bloom argues that the later poet

> holds his own poem so open . . . to the precursor's work that at first we might believe the wheel has come full circle, and that we are back in the later poet's flooded apprenticeship. . . . [A]nd the uncanny effect is that the new poem's achievement makes it seem to us, not as though the precursor were writing it, but as though the later poet himself had written the precursor's characteristic work.[4]

Granted that there are intriguing instances of such possible indebtednesses between one poet and another, it is nonetheless unusual to find any "strong poet" *explicitly* claiming (or even overtly suggesting) a direct association between himself and an earlier poet as "precursor"—in spite of the fact that this is precisely what critics often do, either explicitly or implicitly. Therefore, it is somewhat startling to find R. S. Thomas making such a specific assertion with respect to Wallace Stevens.

In his essay "The Figure of the Youth as Virile Poet," Stevens seems to support the Burckhardtian notion that "Poetry is the voice of religion."[5] If this is so, the contention that Stevens and Thomas shared a theologically based philosophy will not perhaps be a surprising or startling assertion, even though Thomas was a theist and Stevens was an agnostic, if not an atheist. However, in spite of such seemingly different theological or philosophical perspectives, Stevens and Thomas shared a philosophy which, for all the apparent differences, was, I want to claim, really very much the same philosophy. And it was a philosophy with deeply theological trappings, one which worked itself out in both men's thinking—both in their prose (where, in Stevens, it is often most explicit) and in their poetry.[6] It is this theologically focused philosophy, I believe, that caused Thomas, in his late poem "Homage to Wallace Stevens," to assert: "I turn now / not to the Bible / but to Wallace Stevens" (NTF 62).

This is a startlingly straightforward statement, and a rather stunning one, coming from Thomas, whose daily life was and always had been a "turning" primarily to the Bible and to his practice as a parish priest. How did he come to such a conclusion, to such an assertion, and what was the basis of his relationship—and his indebtedness—to Stevens that would allow him to make such a statement? One answer might be based on Thomas's remark, "I think Wallace Stevens comes nearest to expressing the situation, in poetry."[7] This is a paradoxical position for Thomas to take, since, as A. E. Dyson has remarked, Stevens "conjures religious notions away, with unfailing courtesy." Nonetheless, as Dyson also notes, Thomas, "increasingly" came to "conclusions akin to Stevens's," and these "conclusions" "haunt [Thomas's] work." The "echoes" that Thomas "sets up . . . between his poems" and those of Stevens are, Dyson believes, "mutually enriching and elusive." As an instance of the reciprocal relationship between Thomas and Stevens, particularly in terms of what I have referred to as their theological trappings, Dyson says that Thomas's "assertions of God's absence seem as lucid as Wallace Stevens's, though far angrier."[8]

II

I am a fragment, and this is a fragment of me.

—Ralph Waldo Emerson

Thomas published three poems explicitly related to Stevens. Two of them, "Wallace Stevens" (BT 25–26) and "Homage to Wallace Stevens" (NTF 62), directly address Stevens and describe Thomas's indebtedness to him as man, poet and precursor. Another, "Thirteen Blackbirds Look at a Man"

(LP 174–76), is primarily indebted to Stevens poetically; it is Thomas's almost antiphonal response to Stevens's well-known early poem, "Thirteen Ways of Looking at a Blackbird" (*Collected Poetry and Prose* 74–76).

I want to consider each of these poems specifically and in detail, but it is worth noting that Thomas mentions or alludes to Stevens on numerous other occasions, both in his poems and in his prose. In two late poems, for instance, both published in his final book, *No Truce with the Furies* (1995), Thomas mentions Stevens. In "Negative" (NTF 50), he writes: "One word. Say it. / 'No.' No is the word, then? / 'No,' Stevens misled us." And in "Anybody's Alphabet" (NTF 88–92) he writes,

> For Stevens fictions
> were as familiar
> as facts and if far-
> fetched preferable.
> Forfeiting for faith
> fable, he feasted on it.

In addition to these direct references to Stevens, John Powell Ward identifies two other poems that might be related to Stevens: "Winter Starlings" (T 36), which, Ward says, "echoe[s]" Stevens, and "Mrs. Li" (BT 21), which Ward argues has its "direct source in Wallace Stevens" and is "clearly an antiphonal poem to Stevens's "To The One Of Fictive Music." [9] Further, as Tony Brown reports, "In a letter to me of 8 June 2002, Ward draws attention to 'The Conductor' [T 13] published in *Tares* (1961), as possibly owing something to Stevens. This seems a very shrewd suggestion: the poem certainly shares something of the tranquility of poems like 'The Idea of Order at Key West'; it is set on the shore 'at the end of the day' and, as in the Stevens poem, the person makes (or in this case imagines) music in a natural landscape." [10]

On several other occasions Thomas mentioned Stevens in ways that suggest his indebtedness to him. In an interview in 1990 Thomas said that "Literature . . . is the supreme human statement." [11] This seems a clear echo of Stevens's notion of poetry as the "supreme fiction" (see, for example, Stevens's "A High-Toned Old Christian Woman" [*Collected Poetry and Prose* 47], which begins, "Poetry is the supreme fiction, madame.") And Thomas then quoted Stevens's poem "Chocorua to Its Neighbor":

> To say more than human things with human voice,
> That cannot be; to say human things with more
> Than human voice, that, also, cannot be;
> To speak humanly from the height or from the depth
> Of human things, that is acutest speech.
>
> (*Collected Poetry and Prose* 266–67)

Thomas added, "We must remain articulate to the end."[12] Then, in an interview with Graham Turner near the end of his own life,[13] Thomas referred to Stevens's statement that "Poetry must resist the intelligence almost successfully" (see *Collected Poetry and Prose* 910). Also, in a BBC radio program,[14] Thomas mentioned Stevens's "Peter Parasol" (see *Collected Poetry and Prose* 548), as one of several literary texts, that, as Tony Brown[15] reports, "had given him pleasure."

It is also worth remembering that Thomas included Stevens's "Common Soldier," the first of Stevens's 1914–1915 *Lettres d'un Soldat* (see *Collected Poetry and Prose* 538–39), in his edition of the *Penguin Book of Religious Verse* (1963). The second tercet of "Common Soldier" no doubt resonated with circumstances in Thomas's life:

> I have been pupil under bishops' rods
> And got my learning from the orthodox.
> I mark the virtue of the common-place.

III

> . . . *[T]he fictive abstract is as immanent in the mind of the poet,*
> *as the idea of God is immanent in the mind of the theologian. The*
> *poem is a struggle with the inaccessibility of the abstract.*
>
> —Wallace Stevens

Thomas's "Thirteen Blackbirds Look at a Man" (LP 174–76) is obviously and directly indebted to, and will inevitably be associated with, Stevens's "Thirteen Ways of Looking at a Blackbird" (*Collected Poetry and Prose* 74–76). What is perhaps most intriguing about this association is that Thomas, an extremely individual man and poet, at the height of his career, should so obviously indebt himself to any other poet, least of all to a poet as dominant and dominating as Stevens. The fact that Thomas's indebtedness to Stevens is often so subtle as to be easily missed suggests that "Thirteen Ways of Looking at a Blackbird," an atypical poem for Stevens, struck Thomas in such a way that—in his equally atypical poem—he gives us a somewhat disguised reference to a most important aspect of his work.

Stevens said about "Thirteen Ways of Looking at a Blackbird," "This group of poems is not meant to be a collection of epigrams or of ideas, but of sensations."[16] Thomas's "Thirteen Blackbirds Look at a Man" might be described as a collection of epigrams or ideas without sensations. Stevens is, if anything, a poet of "sensations," and Thomas, if anything, is a poet of "ideas." That is, Stevens generally starts with images (sensations) and builds his poem up around them in such a way that it comes to express his idea. Thomas, on the other hand, tends to begin with an idea, a statement he wishes to express, and then he finds images (sensations) to describe the idea that he has in mind. In "Thirteen Blackbirds Look at a Man," then, Thomas forces a reversal on Stevens's "Thirteen Ways of Looking at a Blackbird" so that the focus is turned specifically and insistently toward the man, who is seen from the point of view of the blackbirds, whereas in Stevens's poem the blackbirds symbolize the turnings of the speaker's mind with respect to his own situation. This difference of approach to similar material is typical of the difference in technique between Stevens and Thomas, a difference defined adequately enough as the contrast between the use of sensations and the use of ideas.

But more important than anything else is the fact that, thematically, both poems may best be seen as apocalyptic, in the sense that they participate in and anticipate the final stage of apocalyptic thought, what M. H. Abrams defines as "apocalypse by imagination or cognition."[17]

Notions of apocalypse have attracted, intrigued, even obsessed both Stevens and Thomas. But they have been rather different notions of apocalypse.[18] Whereas, for Stevens, the idea of apocalypse, growing as it does from a theological source, has always been primarily a metaphor, a "poetic idea" to be treated in a "sensational" way, for Thomas the idea of apocalypse is primarily, or even exclusively, associated with a theological and Christian source, and for him it is to be treated, even if metaphorically, as a philosophical or a theological "truth." Even so, both poets might well agree that "the imagination . . . is always at the end of an era," as Stevens said (*Collected Poetry and Prose* 656). However, Thomas and Stevens would no doubt disagree on the way or ways in which that imagination describes the end of that era. For instance, one doubts that Thomas would unreservedly accept the conclusions that Stevens draws from the following premises—although Thomas, surely, would accept the premises:

> The major poetic idea in the world is and always has been the idea of God. One of the visible movements of the modern imagination is the movement away from the idea of God. The poetry that created the idea of God will either adapt it to our different intelligence, or create a substitute for it, or make it unnecessary. These alternatives probably mean the same thing"[19]

But whether or not Stevens and Thomas might come to the same logical conclusions about these matters, surely they have both focused much of their major poetic attention on them. In their companion poems on blackbirds and men the essence of their differences becomes clear, both thematically and stylistically. Since Stevens's poem has been with us for more than fifty years and since it is as well known as almost any of his poems, it might, in the present context, be enough to say that it appears to be, if not the most overt poem (one thinks of "Sunday Morning" and "The Snow Man" of the poems in *Harmonium*), nonetheless one of the many poems in which Stevens, throughout his career, attempted to define the "Nothing that is not there and the nothing that is" (*Collected Poetry and Prose* 8). This itself might be the most definitive of his poetic descriptions of the essence of an apocalyptic moment defined and detailed in terms of "sensation."

"Thirteen Blackbirds Look at a Man" recounts a myth. The setting is an Eden seen from the point of view of a flock of thirteen blackbirds. Thus, immediately, there is a reversal of perspective which points up the contrast between one myth of beginnings and this alternate myth of beginnings. The first section of the poem (each section, like the Stevens poem, a single stanza) sets the scene in a place of Edenic innocence—intruded on, in the final line, by the presence of "a man."

> 1
> It is calm.
> It is as though
> we lived in a garden
> that had not yet arrived
> at the knowledge of
> good and evil.
> But there is a man in it.

Once the knowledge of good and evil has been introduced into this world by the presence of the man, the suggestion seems to be that anything can happen. What does seem to happen is that things immediately diminish:

> 2
> There will be
> rain falling vertically
> from an indifferent
> sky. There will stare out
> from behind its
> bars the face of the man
> who is not enjoying it.

> 3
> Nothing higher
> than a blackberry
> bush. As the sun comes up
> fresh, what is the darkness
> stretching from horizon
> to horizon? It is the shadow
> here of the forked man.

Curiously, after this strong, controlled, and focused beginning, the tone breaks in the central sections of the poem before coming back to insist on its stated theme at the end. In this sense the poem begins and ends better than it middles.[20] Whatever the reasons for the shift of tone in sections seven, eight, ten, and eleven, the myth of the garden spoiled by the presence of the man is clearly the theme of the poem.

A kind of Stevensian "domination of black" (see *Collected Poetry and Prose* 7) runs through the Thomas piece, from the blackbirds to the blackberries they eat, whose seeds, when the birds spit them out, "lie / glittering like the eyes of a man." The man is responsible for the pervasive darkness in the world of the poem, and the blackbirds, their singing disturbed by the man's whistling, "wipe [their] beaks / on the branches / wasting the dawn's / jewellery to get rid / of the taste of a man."

The peaceful repose in the garden has been forever disturbed by the presence of the man:

> 9
> In the cool
> of the day the garden
> seems given over
> to blackbirds. Yet
> we know also that somewhere
> there is a man in hiding.

This man-presence becomes a possibility fraught with terror in the world of blackbirds:

> 12
> When night comes
> like a visitor
> from outer space
> we stop our ears
> lest we should hear tell
> of the man in the moon.

> 13
> Summer is
> at an end. The migrants
> depart. When they return
> in spring to the garden
> will there be a man among them?

Thus the poem ends, on a question. The season in the garden is finished. The "migrants / depart." When the new season comes, when the migrants return in the spring, "will there be a man among them?" The blackbirds obviously fear that there will be, that the man-presence which has intruded upon their peaceful world is there to stay, that, indeed, this ominous presence will be there to usher in the new season when the year, in a world of blackbirds, begins again. The parable, then, is of an inevitably approaching apocalyptic era, an era which will put an end to the repose of all gardens, an era in which the "forked" man's presence intrudes into every stanza and cannot be eradicated, no matter how hard the blackbirds try. Furthermore, the man will be unable to "incubate a solution" to the problem he himself has created.

The man at the end of Thomas's poem, like the blackbird at the end of Stevens's, is an omen of death.

IV

I am too keenly aware that I could not go very far into the subject without speaking too much of myself.

—Paul Valéry

"Wallace Stevens" and "Homage to Wallace Stevens" are explicit with respect to reference to Stevens, and the two poems are clearly related to one another.

"Wallace Stevens" (BT 25–26) begins by describing Stevens's conception and birth:

> On New Year's night after a party
> His father lay down and made him
> In the flesh of a girl out of Holland.
> The baby was dropped at the first fall
> Of the leaf. . . .

Stevens was born on October 2, and thus it is entirely possible that he was "made" on "New Year's night."[21] This rather earthy description of Stevens's conception is quickly followed by an equally "natural" description of Stevens's birth. He was "dropped," like an animal in a field, or like a leaf in autumn during the time of "the first fall / Of the leaf." In either case it is as if he were a "thing" "in a fall in a world of fall."[22]

This child, conceived so arbitrarily,

>   was for years dumb,
> Mumbling the dry crust
> Of poetry, until the teeth grew,
> Ivory of a strange piano.[23]

Stevens, as Thomas imagines him here, prefers not the white keys of his piano ("They were too white"), but the black ones, which are reminiscent of

> The deep spaces between stars,
> Fathomless as the cold shadow
> His mind cast.[24]

The word "Fathomless" is clearly a touchstone word and reference for Thomas. It is a conspicuously Kierkegaardian reference, and, as I have tried to show, Thomas was deeply influenced by Kierkegaard.[25] In particular, Thomas was fascinated by Kierkegaard's metaphor of the "seventy thousand fathoms."[26] But Thomas also seems to be using the word "fathomless" here in terms of multiple meanings. He goes beyond the Kierkegaardian context to suggest that the "cast" (another pun?) of Stevens's mind was both beyond comprehension and, simultaneously, difficult to take "soundings" from. In short, Stevens's mind was, for Thomas, "deep" and "unfathomable" (as Thomas's mind often seems to be to his readers). And thus Thomas here, "In the bleak autumn / Of real time," "without eloquence," eloquently remembers Stevens's birth.

The second section of the poem begins with lines in which Thomas refers directly to Stevens but, again, they might well be applied to Thomas himself—lines which, at least from the first comma on, Thomas must surely have been thinking of in terms of himself as well as of Stevens:

> How like him to bleed at last
> Inwardly, but to the death,
> Who all his life from the white page
> Infected us chiefly with fear
> Of the veins' dryness.

The enjambment of these lines, combined with Thomas's characteristic, indeed quintessential, lines breaks and the way he inevitably emphasizes and compounds the complexities of his meanings by the judicious use of the white spaces at the ends of his enjambed lines, is conspicuously in evidence here. Each of these line-turns amends or revises the anticipated sense of the statement being built up in the previous line, and thus they subtly change the poem's meaning, line by line. The first turn, from "bleed at last" to "Inwardly," simultaneously amends the anticipated meaning, (since the internal bleeding is not fatal, as the initial line of the stanza seems to imply), and it forces an exterior "bleeding" into an "interior," where (it might be argued and assumed) such bleeding would not be immediately harmful, and certainly not likely fatal. Indeed, this "bleeding," as we learn from the continuation of the line, is not fatal, at least not in an "inner" metaphorical sense. And the "bleeding" is also ironic and punningly accurate since we all "bleed inwardly" as our blood circulates through our bodies. And when that internal "bleeding" stops, we do die. But then, in the midst of his sentence, Thomas turns his metaphor to force it away from the literal (whether exterior or interior) and into an aesthetic sense or meaning. The "white page" written on by the "black key" of the pen, or by the type of a typed page, affect and "infect" us with the fear of death itself. More specifically, they affect us with the fear of death by and of literature—the fear that our "veins'" words will run dry, that we will not have blood "bleeding" back to the heart so that it can be pumped out again and be circulated throughout the whole of the body, and throughout the whole of the body of our work, our poems. In this way, we may literally die "inwardly," or at least we may "fear" such an inward death, a loss of literature.

Then Thomas changes the metaphor for a second time—although the abiding sense and presence of a death lingers over the remaining lines of the stanza as well:

> Words he shed
> Were dry leaves of a dry mind,
> Crackling as the wind blew
> From mortuaries of the cold heart.

The words, the "dry crust / Of poetry" mentioned in lines 7–8 of part 1, are here "shed," written, printed, and published, like the "dry leaves of a dry mind" (with its echo of T. S. Eliot). Both Stevens and Thomas, arguably, were men of principally autumnal or wintry minds, and thus their Whitmanian "leaves" of poems (as well as what they have left us) invariably, almost inevitably, "fall" from and into autumnal or wintry seasons from the "mortuaries" of their "cold heart[s]."[27] These "leaves," however, are still animated, still "alive," in the sense that everything falls from, follows from, such seasons—as Stevens reminds us in the imperative opening line of his seminal early poem, "The Snow Man" (see *Collected Poetry and Prose* 8).[28] In Thomas' rendition of this theme, then, he alludes to Eliot's "Gerontion,"[29] in addition to Stevens's "The Snow Man," to "crackle" the dry leaves in the mortuaries of a heart which has been "cold a long time" (*Collected Poetry and Prose* 8). In these kinds of "mortuaries" the self is "ripe, but without taste."

In the final three lines of the poem Thomas changes his metaphor again. He depicts Stevens as "limp[ing] on the poem's crutch" and "taking despair / As a new antidote for love." Here Thomas may well be suggesting a basic contrast between himself and Stevens, this man and poet with whom he knows he shares so much. If Stevens, at the end of Thomas's poem, is stoically "limping" with the help of "the poem's crutch" toward his final assertion of "despair" as an "antidote for love," for Thomas love remains healthy, without the need of any antidote or cure,[30] and it is this love which will provide Thomas with all the "crutch" he will need to continue to write his own poems.

V

Blessings, Stevens . . .

—R. S. Thomas

"Homage to Wallace Stevens" (NTF 62–63) was published in Thomas's final collection of poems, *No Truce with the Furies*. It begins with the surprising, startling, almost sacrilegious statement:

> I turn now
> not to the Bible
> but to Wallace Stevens.

Beyond its initial surprise, this is a serious and, I think, an accurate description of Thomas's poetic and "religious" indebtedness to Stevens. Thomas always acknowledges his debts, and here he is simply saying what has long been true—namely that, as a poet, he reveres, even reverences, Stevens. Even so, Thomas is not above playfully alluding to Stevens (who was an insurance executive in his workaday world) as "Insured against / everything but the muse" and the fitful turnings she might make him make, and asking what Stevens "the word-wizard / [has] to say" for himself.

Then Thomas returns to Stevens, saying for him (and implying that he also said it for himself) that "We walk a void world" in which

> in the absence of the imagination,
> there is no hope.

This "void world" is thus, simultaneously, both Stevens's and Thomas's. But the image also suggests not simply a vacant, empty, or deserted world, but a world which is being voided, or avoided, for the sake of the imagination, for the sake of the imaginative world. Thus, Thomas seems to suggest—both for himself and for Stevens—that the world exists more substantially in the imagination than it does as a physically palpable entity or reality. Furthermore, there is the assertion that without imagination there is "no hope." Hope, for Thomas, would no doubt be linked with faith, as in "the substance of things hoped for, the evidence of things not seen" (Heb 11:1 KJV).[31] (This is a statement that would probably be true for Stevens too, if we take it at face value and outside of its biblical context.)

Next Thomas characterizes Stevens as a "Verbal bank-clerk," an "acrobat walking a rhythmic tight-rope," and a "trapeze artist of the language," and he says that "his was a kind of double-entry / poetics."[32] More pertinently, in terms of Bloom's anxiety theory and in terms of the reciprocal relationships between Thomas and Stevens, this reference suggests a kind of giving and taking (or receiving) between the two poets such that the "debits" and the "cred-its" seem almost to course backward and forward in an even flow between them. And, like Stevens, Thomas too "kept two columns / of thought going" simultaneously, all the while "balancing meaning" between them.[33]

The other two referents are more interesting poetically. Thomas makes his tight-rope walker a literal "acrobat," someone who performs interesting "gym-nastic feats requiring skillful control" and is also "adept at swiftly changing his position" (Webster's) or point of view, in mid-air as it were. In this sense Thomas' "acrobat" is a high-flying trapeze artist dazzling the crowds below him with his jumps and somersaults in mid-air—and, surely, without a net.

In the final comparison he makes between Stevens and himself Thomas turns to a theological metaphor by saying that Stevens's "poetry / was his church," that he "burned his metaphors like incense," and that "his syntax was as high / as his religion." Beyond the suggestion of the fragrant scent or odor released when his metaphors are "burned," Thomas seems to imply (perhaps more pertinently in reference to himself than to Stevens) that some of those metaphors also "incensed" some listeners or hearers (in the sense of causing confusion or even anger) when they were "burned" into the lines of poems. (Certainly it is the case that, on numerous occasions in his often controversial life, Thomas incensed groups or individuals with respect to the stances he took on various social, political, and theological matters.)

The phrase "his syntax was as high / as his religion" contains several puns. Literally, beyond a "connected or orderly system" of words, syntax is also the "harmonious arrangement of parts or elements" (Webster's) of speech which must clearly be evidenced in poetry. Thomas thus seems to be suggesting a reference to Stevens's first book, *Harmonium*, as well as to the fact that Stevens felt that the whole of his poetic career consisted of one single over-arching harmonious movement, "the whole of harmonium."[34] Further, since Stevens had no "religion" save his poetry, Thomas seems to be suggesting that Stevens's "syntax" was as "high" as his, Thomas's, "religion"—as high, that is, in terms of Thomas's position as a priest in the Anglican Church in Wales.

Thomas' poem concludes:

> Blessings, Stevens;
> I stand with my back to grammar
> at an altar you never aspired
> to, celebrating the sacrament
> of the imagination whose high-priest
> notwithstanding you are.

These final lines, beginning with the only break in the poem from the firm left-hand margin, create the sense of a separate stanza or a concluding paragraph in a commemorative address. They directly address Stevens in a most intriguing way, since Thomas uses a word ("Blessings") that has obvious religious connotations, connotations which would certainly be conspicuous for a priest.

This then is an extremely important passage, not only in terms of Thomas's relationship with Stevens, but in terms of his own life, both as poet and as priest. During most of Thomas's ministry the priest, as ministrant to and for the people, faced the altar when he celebrated the Mass. When the church changed the liturgy and the priest was asked to turn around to face the congregation—and thus forced to turn his back on the altar—Thomas refused to participate further in the services. Thomas described his position with respect to the change in the church liturgy in his autobiographical essay, "A Year in Llŷn," this way:

> It pains me greatly, but ever since the Church reformed the Liturgy, I cannot partake of the Sacrament. The new order of the Church in Wales has changed the whole atmosphere of Holy Communion for me. The pinnacle of the original service was when I, as a priest, would say the words of consecration over the bread and wine, with my back to the congregation as one who had the honour of leading them to the throne of God's grace. But now it is the congregation that the priest faces, inviting them to speak, as he breaks the synthetic wafer before them. It is to God that mystery belongs, and woe to man when he tries to interfere with that mystery.[35]

Clearly, these details would seem to be relevant to Thomas's reference in this poem. When Thomas says that he stands with his "back to grammar" he must mean that in turning *to* God, as priest, he turns *away from* the mundane and the human, or even that he turns away from man's grammatical rules of literature and language—all for the sake of the sacred ceremony.[36] And he does this, as priest and poet, before an altar that Stevens "never aspired / to." Even so, in so celebrating Stevens, Thomas defines his own action and activity here as "celebrating the sacrament / of the imagination"—the sacrament of poetry—that same sacrament that Stevens *did* aspire to, and whose "high-priest," Thomas insists—notwithstanding any protests to the contrary—Stevens is.

In short, here at the end of his final poem on and for Wallace Stevens, Thomas, like Stevens himself, turns to and stands before the altar of the imagination—the altar of poetry.

Conclusion

Priests have a long way to go.
The people wait for them to come
To them over the broken glass
Of their vows, making them pay
With their sweat's coinage for their correction.

"Let it be so," I say. "Amen and amen."

— R. S. Thomas, "The Priest"

And what does it come to, Pilgrim,
This walking to and fro on the earth, knowing
That nothing changes, or everything;
And only, to tell it, these sad marks,
Phrases half-parsed, ellipses and scratches across the dirt?
It comes to a point. It comes and it goes.

— Charles Wright, "Skins"

Take the dirt from the old trail up in your hand, Pilgrim,
and throw it into the wind.

— Charles Wright, "Three Poems of Departure"

In the opening line of the title poem of his book *The Southern Cross*, Charles Wright writes: "Things that divine us we never touch." As I have argued elsewhere, Wright here works "an interesting pun on definitions." He does not write *define* but rather *divine*. He is not attempting to "'discover and set forth the meaning of' nor 'fix or mark the limits' for, as the dictionary definition of define defines the word and the process, but rather he intends to 'discover or perceive intuitively' (Webster's); that is, he wishes not simply to describe, but to "look forward to and anticipate" (see my "'Bruised by God': Charles Wright's Apocalyptic Pilgrimages" [*The Wider Scope of English*]). Interestingly enough, at the very end of his literal and symbolic journey through *The Southern Cross* Wright says, "It's what we forget that defines us. . . ." Something along the lines of the implied dichotomy that Wright alludes to here is what I have attempted to do in this book—not simply to "define" and describe R. S. Thomas's long life and career but, rather, to "divine" it. And, thereby, I have also tried to examine Thomas's life and work without forgetting too much, just as Thomas lived his life and wrote his poems within the realm of the divine as he saw it, as he was led to it, and as he was led to do. That was what defined and divined him. In short, I have attempted to follow Thomas in his pilgrimage through his life and work and to make his journey my own.

An obvious poem to look at, then, here at the end of this long journey—both mine and Thomas's—is "Arrival" (LP 203). In it Thomas describes a traveler, "Not conscious / that [he has] been seeking" it, suddenly finding a village "in the Welsh hills / . . . with no road out / but the one [he] came in by." The traveler, in this "hour that is no hour / [he] know[s]," looks into a "dawdling" river that holds a moving mirror for him and in it sees himself as he is:

> a traveller
> with the moon's halo
> above him, who has arrived
> after long journeying where he
> began, catching this
> one truth by surprise
> that there is everything to look forward to.

And so, for now, this journey, this pilgrimage, is over. In the nature of such things, however, here at the end of it one finds that he inevitably returns again to the beginning—or to another beginning. Thus, the end of the journey is often only a brief rest or respite before the beginning of another journey, another pilgrimage. It is indeed almost inevitable that another pilgrimage in or through R. S. Thomas's work will follow this one—but it has been good to have been on *this* pilgrimage with him and to come, if not to an end, at least to this resting place.

First Light
    —for R. S. Thomas (in memory)

I climb the steep stone
steps, glassy with cold,
to enter the empty church.
Faint light swords through
the upper dark. No wind
murmurs. No candles burn.
No God waits there nor wakes.

Last night, quite abruptly,
it began to rain. And then,
before morning, the rain
turned slowly to snow. And
then again, before first
light, almost imperceptibly,
the snow turned back to rain.

                      William Virgil Davis

Notes

Chapter 1

1   Although this is not the place to initiate such an analysis of Matthew Arnold's complete canon, a brief outline of the issues might be helpful. What I am thinking of here are those "writings on religion, to which Arnold gave pride of place when he anthologized himself in 1880" and which, as Keating (7) says, are often "omitted complete" in collections of Arnold's works. Indeed, works like *Literature and Dogma, St. Paul and Protestantism, God and the Bible,* and *Last Essays on Church and Religion* (see Matthew Arnold, *The Complete Prose Works of Matthew Arnold,* ed. R. H. Super [Ann Arbor: University of Michigan Press, 1960–1977], vols. 6, 7, and 8) were not even as crucial in Arnold's time as they may have seemed, since it appears clear that Arnold himself believed that "culture," in addition to literature (or through its direction or lead), would "usurp" religion. This can be seen, for instance, in his essay "A French Critic on Milton" (Arnold 8: 165–87), "an essay on critical method," which Super says "stands in much the same relation to Arnold's later critical essays as 'The Function of Criticism' to the earlier" (419). It contains Arnold's famous "wings of Christianity" passage (". . . pureness and kindness, are, in very truth, the two signal Christian virtues, the two mighty wings of Christianity, with which it winnowed and renewed, and still winnows and renews, the world" [Arnold 8: 184]). Ruth apRoberts says that Arnold's "figure" of the "wings of Christianity" both "borrows a little of the grotesqueness of the Old Testament cherubim and seraphim, and at the same time . . . calls to mind the 'metaphysical' figure of those English poets who wrote in the age of 'Rational Theology.' It can stand as a sort of 'emblem' . . . over the rest of Arnold's career as a literary critic . . ." (267).

2   I am obviously distorting and using Arnold's words out of context here. He is talking, in context, about how rare "great creative epochs in literature" are and he argues that "for the creation of a master-work of literature two powers must concur, the power of the man and the power of the moment, and the man is not enough without the moment. . ." (see Arnold 3: 261).

3   Of course, Arnold also has his defenders. John Holloway, for instance, argues that "Eliot's comments on these suggestions of Arnold's" (he is referring specifically to Eliot's essay on Arnold and Pater) "have exercised more influence than they deserve. . . . Arnold . . . would have denied wanting to preserve the emotions of Christianity without 'the belief'. . . . He thought . . . that religion . . . was doomed before the advance of the scientific temper; while science alone could provide no pattern that would be complete. Hence literature had the brunt to bear by itself. . . . This part of Arnold's work," Holloway insists, "contains some of [Arnold's] most interesting ideas, and because it has been first attacked, then misrepresented, and then neglected, it needs attention" (*The Charted Mirror: Literary and Critical Essays* [London: Routledge & Kegan Paul, 1960] 159, 158). Nathan A. Scott Jr. is even more insistent with respect to Arnold's significance as a religious thinker and even more outraged by Eliot's position and the influence it has had on other readers and critics. He laments that the "deplorable confusion of 'poetry and morals in the attempt to find a substitute for religious faith'—has become the controlling sentiment that informs what is now the well-nigh canonical verdict." He adds that in "the England over which Victoria presided we are bequeathed but three religious thinkers—John Henry Newman, Frederick Denison Maurice, and Matthew Arnold—who, by reason of the relevance of their legacies to contemporary discussions, appear to be genuinely living guides; and it is a considerable oddity of modern intellectual life that Arnold who is, of this great trio, the most truly prophetic figure should, from his own time unto ours, have been regularly responded to in a hostile and dismissive way." Indeed, "[t]he total theory of interpretation, then, which emerges from Arnold's writings of the 1870s—from *St. Paul and Protestantism, Literature and Dogma, God and the Bible*, and the *Last Essays on Church and Religion*—represents a structure of thought which, once it is rescued from the scholiasts, may be seen to be a very considerable achievement, and one that touches with great suggestiveness much that is currently at issue in the intellectual forums of our own period" (*The Poetics of Belief: Studies in Coleridge, Arnold, Pater, Santayana, Stevens, and Heidegger* [Chapel Hil: University of North Carolina Press, 1985] 39, 41, 55).

4   Arnold's phrase, "*The Eternal alone*," is fascinating in terms of its possible implications. Does Arnold mean that God, as "*The Eternal alone*," is alone in his eternality, or does he mean that God is eternally *alone*, that is, that he is not only distant but aloof and isolated, and perhaps even lonely in his solitariness?

5   For the sake of convenience, wherever possible, all references to Stevens's poetry and prose will be to the *Collected Poetry and Prose*, reprinted by *The Library of America* (1997). All of this material is original to *The Collected Poems of Wallace*

Stevens (1954), *The Necessary Angel* (1951), and *Opus Posthumous* (1957), origi-
nally published by Alfred A. Knopf and used with their permission.

6   Tony Sharpe argues that "Sunday Morning" is often "associated with the
compound ghosts of Walter Pater and Matthew Arnold . . ." (*Wallace Stevens:
A Literary Life* [New York: St. Martin's Press, 2000], 47). He adds, "[T]he
early Stevens can be seen as a quarrelsome disciple of Pater, seeking protection
from [his] aesthetic extremism by counterbalancing it with Matthew Arnold's
arguments for the spiritual centrality of poetry, which in turn he leavened with
a Jamesian Pragmatism" (195).

7   For more on this poem and on Thomas's relationship to Stevens, see chapter 9.

8   For my analysis of Thomas's "agnostic faith," see chapter 3.

9   In "The Enigma of Aberdaron," a newspaper article on him by Bryon Rogers,
Thomas is quoted as saying: "I did a television broadcast about the Resurrection
from the point of view of metaphor. I said that it was all to do with language, that
the accounts were just what people felt had happened. It shocked some people. I
had the odd pious letter" (*London Sunday Telegraph Magazine*, November 1975,
27). In the same article Rogers reported that when Thomas was asked about
how his theological positions were reflected in his preaching, he said, "I like
the challenge it puts upon one, to make sense of Christianity" (29). One of
the stumbling blocks for many readers of Thomas's poems is the "challenge"
of attempting to align the message of the poems with the message of the Bible.
Indeed, as Grevel Lindrop, in his own take on this "challenge," has recently
remarked, "one wonders whether the greatest future obstacle to an understanding
of Thomas's poems may not be a simple ignorance of Christianity" ("Purity of
Intent," *PN Review* 31:6 [2005]: 64).

10   Thomas's use of the word "twaddle" in the above statement reminds me of a
passage in Wallace Stevens, who, in referring to C. E. M. Joad's response to
A. J. Ayer's *Language, Truth and Logic*, quotes Joad as saying: "If . . . God is a
metaphysical term, if, that is to say, He belongs to a reality which transcends
the world of sense-experience . . . to say that He exists is neither true nor false.
This position . . . is neither atheist nor agnostic; it cuts deeper than either, by
asserting that all talk about God, whether pro or anti, is twaddle" (see Stevens,
"Imagination as Value," in *Collected Poetry and Prose*, 727). Antony Flew would
agree, or even go further than this. Indeed, he has recently argued that "[i]t
is as atheisitic to affirm the existence of God as it is to deny it" (see *God and
Philosophy* [Amherst, N.Y.: Prometheus Books, 2005], 47). In another essay,
Stevens adds: "From this analysis, we deduce that an idea that satisfies both the
reason and the imagination, if it happened, for instance, to be an idea of God,
would establish a divine beginning and end for us which, at the moment, the
reason, singly, at best proposes and on which, at the moment, the imagination,
singly, merely meditates. This is an illustration. It seems to be elementary, from
this point of view, that the poet, in order to fulfill himself, must accomplish a
poetry that satisfies both the reason and the imagination" ("The Figure of the
Youth as Virile Poet," *Collected Poetry and Prose*, 668). It does seem to be the

case that Thomas, like Stevens, is sympathetic to the basic philosophic positions taken up by "logical empiricism," and/or by the logical positivists. As Thomas says in one of the prose poems in *The Echoes Return Slow*, "The Cross always is avant-garde" (ERS 82). Obviously, he believes its clergy needs to be too. In another prose-poem in *The Echoes Return Slow* Thomas describes the priest preaching, "defend[ing] himself with the fact that Jesus was a poet" (ERS 88).

11 See Arnold's "Preface" to the first edition of his *Poems* (1853); C. B. Tinker and H. F. Lowry, eds. *The Poetical Works of Matthew Arnold* (London: Oxford University Press, 1950), xvii.

12 Arnold, in "Dover Beach," *thinks* of "the turbid ebb and flow / O human misery," but the "Sea of Faith" that he describes is itself at full "ebb," without any evidence of "flow."

13 It is worth nothing that the Aramaic that Jesus would have spoken would have used the words Πέτρος and πέτρα interchangeably with reference to either the proper name or to the common noun. It is also work remembering that Matthew's use of the word ἐκκλησίαν in this passage (from ἐκκλησία, meaning church or assembly) is the Greek usage of the word for church and that Matthew's gospel is the only gospel to use this word in this context. Indeed, neither of the other two synoptic gospels make any mention of this incident or account.

14 One wonders whether Thomas's "falling back" from God, after his "run[ning] / up the approaches" toward him, is intended to suggest that he has been rebuffed by God and whether this "falling back" is a relapse or regression on his part, or simply some inevitably natural phenomenon, like the wavering rhythm of the waves?

15 Barry Sloan, in his mention of "Tidal," describes Thomas's turning "the figure of waves on the shore into a metaphor for the poet's own sea-like advances 'up the approaches of God'" and suggests that "the vicissitudes of [Thomas's speaker's] spiritual state" cause him to "imitate waves by never ceasing to return . . . toward God." Sloan also comments on Thomas's use of the word "spring," suggesting that it "not only refers to high tides, but may be read as a hope that prayer has its own sources, like a well, and that it may be the vehicle whereby the poet will be propelled up to new levels of perception and realization" ("The Discipline of Watching and Waiting: R. S. Thomas, Poetry and Prayer," *Religion and Literature* 34.2 [2002]: 45).

16 In commenting on this poem, and on the "theology" of Thomas's "style," M. Wynn Thomas suggests several interesting details that relate to Thomas's poetic mastery as well as to the mystery of the theological trappings in the poem. He writes: "[T]he line break [between ll. 4 and 5, quoted above] firmly separates 'stone' from 'church,' even as it attaches 'stone' to 'only'—an attachment through parallel form that is actually reinforced by rhyme. 'Stone' is thus enabled to function independently as a self-sufficient noun as well as a qualifying adjective. The line break insists that we give equal weight to the two words, and therefore to the full strangeness of the phenomenon. This is stone

that is also a church—a strange, ironic, combination, which either signifies the mystery of faith (that stone can also be holy); or the absurdity of faith (the church is 'only' an arrangement of stone). And it is also a kind of internal rhyme, caught and emphasized by the line unit, that places the word 'only' into a peculiarly intimate relationship with the preceding word 'full,' so that through the interaction of the two words we hear echoes of 'lonely' and 'forlornly.' Then a later line break again sensitizes us to the quiet intercourse of sounds that breeds hidden meanings: [the] 'sea's / sound' [(ll. 8–9) makes it] 'easy to believe': the line literally enacts or emblematizes its meaning, as the 'sound' of the word 'sea' leads the mind naturally, if insidiously, to think of words like 'easy' and 'believe'" ("Irony in the Soul: The Religious Poetry of R. S[ocrates] Thomas," *Agenda* 36.2 [1998]: 66–67). This, of course, would be in contrast to the sound of the sea that Arnold hears in "Dover Beach."

17 "There are nights that are so still" was originally published in *The Echoes Return Slow* (ERS 79) as an untitled poem; in *The Collected Poems* (CP 457) it was titled "The Other." And as "The Other" it is incised on a stone marker set up outside the church at Aberdaron in north Wales where Thomas served as vicar during his final years in the priesthood.

18 As Justin Wintle says, "Thomas's birds become so much a part of his quest for God that at times God perhaps is a bird, or most like a bird" (*Furious Interiors: Wales, R. S. Thomas and God* [London: Flamingo, 1996], 22). Again, one is reminded of Stevens's birds in "Sunday Morning," and, perhaps more particularly, of Emily Dickinson's poem, "'Hope' is the thing with feathers—" (see *Final Harvest: Emily Dickinson's Poems*, ed. Thomas H. Johnson [Boston: Little, Brown, 1961], 34–35), a poem which catches up any number of strands of the argument I have attempted to weave together in this essay. Surely, there must be those who might accuse Arnold or Thomas (or Stevens) of "sing[ing] the tune without the words" and of "abashing," disconcerting, or making uneasy, the "Hope" in that "little Bird / That kept so many warm," as Dickinson's feathery metaphor has it.

19 I wonder if Thomas is here thinking of, and comparing himself to, the sixth-century Welsh hermit, Saint Govan, who lived in a small stone chapel on the Pembrokeshire coast in south Wales? Certainly, in this tiny chapel at the base of a steep rocky cliff, which legend has it miraculously closed around the saint to protect him, St. Govan was both the "hermit of the rocks" and "habited with the wind and mist."

Chapter 2

1 In spite of his strong opinions and fierce nationalism, Thomas did not endorse or support Plaid Cymru, "The Party of Wales" (Cymru is the Welsh name for Wales), because it, in turn, acknowledged the British role, and rule, in Wales. Even so, Thomas's relationship to Plaid Cymru is a rather complicated one—far too complicated to describe briefly here.

2   Gwydion was named after a character in the medieval collection of Welsh tales known as *The Mabinogion*. In *The Mabinogion* (trans. Gwyn Jones and Thomas Jones [Rutland, Vt.: Charles E. Tuttle, 1989], 57) Gwydion is described as "the best teller of tales in the world." In "Abercuawg" Thomas describes his son's name in the context of "the inherent power of words"; he translated the above passage from *The Mabinogion* as "the best story teller in the world" (see *R. S. Thomas: Selected Prose*, ed. Sandra Anstey [Bridgend: Poetry Wales Press, 1986], 165).

3   It does seem to be clear, however, that Thomas often gave precedence to poetry—perhaps because he believed that words were the most important means of dealing with all matters: literally, literarily, and theologically. And he had, of course, a very ready justification for believing this for, as The Gospel According to St. John asserts, "in the beginning was the word."

4   R. S. Thomas, "Former Paths," in *R. S. Thomas: Autobiographies*, ed. Jason Walford Davies (London: J. M. Dent, 1997), 5.

5   Bird watching would remain an important avocation for Thomas throughout his life.

6   For more on Thomas and his treatment of "the machine," see chapter 8.

7   *Hiraeth* is an almost untranslatable Welsh word used to describe the nostalgia or longing for a time or a place long past.

8   John Powell Ward, *The Poetry of R. S. Thomas* (Bridgend: Seren, 1987), 34.

9   R. S. Thomas, "Abercuawg," in *R. S. Thomas: Selected Prose*, ed. Anstey, 167.

10 R. S. Thomas, "Autobiographical Essay," in *Miraculous Simplicity: Essays on R. S. Thomas*, ed. William V. Davis (Fayetteville: University of Arkansas Press, 1993), 10.

11 R. S. Thomas, "Abercuawg," in *R. S. Thomas: Selected Prose*, ed. Anstey, 167.

12 Some of these folk elements are vividly evident in Thomas's long radio play "The Minister" (see M), which was written for the BBC in Wales as part of a series of very successful dramas the BBC produced. Perhaps the most famous of these was *Under Milk Wood*, by Thomas's namesake and fellow Welshman, Dylan Thomas.

13 "Gifts," (P 17), another poem published during this period, is perhaps Thomas's most explicitly personal poem.

14 "*Souillac: Le Sacrifice d'Abraham*" both anticipates Thomas's later poems on paintings and, in concentrating on the Abraham-Isaac story, deals with the theme of the relationship between fathers and sons, an important one in Thomas's work. For more on this poem and the father-son relationship see chapter 7.

15 Thomas read Kierkegaard closely throughout his life, as he made clear in his essay "The Creative Writer's Suicide" (see *R. S. Thomas: Selected Prose*, ed. Anstey, 175–82). In several other poems, including the important "S. K.," in *No Truce with the Furies* (see NTF 15–17), Kierkegaard provided Thomas with several of his central metaphors. For more on Thomas and Kierkegaard see chapter 9.

16 Morgan's translation of the Bible into Welsh was instrumental in cementing Welsh as the official language (thereafter so recognized throughout the British Isles) in terms of all official matters having to do with religion conducted in

Wales—even if English was to remain the official language in terms of politics and bureaucracy.

17 For more on Thomas and the poetry of the apocalyptic mode, see chapter 4.

18 See Jason Walford Davies' translation of "No One," in *Autobiographies*, ed. Davies, 76–77.

19 In spite of this, as Thomas was later to say in "Nuance" (NTF 32), we "must not despair"; rather, we must remember that even an "invisible" God can be "inferred." Perhaps only Thomas would not "despair" under such circumstances.

20 For more on Thomas and "the machine," see chapter 8.

21 The *eisteddfod*, a Welsh-language competition involving both poetry and music, is an annual "assembly of poets" begun in the twelfth century.

22 See *R. S. Thomas: Selected Prose*, ed. Anstey, 163, 166, 171.

23 And, of course, as previously mentioned, Thomas had already written "*Souillac: Le Sacrifice d'Abraham*" (BT 43) in anticipation of these later ekphrastic poems.

24 Ward, *Poetry of R. S. Thomas*, 111 (1987 ed.). Ward argues that the reaction that rose up against the Impressionist painters supported the charge that, by concentrating only on the surface of reality, these painters seemed to "omit" the "inside," whereas, somewhat ironically, Thomas, after "having sought . . . nothing less than the heart of reality itself (God)," turned in his poems on paintings to the "immediate world of . . . appearance[s]."

25 See Davis, *Miraculous Simplicity*, 1.

26 An exception to this would be the several masterfully lyrical poems Thomas wrote for his wife, Elsi—as, for instance, the final poem in the collection, "I look out over the timeless sea" (ERS 121), or "Comparisons" (R 57), published in Thomas's posthumous volume, *Residues* (2002).

27 "There are nights that are so still" was included in Thomas's *Collected Poems* as "The Other" (CP 457).

28 This is an interesting pun, implying "one turn" as well as "turned toward," and no doubt meant to be taken both literally and personally as well as poetically and globally.

29 For more on Thomas's use of this passage in *Genesis,* see chapter 3 n. 22.

Chapter 3

1 This parable by Antony Flew ("Theology and Falsification," *New Essays in Philosophical Theology*, ed. Antony Flew and Alasdair Macintyre [London: SCMP, 1955], 96) was "developed from a tale told by John Wisdom in his haunting and revelatory article 'Gods'" (see *Philosophy and Psycho-Analysis* [New York: Philosophical Library, 1953]). Flew's version of Wisdom's parable initiated a spate of responses and commentaries: see, for example, Hare (99–103), Mitchell (103–5), and Crombie (109–30) in *New Essays*, and Frederick Ferré (*Language, Logic and God* [New York; Harper & Brothers, 1961], 32, 50–52, 131–35, *passim*). Flew, in a final response to the positions taken with respect to his parable, suggests that "philosophers of religion" might well remember George Orwell's

1984 and his notion of "*doublethink*," the "power of holding two contradictory beliefs simultaneously, and accepting both of them" (*Nineteen Eighty-Four* [New York: Harcourt, Brace, 1949], 215). Flew adds, "[p]erhaps religious intellectuals . . . are sometimes driven to doublethink in order to retain their faith in a loving God in face of the reality of a heartless and indifferent world" (108).

2   In "Homage to Wallace Stevens" (NTF 62), in *No Truce with the Furies*, his final collection of poems, Thomas said of Stevens, "His poetry / was his church." And, in defining his relationship to Stevens, Thomas added: "I turn now / not to the Bible / but to Wallace Stevens." For more on Thomas's indebtedness to Stevens, see chapter 10.

3   See chapter 1, which I am here closely paraphrasing, and, in part, directly quoting from.

4   Davies, *Autobiographies*, 84.

5   For Thomas's full statement, see above p. 8. For more comments along these same lines see Thomas's BBC Radio 4 interview with R. E. T. Lamb ("Religion in Its Contemporary Context: the Poetry of R. S. Thomas [The Artist and His Vision]" [1971]) as well as his interview with Naim Attallah ("R. S. Thomas," *The Oldie* 79 [1995]: 12–15). As these interviews, given over a considerable length of time, suggest, Thomas held consistent views for a long time.

6   This is not, obviously, the place to launch into an analysis or a defense of Thomas's poetics, but I do hope to show, in what follows, some of Thomas's poetic fingerprints on the poems I discuss.

7   This is not the place to try to analyze the complexities of church-chapel relationships and conflicts in modern times, nor indeed in past Welsh history, although certainly it is the case that the "history of literature in modern Wales cannot be understood without detailed attention to the contribution and influence of Nonconformity, and the reaction against it" (*The New Companion to the Literature of Wales*, ed. Meic Stephens [Cardiff: University of Wales Press, 1998], 533). Still, it is worth noting that Thomas, himself embroiled in some of this controversy, comments quite movingly on the role of the (at least historical) chapel in Wales in his short essay "Dan Gapel" (trans. by Catherine Thomas and published in English as "Two Chapels," in *R. S. Thomas: Selected Prose*, ed. Anstey, 43–47). In this essay Thomas describes his visit to two deserted, isolated, and "remote" chapels in "wild romantic settings." They are Maes-yr-Onnen, situated on "high ground overlooking the river Wye," and Soar-y-Mynydd, sheltered "behind a row of cooper beaches" in a silence broken only by the "thin, complaining voice of the stream and the constant drip of moisture from the trees" (45). Thomas calls these two chapels, respectively, "The Chapel of the Spirit" and "The Chapel of the Soul." At the "Chapel of the Spirit," Thomas, lying on the grass and letting his mind "wander back into the past" to "two and a half centuries earlier" has a vision in which he feels that he can "comprehend the breadth and length and depth and height of the mystery of the creation," and in which he feels everything ("no beginning and no end") "welling up endlessly from immortal God" (44). Thomas adds, "It might have been the first day of

Creation and myself one of the first men. Might have been? No, it *was* the first day. The world was recreated before my eyes. The dew of its creation was on everything, and I fell to my knees and praised God—a young man worshipping a young God, for surely that is what our God is" (44, italics are original). At the other chapel, "The Chapel of the Soul," Thomas had another vision, which he describes as "a glimpse of the spirit of man; here, I saw the soul of a special type of man, the Cymro or Welshman. For the very source of Welsh life as it is today is here in the middle of these remote moorlands of Ceredigion. And it is in places of this sort that the soul of the true Welshman is formed" (46). Thomas concludes, "If I had to choose between the two chapels, I would no doubt prefer the second" (46). Then he asks, "What, then is the purpose of this rambling essay?" And he answers, "It is an attempt to describe what Wales means to me, and also to discover the true soul of my people. . . . Here, in the soil and the dirt and the peat do we find life and heaven and hell, and it is in these surroundings that a Welshman should forge his soul" (46–47). The nostalgic theme that runs through this essay is evident too in Thomas's poem "The Chapel" (LS 19).

8   In a late interview Thomas said, ". . . [A]s a country priest I was very much on my own and I would find myself kneeling in an empty church and all those sort [*sic*] of things and . . . I began to become interested in the unseen God, the unknown God and I linked this up with life in a rural area where these parishioners of mine were out in the fields" (see "R. S. Thomas in Conversation," Interview with Molly Price-Owen, *The David Jones Journal* (2001): 94). Thomas specifically relates this comment to the period of his priesthood in Manafon (1942–1954). "In a Country Church" (SYT 114) was published in Thomas's 1955 volume *Song at the Year's Turning*.

9   Thomas is rather notorious for his interchangeable use of the first and the third person—in his poems and even in his autobiographical writings. Thomas's autobiography, *Neb* (which means "No One"—although it can also mean "Someone"), was originally written and published, in Welsh, in the third person (see the Gwasg Gwynedd edition, 1985). Thomas himself then "translated" this autobiography into English and shifted the pronoun from the third to the first person (see "Autobiographical Essay," in *Miraculous Simplicity*, ed. W. V. Davis, 1–20). This essay was subsequently retranslated, again in the third person, by Jason Walford Davies (see "No-One," in *Autobiographies* [1997], 27–29).

It is no doubt worth remembering, as I have tried to show elsewhere (see "R. S. Thomas, *The Odyssey*, and Derek Walcott: A Note on the Use of 'No One,'" *Notes on Contemporary Literature* 35:4 [2005]: 6–7), that Odysseus used a similar pun to deceive the Cyclops Polyphemus in book 9 of *The Odyssey* when he referred to himself as "nobody," and that Derek Walcott's autobiographical protagonist, Shabine, in "The Schooner *Flight*," says: "I have Dutch, nigger, and English in me, / and either I'm nobody, or I'm a nation" (*Collected Poems 1948–1984* [New York; Farrar, Straus & Giroux, 1986], 346). And, therefore, as I have tried to show, "Although there is no way to be certain about the possible interconnections between or among these parallel uses of 'nobody' and 'No

One' (even though it would seem as if Walcott and Thomas are both clearly remembering Homer), one can imagine that Thomas, in referring to himself as 'No One' or 'nobody' might also, like Homer and Walcott, have been thinking of himself as a 'nation,' or at least as a national representative for Wales—since Thomas was a fiercely outspoken advocate for Wales, for all things Welsh, and especially for the Welsh language, which he saw as equivalent to, and necessary for, the survival of the nation itself, in much the same way that Walcott in *Omeros* attempted to recreate and substantiate the collective history of the Caribbean Islands, and Homer in his epics that of the Greeks" (7). Thus, whatever might be behind Thomas's use of the word *neb* to define himself, surely it is the case, as Davies points out, that "[o]nly a writer who knows, at a deep impersonal level, that he is *someone* can afford to call himself 'no-one'" (*Autobiographies*, xiii).

A similar bifurcation in Thomas's treatment of autobiography can be seen in his important collection, *The Echoes Return Slow* (1988), in which prose paragraphs (really prose poems) and parallel poems in lines alternate with one another, sometimes in the first person, sometimes in the third. For treatments of the autobiographical trappings in Thomas's poetry, see M. Wynn Thomas, "'Songs of Ignorance and Praise': R. S. Thomas's Poems about the Four People in his Life," in *Internal Difference: Twentieth Century Writing in Wales*, ed. Thomas (Cardiff: University of Wales Press, 1992), 130–55; and Marie-Thérèse Castay, "The Self and the Other: The Autobiographical Element in the Poetry of R. S. Thomas," in *The Page's Drift: R. S. Thomas at Eighty*, ed. M. Wynn Thomas (Bridgend: Seren, 1993), 119–47.

10   This lack of response can be found in other Thomas poems as well. Compare, for instance, "One Way" (BHN 95), "The Presence" (BHN 107), and "Suddenly" (LP 201). Merchant describes the setting of "In a Country Church" (SYT 114) as the typical setting of Thomas's "bitterest struggles with himself, where despite all prayer and the presence of the symbols of traditional beauty and grace, 'no word came'" (23). Shepherd, in a reading of "In a Country Church" which is quite different from my own, contrasts Thomas's poem to St. Ignatius's statement (quoted from Simon Tugwell's formulation): "God is one, in a mystery of his own being; but from his primordial Silence there comes a Word." Shepherd further suggests that in "In a Country Church" Thomas creates "an antithesis to the experience of Pentecost." In place of the "mighty rushing wind" which "stirred the saints," here the wind only "saddens" these "grave saints." Shepherd sees the poem as arguing against the possibility of any "private interpretation" of the first stanza and, in terms of the second stanza, as leaving the reader "little room" for any "private reading" of the poem. Indeed, she argues that the question which opens the second stanza "reveals that the narrator . . . has difficulty . . . making sense of the situation" (128–29).

11   Only one of the three synoptic gospels specifically says that Jesus "knelt down and prayed" in the garden (see Luke 22:41 RSV). Mark says that Jesus "fell on the ground and prayed" (14:35), while Matthew says that Jesus "fell on his face and prayed" (26:39). Ben Astley suggests an intriguing, if (perhaps) rather far-

fetched reading of this "complex compound" image by arguing that a man on his knees may be praying, or he may be "a man awaiting his own execution." This is, according to Astley, an acknowledgment that "registers the fact that authentic religious experience requires one to die to one's self." And since "no word came" to the "one kneeling down" in Thomas's poem, the very "suspension of presence signals the precondition for, not the obstacle to, religious experience" ("Iago Prytherch and the Rejection of Western Metaphysics," *Welsh Writing in English* 5 [1999]: 108–9).

12 See "The Empty Church" (F 35). Also see my consideration of "The Shadow" below.

13 This is one instance among many where Thomas's rather unique use of the line break and enjambment either suspends the meaning or causes it to shift focus or direction. The resulting inevitable ambiguities are clear evidence of Thomas's unique way of thinking—a habit of mind no doubt, as well as an increasingly conspicuous device in his poetry. In Thomas's poems we see and watch him thinking.

14 In this sense the basic distinction might be compared to the distinction between transubstantiation and consubstantiation, with Thomas here simply taking the traditional Protestant position. And, of course, this interpretation would be in keeping with Thomas's position with respect to metaphors and symbols, as mentioned above.

15 In a late interview Thomas, acknowledging that he was always "a loner," says that he had "always sought out lonely places" because he felt "closer to God in lonely places" (see Thomas's interview with Graham Turner, *The Daily Telegraph* [December 4, 1999], 1, 7).

16 Cf. "The Belfry" (P 28):

> Always,
> Even in winter in the cold
> Of a stone church, on his knees
> Someone is praying, whose prayers fall
> Steadily through the hard spell
> Of weather that is between God
> And himself.

In his 1972 BBC TV interview with John Ormond, Thomas described the "loneliness and quietness" in an empty church, and added: ". . . one projected this image of oneself kneeling, . . . or entering the village church and just waiting, waiting but nothing happening" ("R. S. Thomas: Priest and Poet." Reprinted in in *Poetry Wales* 7.4 (1972): 51).

17 As I have argued elsewhere, in "The Empty Church" (F 35) the "stone trap" of the church "is to the world what the heart (also stone) is to man: both are traps to catch God." And man's "prayers are like flint struck on his stone heart in the hope of creating a spark which will ignite—if only to create an illusion—'the shadow of someone greater than I can understand' on the empty wall of the church" (see chapter 2). One is reminded of Othello's famous line: ". . . my heart

is turned to stone, I strike it and it hurts my hand . . ." (*Othello* IV.i.192–93). It might even be the case that Thomas is here also thinking of one of Shakespeare's most enigmatic sonnets, # 94 (see *Shakespeare: The Complete Works*, ed. G. B. Harrison [New York: Harcourt, Brace & World, 1952], 1612):

> They that have power to hurt and will do none,
> That do not do the thing they most do show,
> Who, moving others, are themselves as stone,
> Unmovèd, cold, and to temptation slow—
> They rightly do inherit Heaven's graces. . . .

18 We know that Thomas read George Steiner's work closely (see, e.g., his *Autobiographies* 161, 164). In a late interview Thomas said, "I read every morning, something of substance, philosophy or theology, people like George Steiner and Paul Tillich, just to keep the mind ticking over. If an idea came, I'm certainly ready to pursue the mosquito" (see interview with Graham Turner 1). Thomas would, no doubt, agree with Steiner's notions of "real presences." *Real Presences* is a book that, as M. Wynn Thomas attests, Thomas "particularly admired" ("'Time's Changeling': Autobiography in *The Echoes Return Slow*," in *Echoes to the Amen: Essays After R. S. Thomas*, ed. Damian Walford Davies [Cardiff: University of Wales Press], 203) and one which Thomas commented on in terms of his own understanding of "the contemporaneity of the Cross." Thomas wrote, "It was heartening to read a while ago George Steiner's 'Real Presences,' and to watch a fine mind surveying linguistics, philosophy and science in a civilized way and yet tentatively suggesting a not dissimilar conclusion" than that of the "valid and timeless symbol" of "the contemporaneity of the Cross" (Clare Brown and Don Paterson, eds., *Don't Ask Me What I Mean: Poets in Their Own Words* [London: Picador, 2003], 284). In *Real Presences* (Chicago: University of Chicago Press, 1991) George Steiner himself had written: "In so far as they are language . . . all 'proofs' of the existence or non-existence of God are unbarred to negation. In the city of words, equal legitimacy attaches to the conviction that the predication of God's existentiality lies at the very source of human speech and constitutes its final *dignitas*; and to the view of the logical positivists that such predication has the same status as nonsense rhymes. Grammatical postulates and demonstrations of God's existence . . . can have validity only inside closed speech systems. . . . In natural and unbounded discourse God has no demonstrable lodging. This is the obstinate dilemma at the heart of Kant's cautionary metaphysics. Negative theology, this is to say the postulate of His non-being, is as legitimate in respect of word and proposition as is the dogma of His presence. Hence the symmetrical abyss within genuine faith and genuine denial; hence the potential anarchy of spirit on either side of the free spaces of utterance" (57–58). Steiner summarizes his position this way: "The ontologically linguistic, discursive substance of interpretations and value-judgments in aesthetics makes verification and falsification logically as well as pragmatically impossible. No proposition in poetics and aesthetics can, in any rigorous sense, be refuted" (68).

19 Not to be confused with another poem also entitled "Questions" (EA 39).

20 I take this phrase from George Mackay Brown's poem "The Poet." (*Selected Poems: 1954–1983* [London: John Murray, 1991], 24).

21 In "A Year in Llŷn" Thomas mentions his "rereading" of Beckett and points out differences between himself and Beckett: "I can see the intricate skill and originality of the man, and realize that he is expressing the contemporary condition of mankind in the large towns of the West, but how on earth can I cherish the same ideas in Llŷn, of all places? Although there are problems here, and the Welsh language and culture are under pressure, how, surrounded by the beauty of Llŷn can one lose hope and consider life meaningless? That would be blasphemy. Beckett must be true to his vision as a creative writer, but that does not impair my right to my own vision either. The Irish Sea has been polluted, the aeroplanes roar above our heads, preparing for the next war; but this is the work of man. Seeing the dew in the morning and the beauty of the sea at sunset; listening to the silence after the aeroplanes have ceased their tumult, I have just as good a right to my faith as he has to his atheism" (*Autobiographies*, ed. Davies, 156). For more on Beckett and Tillich and the notion of "waiting" see my "The Waiting in 'Waiting for Godot'" (*The Cresset* 34.4 [1971]: 10–11).

22 I am indebted to Tony Brown for pointing out that Thomas's abrupt opening of this poem, "Face to face," might well be a reference to the account in Genesis 32:24-30 of Jacob's wrestling with the angel. It does seem plausible that Thomas may have this biblical story in mind, both here at the outset of his poem and also in terms of the lines referring to "your name / vouching for you . . ." (ll. 7–8). In the biblical account, Jacob is required to give his name, Jacob (יַעֲקֹב), which in Hebrew means "one who follows" or "follows after." Jacob is then given a new name by the angel he has wrestled with. His new name, he is told, is to be Israel (יִשְׂרָאֵל), which in Hebrew means "ruling with God" or "God rules." Thus, under either name, Jacob or Israel, his name "vouches" for him. And, of course, the name of the place where the encounter occurred, where Jacob met God "face to face," was called Peniel (פְּנִיאֵל), which in Hebrew literally means "the face of God." In addition, I think it is entirely possible that Thomas may here also be remembering another biblical account, Paul's defense of himself and his conversion in the Book of Acts. Specifically, he may have in mind Paul's particular testimony before King Agrippa at Caesarea, when Paul demanded that he be permitted to confront his accusers "face to face" (see Acts 25:26). Paul's defense here is often considered to be the model of a classic defense of Christianity itself. For more on the phrase "face to face" and its significance for Thomas's thinking, here and elsewhere, see below.

23 It is worth remembering here another poem, "Llananno" (LS 62), which makes use of the same phrase, "Face to face," but which comes to quite a different conclusion:

> Face to face
> with no intermediary
> between me and God, and only the water's

quiet insistence on a time
older than man, I keep my eyes
open and am not dazzled,
so delicately does the light enter
my soul from the serene presence
that waits for me till I come next.

24 Wynn Thomas, in commenting on an earlier version of this essay, delivered as
a lecture at the University of Wales at Swansea, pointed out that, paradoxically,
poetry is a way of "undoing" language "by forcing it to witness against its ordi-
nary self—the self that sustains our 'ordinary' reality." This is an astute observa-
tion, one which seems apt here, and elsewhere in Thomas, since it suggests, I
think rightly, that, for Thomas, poetry is often a way of simultaneously "doing"
and "undoing" language.

25 For more on Thomas and Kierkegaard, see chapter 9.

26 In *The Origin of Consciousness in the Breakdown of the Bicameral Mind* (Boston:
Houghton Mifflin, 1976), Julian Jaynes suggests a theory for the source of poetry
as an outgrowth of man's "nostalgia for the absolute" in a world from which the
divine (and the oracles which are thought to issue messages from the divine,
from God) has withdrawn. Jaynes summarizes his argument this way: "Poetry
begins as the divine speech of the bicameral mind. Then, as the bicameral mind
breaks down, there remain prophets. Some become institutionalized as oracles
making decisions for the future. While others become specialized into poets,
relating from the gods statements about the past" (374). And then Jaynes asks:
"Why as the gods retreated . . . into their silent heavens . . . did not the dialect
of the gods simply disappear? Why did not poets simply cease their rhapsodic
practices as did the priests and priestesses of the great oracles?" (375). "The
answer," he says, "is very clear. The continuance of poetry, its change from a
divine given to a human craft is part of [the] nostalgia for the absolute. The
search for the relationship with the lost otherness of divine directives would not
allow it to lapse" (375). This hypothesis would be one, I suspect, that Thomas
would support, and perhaps even endorse. (For Jaynes's more recent thinking on
this topic see his "Consciousness and the Voices of the Mind" [1986].)

27 In "The New Mariner" (BHN 99) Thomas describes himself as an astronaut on
an "impossible" journey to the "far side of the self," sending out "probes" into
the "God-space" and returning "with messages / [he] cannot decipher."

28 Thomas has another poem called simply "Shadows" (F 25) that anticipates "The
Shadow." "Shadows" describes a "darkness" that implies presence and creates a
"splendour"; the poem also speaks of "the language of silence." (For more on
"Shadows" see chapter 4.)

29 Rowan Williams points out that Thomas "push[es] together" the words
"redemption" and "shadow" in a single line of this poem. He adds, "[T]he words
(the poet) are shadowed by the possibility that there is no atonement" (*The Page's
Drift*, ed. M. W. Thomas, 91). Justin Wintle, noting Thomas's use of "charmed"
in the poem ("I am charmed here") says, "The poet remains charmed by the

beauty of what he sees, but he is also charmed in another way. A spell has been put on him, perhaps by the sheer scale of the time-spans involved at Braich-y-Pwll" (*Furious Interiors*, 321).

30 Wintle suggests that the "environs" of Braich-y-Pwll (at the very tip of the Llŷn peninsula, near where Thomas lived toward the end of his life) "satisfied Thomas's emotional and mental needs. In the very remoteness of Pen Llŷn there was a proximity to the ultimate truths and values the poet sought. If the landscape, suspended between sea and sky, seemed precarious, it also contained, as Thomas had perhaps already discovered, some of the oldest rocks in Europe: the pre-Cambrian outcrops of Braich-y-Pwll, in the shadow of Mynydd Mawr. Throwing his own shadow against them, Thomas could test his faith and his intellect against the manifest paradoxes before him" (*Furious Interiors*, 320).

31 "Nobody" seems to be another pun, suggesting both "no one" in the sense of an unimportant person—as Thomas always insisted he was—and, at the same time, a "person," in the sense, for instance, of the third person of the Trinity, a spirit without a "body."

32 See *Pietá* 36.

33 See *The Echoes Return Slow* 109.

Chapter 4

1 Thomas J. J. Altizer, "Imagination and Apocalypse," *Soundings: An Interdisciplinary Journal* 53.4 (1970): 398.

2 A. M. Allchin, "The Poetry of R. S. Thomas: An Introduction," *Theology* (November 1970): 490.

3 R. S. Thomas, "A Frame for Poetry," *The Times Literary Supplement*, 3 March 1966: 169.

4 See Ormand, "R. S. Thomas: Priest and Poet," in *Poetry Wales* 7.4 (1972): 52–53. For Thomas's full statement of the relationship between his roles as a priest and poet see pp. 7–8.

5 See *The Collected Poems of Theodore Roethke* (New York: Doubleday, 1975), 129.

6 Theodore Roethke, "Open Letter," in *On the Poet and His Craft*, ed. Ralph J. Mills Jr. (Seattle: University of Washington Press, 1965), 39.

7 See my "The Escape into Time: Theodore Roethke's 'The Waking,'" *Notes on Contemporary Literature* 5.2 (1975): 2–10, for more on this theme in Roethke.

8 Roethke, "On 'Identity,'" in *On the Poet and His Craft*, ed, Mills, 25.

9 R. S. Thomas, "Introduction," *The Penguin Book of Religious Verse* (Harmondsworth: Penguin, 1963), 9.

10 Roethke, "On 'Identity,'" in *On the Poet and His Craft*, ed, Mills, 26. Cf. Thomas's acknowledged debt to a poem like Francis Thompson's "The Hound of Heaven."

11 Both Roethke and Thomas might best be described as "nature mystics." Indeed, Thomas so described himself in the BBC film of 1972. Later, Thomas

again attempted to define his mystical tendencies—and to deal with the "misunderstanding and misinterpretation on the part of the critics" in terms of this notion ("R. S. Thomas talks to J. B. Lethbridge," *Anglo-Welsh Review* 74 [1983]: 47–48).

12 As Martin Buber says, "The apocalyptic writer has no audience turned towards him; he speaks into his notebook. He does not really speak, he only writes; he does not write down the speech. He just writes his thoughts—he writes a book" ("Prophecy, Apocalyptic, and the Historical Hour," *Pointing the Way* [New York: Harper & Brothers, 1957], 200).

13 See note 9 above. Cf. "R. S. Thomas talks to J. B. Lethbridge," 55.

14 A. E. Dyson, *Yeats, Eliot and R. S. Thomas: Riding the Echo* (London: Macmillan, 1981), 304. This image of the cross, as I have tried to show, goes back in Thomas's work to the seminal and explicit reference in "Amen," in *Laboratories of the Spirit* (LS 5). Dyson considers "Amen" to be one of the two poems in *Laboratories of the Spirit* (the other is "Rough" [LS 36]) which he "cannot pretend fully to understand," although he does see it as "a poem poised at a cross-roads" (312, 317).

15 For a more detailed analysis of "In Church" and "The Empty Church," see chapter 3.

16 For more on Thomas's use of imagery of reflection, see chapter 5.

17 Calvin Bedient, *Eight Contemporary Poets* (London: Oxford University Press 1974), 67.

18 Thomas's poem "Waiting," referred to here, should not be confused with two other poems also entitled "Waiting" (see BHN 83 and WA 48). For more on "Waiting" (F 32), see above pp. 53–55. Cf. W. S. Merwin: "In an age when time and technique encroach hourly, or appear to, on the source itself of poetry, it seems as though what is needed for any particular nebulous unwritten hope that may become a poem is not a manipulable, more or less predictably recurring pattern, but an unduplicatable resonance, something that would be like an echo except that it is repeating no sound" ("On Open Form," in *Naked Poetry: Recent American Poetry in Open Forms*, ed. Stephen Berg and Robert Mezey [Indianapolis: Bobbs-Merrill, 1969], 270–71). Cf. my essay on Merwin as an apocalyptic poet: "'Like the Beam of a Lightless Star': The Poetry of W. S. Merwin," *Poet and Critic* 14.1 (1982): 45–56.

19 Cf. "The central and stubborn meaning of Thomas's work is . . . the ambiguity of reflection. Existence and action, as Jaspers remarks, display an 'endless ambiguity': 'anything can mean something else for reflection.' Only eternal knowledge is finite—which helps explain why Thomas, one of the most restless of men, refers himself to it" (Bedient 67).

20 Thomas here sounds like Wallace Stevens, a poet he was clearly fond of and had been influenced by, as I have tried to show elsewhere—see chapter 10. Thomas had said that, for him, there is no "newer voice" in English poetry than Stevens, who "comes nearest to expressing the situation" of the moment ("R. S. Thomas talks to J. B. Lethbridge," 56).

21 In terms of this poem, it is interesting to remember that Thomas lived at the very tip of the Llŷn peninsula in northern Wales, near Aberdaron, above Porth Niegwl, "The Mouth of Hell."

22 See notes 9 and 11 above.

23 Thomas, at about the same time these poems were written, was thinking of Kierkegaard in another context. In a lecture he delivered in 1977, entitled "The Creative Writer's Suicide," he said, "In his book, *The Present Age,* Kierkegaard posed a profound and important question: Does man have a right to let himself be killed for the sake of truth?" Thomas uses this Kierkegaardian question as the basis for his talk on "the creative writer." It is clear that much of what he says there has a direct bearing on his own work. (See R. S. Thomas, "The Creative Writer's Suicide," *Planet* 41 [1978]: 30. Cf. also Thomas's poem "Kierkegaard" [P 18–19] and his reference to Kierkegaard in the BBC television documentary mentioned above, as well as "R. S. Thomas talks to J. B. Lethbridge" 54–55.) For more on Thomas and Kierkegaard see chapter 9.

Chapter 5

1 See R. S. Thomas, "Autobiographical Essay," in *Miraculous Simplicity*, ed. W. V. Davis, 17.

2 Cf. Thomas's "Hark" (MHT 38): "You were wrong, Narcissus. / The replica of the self / is to be avoided. Echo / was right, warning you against // the malevolence of mirrors." ("Hark" is one of many poems that Thomas chose to exclude from his *Collected Poems*. It almost seems as if he wanted to "hide" some of his most important poems. Indeed, such a procedure might be seen as an instance of the "presence of absence" in his work. This curious habit, together with the fact that Thomas sometimes used the same title for more than one poem, and that he frequently revised poems from one published version to another, increases the complications of reading and commenting on his work.)

3 As a slight variation on this theme, there are numerous mirror-like windows in Thomas's poems, windows which give off glimpses of a "reflected" place or person and of the semi-hidden self which stares through them, the window being, or becoming, a mirror—both a means of seeing the self as it is and also a means of seeing beyond the self.

4 I have no knowledge that Thomas read Levinas, although, given Thomas's eclectic habit of mind and his wide-ranging reading in many fields, especially in philosophy and theology, and because Levinas would be, for Thomas (as indeed Thomas would be for Levinas), an illuminating, mirror-like thinker, it would be surprising if he had *not* read him—and *vice versa*. We do have Thomas's testimony that he "engage[d] with philosophy / in the morning[s]" ("Present" [F 9]) and there are numerous references to philosophers and philosophic thought scattered throughout his work. The poem "I" (MHT 58, not to be confused with another poem entitled "I" (YO 29), for instance, begins, "Kierkegaard hinted,

Heidegger / agreed. . . ." For more on Thomas's relationship to philosophy and philosophers—especially to Søren Kierkegaard—see chapter 9.

5   Levinas says that in his *Phenomenological Psychology* Husserl shows that "the sub-jective modes of appearing of the world and of nature, the *Erscheinungeweisen* or the aspects of the real are still a part of being" in such a way that the "'sphere of the world swims in the subjective'" (Emmanuel Levinas, *Of God Who Comes to Mind*, trans. Bettina Bergo [Stanford: Stanford University Press, 1998], 17–18). Speaking of the essay I have here quoted from, the anonymous cover blurb for this collection of Levinas's work suggests that this essay "illuminates Levinas's re-lation to Husserl and thus to phenomenology, which is always his starting point, even if he never abides by the limits it imposes."

6   Colin Davis, *Levinas: An Introduction* (Notre Dame: University Notre Dame Press, 1996) 28. As Davis says, "The rest of Levinas's philosophical career will, then, be dominated by one question: what does it mean to think of the Other as Other?" (33). Levinas said, "The relationship with the other is not an idyl-lic and harmonious relationship of communion or a sympathy [*sympathie* is Levinas's translation of Husserl's *Einfühlung*] through which we put ourselves in the other's place; we recognize the other as resembling us, but exterior to us; the relationship with the other is a relationship with a Mystery" (Emmanuel Levinas, *Time and the Other*, trans. Richard A. Cohen [Pittsburgh: Duquesne University Press, 1987], 75). Davis says that "This passage indicates the crux of Levinas's dispute with phenomenology . . ." (*Levinas: An Introduction*, 31). In my summaries of Levinas's thinking, here and elsewhere, I am indebted to Davis's lucid summarizations of Levinas's thought.

7   Levinas, *Of the God Who Comes to Mind*, 24.

8   Levinas, *Of the God Who Comes to Mind*, 26. Cf. "Between me and the other there gapes a difference which no unity of transcendental apperception could recover" (71). Such a "gape" is also a "gap." For more on Thomas and the use and significance of gaps in his poetry, see chapter 6.

9   Emmanuel Levinas, *Totality and Infinity: An Essay on Exteriority*, trans. Alphonso Lingis (Pittsburgh: Duquesne University Press, 1969), 69. Cf. "The intelligibil-ity of transcendence is not ontological. The transcendence of God can neither be said nor thought in terms of being" (Levinas, *Of the God Who Comes to Mind*, 77).

10 Emmanuel Levinas, "The Trace of the Other," in *Deconstruction in Context: Literature and Philosophy*, ed. Mark C. Taylor (Chicago: University of Chicago Press, 1986), 354–55.

11 Levinas says, "The self is the site where the Same identifies itself as such" (see Colin Davis, *Levinas, An Introduction*, 42).

12 Levinas argues that "God is not simply the 'first other' [*premier autrui*] or the 'other par excellence' [*autrui par excellence*] or the 'absolutely other' [*absolument autrui*], but other than the other, other otherwise, other by an alterity prior to the alterity of the other [*autre qu'autrui, autre autrement, autre d'altérité préalable à l'altérité d'autrui*], prior to the ethical obligation to the neighbour, transcendent

to the point of absence . . ." (see *En découvrant l'existence avec Husserl et Heidegger* [Paris: Vrin, 1974], 199–202; *De Dieu qui vient á l'idée* [Paris: Vrin, 1992], 115). Cf. Levinas, *Of the God Who Comes to Mind,* 69. The word "trace" is a particularly important word for Levinas and within the phenomenological/philosophical movement that he champions. It is also a word that links these philosophical considerations with specifically literary ones. Such a linkage has perhaps been most overtly made and detailed by Jacques Derrida (a student of Levinas), who brings these two disciplines together through his deconstructive approach to both. Derrida is indebted to Levinas as well as having been, later on, an influence on him. The first and arguably the most incisive analysis of *Totality and Infinity* is Derrida's "Violence and Metaphysics: An Essay on the Thought of Emmanuel Levinas" (*Writing and Difference,* trans. Alan Bass [Chicago: University of Chicago Press, 1978], 79–153). As Colin Davis says, "Derrida's engagement with Levinas clearly does go far deeper than a simple critique. His intense and ongoing studies of Husserl and Heidegger put him in an almost unique position to assess Levinas's relationship to his most evident sources. Most importantly, Derrida's essay is also to some extent an act of philosophical self-recognition, as Levinas's ambiguous relationship to the language and values of the philosophical tradition is a reflection of Derrida's own position. Derrida perceives that Levinas's writing anticipates the difficulties faced by deconstruction. According to Feron, 'The essential point of Derrida's argument consists in recognizing that philosophical discourse can only say the Other in the language of the Same' (Étienne Feron, *De l'idée de transcendance á la question du language: L'Itinéraire philosophique d'Emmanuel Levinas* [Grenoble: Jérôme Millon, 1992], 260); and this can be taken to summarize Derrida's dilemma as much as that of Levinas" (see Colin Davis, *Levinas: An Introduction,* 66). Derrida's essay appeared before Levinas's *Otherwise than Being or Beyond Essence,* and some critics argue that, in that book, Levinas attempted to take Derrida's criticism of his earlier work into account. At the very least, it seems certain that Derrida influenced Levinas's later thought and brought it more specifically into the realm of literary criticism per se. In another crucial text, *Of Grammatology* (trans. Gayatri Chakravorty Spivak [Baltimore: The Johns Hopkins University Press, 1976]), Derrida traces the word "trace" through the philosophy of Heidegger and Levinas before coming to his own conclusions with respect to it in terms of this tradition. Derrida describes this trace as a metaphysical concept based on the notion of presence. For him, "the word designates something of which the metaphysical concepts of trace and presence are the erasure." Therefore, it "names an originary tracing and effacement" and becomes "the trace of effacement"; "it names something of which . . . self and Other are the erasure . . ." (Rodolphe Gasché, *The Tain of the Mirror: Derrida and the Philosophy of Reflection* [Cambridge: Harvard University Press, 1986], 186–87). For more on the relationship between Derrida and Levinas, see Levinas's "Jacques Derrida: Wholly Otherwise" in *Proper Names,* trans. Michael B. Smith (Stanford: Stanford University Press, 1996), 55–62; Robert Bernasconi, "The Trace of Levinas in Derrida," in *Derrida and Différence,* ed. David Wood and Robert Bernasconi (Evanston: Northwestern University Press,

1988), 13–29; Robert Bernasconi and Simon Critchley, eds. *Re-Reading Levinas* (Bloomington: Indiana University Press, 1991), 3–10, 11–48, 162–89, *passim*; and Simon Critchley, *The Ethics of Deconstruction: Derrida and Levinas* (Blackwell: Oxford University Press, 1992).

13 See Colin Davis, *Levinas: An Introduction*, 99.

14 See Colin Davis, *Levinas: An Introduction*, 100. As Levinas says, "One may wonder whether the true God can ever discard His incognito" (*Entre Nous: On Thinking-of-the-Other*, trans. Michael B. Smith and Barbara Harshav [New York: Columbia University Press, 1998], 56). Cf. ". . . [O]ne may wonder whether the incognito should not be the very mode of revelation . . ." (Levinas, *Proper Names*, 78.]

15 Emmanuel Levinas, *A l'heure des nations* (Paris: Minuit, 1988), 204.

16 There are several other instances of images of "cracked mirrors" in Thomas's canon, but perhaps the most interesting in terms of my purposes here is one that combines several references to be noted later. This reference occurs in a poem called "Pardon" (EA 29). The reference is to "homo sapiens, that cracked mirror, / mending himself again and again like a pool." Another early poem makes a similar, equally interesting and complex use of this imagery; in it Thomas describes "an old farmer" who "plays" the "neglected music" of a woman's "thin body" as she, watching him, sees in the mirror of "his eye / The light of the cracked lake // That once she had propped to comb / Her hair in" (T 22, not to be confused with another important poem also entitled "Once," H'm 1.)

17 See Genesis 1:3-31, esp. 26-27: "Then God *said*, 'Let us make man in our image, after our likeness. . . .' So God created man in his own image. . ." (italics added). It would seem obvious that Thomas initially found his metaphor of the mirror, and based his subsequent contemplations on it, in this biblical passage.

18 *Mass for Hard Times* is obviously a book that, in several ways, itself serves as a mirror or a "counterpoint" to *Counterpoint*.

19 See chapter 9. It is perhaps worth mentioning the not surprising fact that Levinas has also often mentioned Kierkegaard, a philosopher who has clearly interested him. See, for instance, Levinas's essay, "Kierkegaard: Existence and Ethics," in which he remarks that "Kierkegaard's philosophy has marked contemporary thought so deeply that the reservations and even the rejections it may elicit are yet forms of that influence" (*Proper Names*, 71). And, he adds, no one "has developed with greater rigor" than Kierkegaard the "phenomenology" of "the correlate of truth crucified" (*Proper Names*, 70). In "A Propos of 'Kierkegaard *vivant*'" Levinas says, "Thus Kierkegaard brings something absolutely new to European philosophy: the possibility of attaining truth through the ever-recurrent inner rending of doubt. . ." (*Proper Names*, 77).

20 The fact that Thomas, who is usually referred to by his initials, chooses to refer to Kierkegaard as "S. K." suggests Thomas's indebtedness to Kierkegaard. For more on Thomas's relationship to Kierkegaard, see chapter 9.

21 Thomas may well be thinking here of Martin Buber, a thinker to whom he frequently refers. Likewise, Levinas regularly mentions Buber, especially in terms of

his seminal book *Ich und Du* (*I and Thou*) [Ronald G. Smith, trans. Ediburgh: T&T Clark, 1937]. However, as Colin Davis points out, "Levinas rejects Buber's I-Thou "relationship because it implies too much familiarity with the Other, which should be addressed with the more formal *vous*; but this *vous* is in turn too familiar, too direct an address for God. God is glimpsed only in the third person, neither a presence nor an absence, but a trace (*En découvrant l'existence avec Husserl et Heidegger*, 199–202), infinitely close and absolutely distant" (see Colin Davis, *Levinas: An Introduction*, 99). See also Levinas's essays on Buber: "Martin Buber and the Theory of Knowledge," and "Dialogue with Martin Buber" (in Levinas, *Proper Names*, 17–35 and 36–39).

Chapter 6

1   John W. Kronik, "Editor's Column," *PMLA* 107:1 9.
2   *Neb* was written in the third person, in Welsh; it has been translated into English by Jason Walford Davies (see *R. S. Thomas: Autobiographies*). Thomas himself, however, translated a portion of this autobiography—in the first person (see *Miraculous Simplicity*, ed. W. V. Davis).
3   See n. 2 above as well as Thomas's comments in a recent interview:

> I was asked to write *Neb*. It would never have occurred to me to write an unsolicited autobiography, because I am of no importance as a person and have never been at or near the centre of so-called important events. . . . If there be such an unwise person in the future as to undertake to write a biography of me, he is welcome to enter the morass of trivia which may or may not be open to him. I don't consider it of any importance. Hence the title I gave the short account which I wrote myself. I was approached some while ago for permission to write such by a professional biographer. He did not consider his lack of Welsh an impediment, but how else could he have found out my size in shoes? (see Ned Thomas and John Barnie, "Probings: An Interview with R. S. Thomas," *Planet* 80 [1990]: 36).

The "unwise person" Thomas refers to here must be either Justin Wintle or Byron Rogers. Wintle's biography of Thomas is called *Furious Interiors*. As my book was going to press, a new biography of Thomas, *The Man Who Went into the West: The Life of R. S. Thomas*, by Byron Rogers, was published.
4   Thomas's habit of using a single word as title more than once, along with his practice of failing to reprint some of his strongest poems in the several selections he has made of his work (and, one suspects, of keeping some strong poems out of even the various individual volumes as they have appeared), makes for complex bibliographic and critical complications. More than for most contemporary poets, a complete edition of Thomas's poems and a definitive bibliography are needed.
5   *Webster's Ninth New Collegiate Dictionary* (1985), 492.

6   Here at the beginning of our consideration of *Frequencies* at least two of
     Thomas's earlier poems need to be remembered in terms of the larger context
     of "The Gap." First, and most immediately, there is that other, earlier poem,
     also entitled "The Gap," in *Laboratories of the Spirit* (LS 37). This poem begins
     with a description of an Edenic world: "The one thing they were not troubled /
     by was perfection. . . ." In this paradise, "Their hand" (as if Adam and Eve are
     truly one) "moved in the dark / like a priest's, giving its blessing." And then,
     "their work / finished," they "withdrew . . . / leaving the interrogation of it /
     to ourselves." This, of course, "was before / the fall." And "Somewhere between
     them and us / the mind climbed up into the tree / of knowledge, and *saw* . . ."
     (my italics).
         In an even earlier poem, "The Gap in the Hedge" (AL 15), we find Thomas's
     peasant paradigm, Iago Prytherch, "framed in the gap / Between two hazels with
     his sharp eyes, / Bright as thorns, watching the sunrise." This vivid image of
     Prytherch has remained in the speaker's mind: "he's still there / At early morning,
     when the light is right." There is a double frame here. First, the title of the
     poem, "The Gap in the Hedge," (note that "hedge" contains the word "edge")
     provides the initial frame or vantage point for the vision of Prytherch, who is
     first seen through a gap of hedge. Then, a second frame, Prytherch is described
     as being "framed in the gap / Between two hazels." The symbolic suggestion,
     and even the double remove (which deepens the distance as it accentuates the
     image), clearly implies a parallel between Prytherch and Christ, each of whom
     is here "framed" in memory and imagination, between two trees. But beyond
     that framing, and behind this poem, Thomas surely has in mind and wants us to
     remember that greater "gap" between God and man, filled and framed by Christ
     on his cross. (In spite of the Welsh tradition of *cynghanedd*, it is, of course, no
     accident that the poem is written in rhymed couplets, approximately like the
     Welsh *cywyddau*.)
         Furthermore, if this obsession with "gaps" has been obvious since the begin-
     ning of Thomas's career, it is equally evident in his more recent work. For
     instance, in "Bleak Liturgies" (MHT 59–63), written twenty years after "The
     Gap," we find the line, "The gaps in belief. . . ." Clearly then, this word "gaps"
     and the various literal and metaphoric meanings it suggests, have continued to
     obsess Thomas—even as they obsessed him early on.

7   It is worth mentioning that the Welsh words *adwy* and *bwlch* can both be translated
     as "gap" or "pass." In addition, the feminine *adwy* can be translated "breach" and
     the masculine *bwlch* as "notch." The connotative differences between a "gap"
     and a "pass," a "breach" and a "notch," are, no doubt, as important to Thomas
     as they ought to be to his readers—even in English. This is, of course, only a
     small instance of the much greater problem Thomas faced throughout his life
     as an "Anglo-Welsh" poet. He often commented on the complexities of his life
     and poetry in terms of this issue, but in this specific instance it is perhaps most
     important to remember his comments in his essay "Words and the Poet": "One
     of the problems of an Anglo-Welsh poet . . . is that of having to try to transpose

the raw material of his imagination and experience into the alien medium of English speech which has no exact equivalents for *mynydd* [mountain] and *bwlch, cwm* [valley] and *hafod* [upland farm]; poetry being, as all will allow, in the last resort untranslatable. I mention that as personally applicable" ("Words and the Poet," in *R. S. Thomas, Selected Prose*, ed. Anstey, 80–81).

8   Thomas and Barnie, "Probings: An Interview with R. S. Thomas," 45.

9   "The Porch" (F 10), set "in a church porch," may well be indebted to George Herbert's "The Church Porch." Thomas had long been interested in Herbert, and there are many connections between them, as has frequently been noted (see, for instance, William J. McGill's *Poet's Meeting: George Herbert, R. S. Thomas, and the Argument with God* [Jefferson, N.C.: McFarland, 2004]). In the "Introduction" to his selection of Herbert's poetry, Thomas, in defining Herbert's dominant theme, identifies his own dominant theme: "What he [Herbert] had was an argument, not with others, nor with himself primarily, but with God . . ." (see *A Choice of George Herbert's Verse*, 12).

10 See Dionysius the Areopagite, *The Divine Names and the Mystical Theology*, trans. C. E. Rolt (London: SPCK, 1940), 194, 196.

11 Thomas's poem "Abercuawg" (F 26–27) has its obvious parallel in his essay with the same title, originally delivered at the Eisteddfod in 1976. The original essay, in Welsh, can be found in Sabine Volk, *Grenzpfähle der Wirklichkeit: Approaches to the Poetry of R. S. Thomas* (Frankfurt am Main: Peter Lang, 1985), 259–73. Volk (her work revised by Thomas himself) has translated portions of this essay. A translation of the complete essay is included in *Selected Prose* (1986), ed. Anstey, 163–74. For additional details concerning the translation of "Abercuawg," see Volk, 68 n. 3. In terms of our present purposes here it is interesting to note that "Abercuawg" is itself a kind of "gap." In searching for it "[w]e are searching . . . within time, for something which is above time, and yet, which is ever on the verge of being. . . . [W]e can never become conscious of absence as such, only that what we are seeking is not present" (*Selected Prose*, ed. Anstey, 171–72). As Volk indicates, "Abercuawg" is a "key symbol" for Thomas "since it is almost an empty form . . ." (69). In talking about Abercuawg, Volk refers to the "gap between the word and the fact" (70) and quotes Thomas: "For such a place I am willing to sacrifice, perhaps even as much as my life" (71). (Anstey translates this passage, "For such a place I am ready to make sacrifices, maybe even to die" [*Selected Prose* 166]). Finally, as Thomas himself says, "Welsh is perhaps superior to English in this matter. 'Nothing is nothing' is an ambiguous proposition, to say the least. But *'Dim ydyw dim'* is quite clear and final. What the English suggests is: 'Nothing is without existence.' And in the light of this it would be possible to assert that Abercuawg exists. But a Welshman can say *'Nid yw Abercuawg yn bod'*" (see *Selected Prose*, ed. Anstey, 167–68).

12 For more on "Waiting" see chapter 3. In one of the prose poems in *The Echoes Return Slow*, Thomas asks, "[I]s the meaning, then, in the waiting?" (ERS 42). Later in the same book, he seems to answer himself: "You have to imagine / a waiting that is not impatient / because it is timeless" (ERS 81). Rather obviously,

Thomas might well agree with his fellow cleric Paul Tillich, in whose sermon "Waiting" we find the following sentences: "Waiting means *not* having and having at the same time." "The fact that we wait for something shows that in some way we already possess it." "If we wait in hope and patience, the power of that for which we wait is already effective within us." "We are stronger when we wait than when we possess." "Let us not forget, however, that waiting is a tremendous tension. Waiting is not despair. It is the acceptance of our not having, in the power of that which we already have" (see *The Shaking of the Foundations* [New York: Charles Scribner's Sons, 1948], 149–52; cf. Thomas's poem "Emerging" [F 41] discussed below).

13   Thomas knows Eliot's poetry and criticism equally well, and the echoes and direct references to Eliot (and, indeed, to Yeats, Wordsworth, etc.) in his work are numerous, and have become increasingly frequent. Here, of course, I am thinking of Eliot's "The Love Song of J. Alfred Prufrock."

14   Thomas often had Kierkegaard in mind and specifically alludes to him on several occasions, both in his poems and in his prose works. The two most significant specific references in the poetry, before "Balance" (F 49), are "Kierkegaard" (P 18–19) and "A Grave Unvisited" (NHBF 9). In the former, Kierkegaard, "wounded," "crawled / To the monastery of his chaste thought / To offer up his crumpled amen" (i.e., Kierkegaard, like Thomas, is already "experimenting with" his "amen"). "A Grave Unvisited" is even more explicit, and it makes clear several parallels between Thomas and Kierkegaard. Thomas notes at the outset of the poem that he has "Deliberately not" visited Kierkegaard's grave in Copenhagen (although he has been there). Even though the Danes have done "What they could do to anchor him / With the heaviness of a nation's / Respectability" (like Wales has Thomas?), Thomas asks, "would he have been / There to receive this toiling body's / Pilgrimage. . . ?" What is important for Thomas is to "go / Up and down with him in his books, / Hand and hand like a child / With its father, pausing to stare / As he did once at the mind's country." And, although its occasion and thesis are clearly removed from the context of these particular poems, in "The Creative Writer's Suicide," a lecture he delivered in 1977, Thomas refers specifically to Kierkegaard's *The Present Age,* the thesis of which he wants, he says, to use "as a springboard" for his address. In *The Present Age* (trans. Alexander Dru [New York: Harper & Row, 1962] Kierkegaard speaks of "the infinite freedom of religion" and "the religious courage which springs from . . . individual religious isolation" and argues that "in the reality of religion and before God" each man must learn "to be content with himself," "to dominate himself, content as priest to be his own audience, and as author his own reader" (53, 54, 57). Clearly Thomas took much of Kierkegaard to heart. Kierkegaard, Thomas notes, "defined a poet as one who suffers. It is in his anguish that he opens his mouth" (see *Selected Prose,* ed. Anstey, 178). For more on Thomas and Kierkegaard, see chapter 9.

15   This initial question alludes both to the Christmas eve story and to the church festival of January 6th commemorating the coming of the Magi as a manifes-

tation of Christ to the gentiles. The tradition, in England, of the three Kings bringing the symbolic offerings of gold, frankincense and myrrh to the Chapel Royal on the feast day is also apparently alluded to in the first several lines of the poem.

16   Bardsey Island, also known as the "Isle of 20,000 Saints," was the site of the earliest Christian settlement in Wales. Founded by St. Cadfan in the sixth century, it became a famous place of pilgrimage in the Middle Ages.

17   Cf. "Retirement" (EA 38), where Thomas, in the first person, uses almost identical imagery.

Chapter 7

1   See chapter 9 and elsewhere.

2   As quoted in Walter Lowrie, *Kierkegaard* (New York: Harper & Brothers, 1962), 11. It is interesting to note, especially in the context of Thomas's poem on this story, that Joakim Garff, Kierkegaard's most recent biographer, argues that *Fear and Trembling* "is obsessed with the importance of language, with nonverbal communication, with signals, and with the far-reaching significance of the silent gesture" (see *Søren Kierkegaard: A Biography* [Princeton: Princeton University Press, 2005], 252).

3   See Lowrie, *Kierkegaard,* 11–12.

4   The ekphrastic tradition has a long history. Although it was originally thought of rather exclusively as "the Greek rhetorical exercise of evocative description," there are classical, literary and historical components involved in the practice of *ekphrasis*. Indeed, it has recently been defined as a reciprocal tradition that "sets the arts in friendly and mutually supportive competition" with one another (see David Rosand, "Ekphrasis and the Generation of Images," *Arion* 1.1 (1990): 61). The first verbal expression of *ekphrasis* may well be Simonides of Ceos's (ca. 556–467 B.C.) statement, "Painting is mute poetry, and poetry a speaking picture" (see Jean Hagstrum, *The Sister Arts: The Tradition of Literary Pictorialism and English Poetry from Dryden to Gray* [Chicago: University of Chicago Press, 1958], 10). Since at least Horace's *ut pictura poesis, ekphrasis* (or *ecphrasis*), the literary effort to recreate a work of visual art, has been a common practice among poets. Even so, as John Hollander has shown in his detailed study of both the history and practice of *ekphrasis*, over the centuries the term has come "to stand for an agenda of far more wide-ranging comparisons and contrasts" than was historically the case (see *The Gazer's Spirit: Poems Speaking to Silent Works of Art* [Chicago: University of Chicago Press, 1995], 6). Initially popular in ancient times and in classical literature, the *ekphrastic* tradition was rediscovered and revived in the Renaissance. It then became popular again in the nineteenth and twentieth centuries. And, as Hollander indicates, there was "a good deal of such poetry addressing a wide range of good and bad, great and obscure, unglossed and overinterpreted works of art . . . taking up a range of stances toward their objects" during the last several centuries. Still, *ekphrasis* "has been

until the last decade or so a technical term used by classicists and historians of art to mean a verbal description of a work of art." However, "in recent literary theory, considerations of ecphrasis have concerned the ways in which space and time are involved in the various mutual figurations of actuality, text and picture" (Hollander 4–5). Several pioneering studies of the *ekphrastic* tradition might be mentioned: Renasselaer W. Lee's "*Ut Pictura Poesis*: The Humanistic Theory of Painting" (*Art Bulletin* 22 [1940]: 197–269); Hagstrum's *The Sister Arts*, referred to above; and Murray Kreiger's "*Ekphrasis* and the Still Movement of Poetry: or *Laokoön* Revisited." (Kreiger's essay was reprinted as an appendix to his more comprehensive *Ekphrasis: The Illusion of the Natural Sign* [Baltimore: The Johns Hopkins University Press, 1992].)

    With respect to R. S. Thomas, it is worth noting that Thomas's first wife was the artist Mildred E. Eldridge and that he published two substantial collections of poems on paintings: *Between Here and Now* (1981), which contains a collection of thirty-three lyric poems based on the French Impressionist paintings reproduced in Germain Bazin's *Impressionist Paintings in the Louvre* (London: Thames & Hudson, 1958), and *Ingrowing Thoughts* (1985). Thomas also, of course, wrote other individual poems on paintings or on other works of art. Even so, in spite of Thomas's obvious interest in and his contributions to the *ekphrastic* tradition, "*Souillac: Le Sacrifice d'Abraham*" remains unique. Gwydion Thomas, R. S. Thomas's son, has recently remarked that his father's poem "could not have been written without his mother's input" (see "Quietly as Snow," Gwydion Thomas's interview with Walford Davies in *New Welsh Review* 64 [2004]: 45). This is, no doubt, the case.

5   Perhaps the most obvious and best known depictions of this biblical story are those created by Ghiberti and Brunelleschi in the competition for the commission to design the bronze doors of the Baptistery in Florence. In both Ghiberti's and Brunelleschi's competitive panels Isaac is depicted as kneeling on an altar.

6   Meyer Schapiro, *Words and Pictures: On the Literal and the Symbolic in the Illustration of a Text* (The Hague: Mouton, 1973), 14.

7   Schapiro continues, "On the other side of the pillar are three superposed scenes of a boy fighting with an old man; in the lowest the boy resists, in the second they struggle, at the top the boy submits; but at that point the victorious old man is himself devoured by a monster" (*Words and Pictures*, 14–16).

8   See Shapiro, *Words and Pictures*, 16.

9   Meyer Schapiro, "The Angel with the Ram in Abraham's Sacrifice: A Parallel in Western and Islamic Art," *Ars Islamica* 10 [1943]: 144–45.

10   See Meyer Schapiro, "The Sculptures of Souillac," in *Medieval Studies in Memory of A. Kingsley Porter*, ed. Wilhelm R. W. Koehler, 2 vols. (Cambridge: Harvard University Press, 1939), 384.

Chapter 8

1   See Thomas's interview with Ned Thomas and John Barnie in *Miraculous Simplicity*, ed. W. V. Davis, 36–39. These are not isolated remarks. Thomas has often mentioned contemporary science and compared the work of physicists to the work of poets, as he does, for instance, in another wide-ranging lecture:

> By shifting the emphasis away from matter as something solid to something closer to a field of force, contemporary physicists have come to realize just how mysterious the universe is, and that we need qualities such as imagination and intuition and a mystical attitude if we are to begin to discover its secrets. . . . Contemporary physics' vision of the nature of being is . . . similar to that of a poet or a saint. The physicist believes in a living web, which connects everything in the entire universe. All living things are related to each other, and no part of the universe can be harmed or abused without awakening echoes throughout the whole web. This is the voice heard by the author of the Book of Revelation: "Hurt not the earth." And here we have physics confirming the declaration of the English poet Francis Thompson who said: "Thou cant not stir a flower / Without troubling of a star."
>
> The West has been under the thumb of reason for a very long time. Because of this we divide everything into A and not-A. Nothing can be A and not-A at the same time. However, contemporary physics contradicts this by showing how matter is both a wave and a particle at the same time, and by describing the strange behaviour of one of the elements of life, the electron. We are gradually beginning to see how the scientific mind works. Some of the most abstruse and complex problems of nature have been solved, not by means of a process of reasoning, but as a result of a sudden intuition which was closer to the vision of an artist or a saint than anything else. . . . So, in the long run, what emerges from the vision of contemporary physics is a picture of the world as a living being of which we all form a part. This is the unity of being of which we must be aware, if we wish to survive (see "Unity," in *R. S. Thomas: Selected Prose*, ed. Anstey, 147–48; the Thompson reference is to "The Mistress of Vision.")

2   See Barnie's review of Thomas's *Later Poems 1972–1982, Poetry Wales* 18 (1983): 90–91. Cf. Ned Thomas, "This side of his work ["where the poet turns his gaze on modern technology"] has been less discussed—the poems are difficult, and it is often more convenient for critics in England to categorize R. S. Thomas as a Welsh, religious, country poet—a triple relegation to margins where he can be allowed to reign supreme—than to take him on his own philosophic terms. When the critics do refer to his poems about science and technology, there is a tendency to depict the poet as the simple enemy of progress" ("R. S. Thomas: The Question about Technology," *Planet* 92 [1992]: 55).

3   Although I have no specific knowledge that Thomas knew the work of Norbert Wiener, I suspect, knowing Thomas's habit of reading widely in popular scientific literature, that he may well have read him—or that he would have immediately

found him interesting. It is also teasingly interesting that Wiener—at about the same time that Thomas was writing his first poems in which man confronts "the machine," published his fascinating book *The Human Use of Human Beings: Cybernetics and Society* (New York: Avon, 1950)—a book in which he argued that "society can only be understood through a study of the messages and the communication facilities which belong to it," and that in the future the "development of these messages and communication facilities . . . are destined to play an ever-increasing" role in society (25). Cybernetics, the "theory of messages" (106), is thus crucial to the effective understanding and operation of society, and, as Wiener points out, both man and machine are "communicative organisms" and "the communication characters of man and of the machine impinge upon one another" (185)—further, these reciprocal exchanges impact upon society as a whole.

4   It should be noted that Thomas's first significant reference to "the machine" occurs early on in his second book, *An Acre of Land* (1952), in "Cynddylan on a Tractor" (AL 26):

Ah, you should see Cynddylan on a tractor.
Gone the old look that yoked him to the soil;
He's a new man now, part of the machine,
His nerves of metal and his blood oil.

Jeremy Hooker argues that, early on, Thomas "develops his idea of the machine . . . into a mythology of evil." He adds, "the poems concerned with this theme are metaphorical statements of the cause of man's estrangement from God and from his own nature as his worship of the machine. At first, it may appear that R. S. Thomas's idea of the machine is an abstraction scarcely less injurious to creative thought than the abstracting tendency of the mechanical principle itself; that the dramatic form of the metaphors merely conceals the dogged repetition of a prejudice. On further acquaintance, however, one can see that the machine, if it does reflect an outlook as obdurate as the mechanical principle it stands for, is also being used as a flexible symbol for the processes by which man is divorced from his humanity by the false idols he creates" (Hooker, *The Presence of the Past: Essays on Modern British and American Poetry* [Bridgend: Poetry Wales Press, 1987], 33). Similarly, Ned Thomas indicates that "From quite early on in [Thomas's] poetry we find words and phrases with a scientific and technical ring to them, . . . but by the later volumes, terms such as virus, molecule, cell, gene, frequency, equation are part of the way he apprehends reality—or . . . explores it. He uses the words of science for their ability to probe beyond what is apparent to our ordinary senses and to our common sense, but the probings are redirected from the purpose of understanding and controlling the physical world to serve his own research into the great question of Being" ("R. S. Thomas: The Question about Technology," 59–60).

5   In this category I would include those poems in which "the machine" is seen as a God and in which it is frequently depicted as if it were some kind of contemporary version of the old notion of the *deus ex machina*. These poems

constitute a fascinating sequence which, to my knowledge, has never been sufficiently explored.

6   As Patrick Deane has remarked, Thomas's "poems come to resemble those of the English metaphysicals in the deliberateness with which contemporary science and technology are yoked in the service of theological speculation. . . . A sense of failure is there in Thomas's poems even from his first attempts to break with rustic idealism and march with science to the door of heaven. . . ." (see "The Unmanageable Bone: Language in R. S. Thomas's Poetry" in *Miraculous Simplicity*, ed. W. V. Davis, 211, 214). Cf. Barbara Hardy: "[Thomas's] Christianity is set in the world of mathematics and science, co-habits with equations, is forced to wear the garb of machinery, lasers, silicon, in ways which deprecate science but use it also. . . . Thomas's god . . . is defined advantageously in scientific language. . . . [and] is imagined in litotes, meiosis, occupation, and the topos of inexpressibility, not occasionally, as in Milton, but habitually. He is absent or angry, not occasionally, as in Hopkins, but almost always. He isn't loving, or comforting or close" (see "Imagining R. S. Thomas's Amen," *Poetry Wales* 29 [1993]: 22). In short, as Grevel Lindrop suggests, ". . . for Thomas the notions of Scientist and Machine are dangerously enticing because they represent forms of the selfless purity and coherence which are sought and not always found in the religious life" (see "The Machine Speaks," TLS [16 December 1983]: 1411).

7   This poem "Emerging" ("Not as in the old days I pray," LS 1) should not be confused with another poem, also entitled "Emerging" ("Well, I said, better to wait," F 41) published in *Frequencies* (1978). (This is only one of several instances in which Thomas uses the same title for several poems.)

8   "At It" was originally published as "The Verdict" in *Encounter* 50:3 (1978): 3.

9   Cf. one of Thomas's later poems, entitled "Visions," (*Frieze* 24) in which he defines his "vision" this way: "The mathematical god, anticipated / by his statistics, crucified / over again by secondary / causation, shedding from an articulated / cross tears of oil."

10   In "The New Mariner" (BHN 99), Thomas describes himself as an "astronaut" on an "impossible journey," sending his "probes" out into "the God-space" and returning with "messages" he "cannot decipher."

11   See *Poetry Wales* 28 (1992): 3.

12   See Thomas's interview with Ned Thomas and John Barnie in *Miraculous Simplicity*, ed. W. V. Davis, 40.

Chapter 9

1   *Selections from Ralph Waldo Emerson*, ed. Stephen E. Whicher (Boston: Houghton Mifflin, 1957), 46.

2   R. S. Thomas, "A Frame for Poetry," in *R. S. Thomas: Selected Prose*, ed. Anstey, 90.

3   See John Ormond, "R. S. Thomas: Priest and Poet." Transcript of the BBC TV film in *Poetry Wales* 7.4 (1972): 53.

4   See Thomas, "The Creative Writer's Suicide," in *Selected Prose*, ed. Anstey, 177.
5   Howard V. Hong and Edna H. Hong, eds. and trans. *Søren Kierkegaard's Journals and Papers,* Part I (Bloomington: Indiana University Press, 1970–1978), 358–59.
6   "R. S. Thomas Talks to J. B. Lethbridge," 55.
7   "R. S. Thomas Talks to J. B. Lethbridge," 51.
8   "R. S. Thomas Talks to J. B. Lethbridge," 54.
9   Søren Kierkegaard, *Concluding Unscientific Postcript*, trans. David F. Swenson and Walter Lowrie (Princeton: Princeton University Press, 1944), 182.
10 R. S. Thomas, letter to William V. Davis, 13 April 1996.
11 Thomas, "The Creative Writer's Suicide," in *Selected Prose*, ed. Anstey, 178.
12 See, e.g., Søren Kierkegaard, *Either/Or: A Fragment of Life*, trans. David F. Swenson, vol. 2 (New York: Doubleday, 1959), 150, *passim*.
13 Søren Kierkegaard, *Stages on Life's Way,* trans. Walter Lowrie (Princeton: Princeton University Press, 1940), 430.
14 Thomas, "The Creative Writer's Suicide," in *Selected Prose*, ed. Anstey, 177.
15 See M. Wynn Thomas, "R. S. Thomas: The Poetry of the Sixties," in *Internal Difference,* ed. M. W. Thomas, 116. In "Irony in the Soul," 49–69, however, Wynn Thomas does attempt to deal with R. S. Thomas's use of "Kierkegaardian irony." Tony Brown, another critic who deals with Thomas and Kierkegaard, makes reference to Thomas's poem "Balance" in terms of Kierkegaard's consideration of "authentic existence" and of both writers' "search for truth" (see "'Over Seventy Thousand Fathoms': The Sea and Self-definition in the Poetry of R. S. Thomas," in *The Page's Drift*, ed. M. W. Thomas, 165–66). I have also pointed out direct parallels between Thomas and Kierkegaard, both in terms of the early poems obviously indebted to Kierkegaard and in terms of the correspondences between "The Creative Writer's Suicide" and *The Present Age* (see chapter 4 above, especially n. 23).
16 Moelwyn Merchant, *R. S. Thomas* (Fayetteville: University of Arkansas Press, 1990), 54.
17 See below for the significance of mirrors in Thomas. Thomas, of course, was always chary with biographical details and always shunned references to biography, both in his prose writings and in his poems. In "Biography" (EA 17–18), for instance, he writes: "A life's trivia: commit them / not to the page, but to the waste-basket / of time." Nonetheless, biographical references, allusions, and explicit "facts" did begin to appear late on, even in Thomas's poetry, most specifically in, and following, *The Echoes Return Slow* (1988). Likewise, critics have recently begun to explore Thomas's life and his veiled treatment of it in his poems. See, for example, M. Wynn Thomas, "Songs of 'Ignorance and Praise': R. S. Thomas's Poems about the Four People in his Life," in *Internal Difference,* ed. M. W. Thomas, 130–55; Castay, "The Self and the Other," in *The Page's Drift,* ed. M. W. Thomas, 119–47, and Barbara Prys Williams, "'A Consciousness in Quest of Its Own Truth': Some Aspects of R. S. Thomas's *The Echoes Return*

Slow as Autobiography," *Welsh Writing in English: A Yearbook of Critical Essays* 2 (1966): 98–125.

18 An emphasis on pilgrimage, as I have tried to show, runs throughout Thomas's work and perhaps comes to climax in his poem "Pilgrimages" (F 51–52), a poem that, although it clearly refers directly to pilgrimages made to Bardsey Island, off the coast of the Llŷn peninsula across the strait from Aberdaron, the place where Thomas served his final parish, also seems to be related to Kierkegaard as well—even though this is never stated directly in the poem. (I have mentioned these parallels elsewhere: see chapters 3 and 5.)

19 See M. W. Thomas, *Internal Difference,* 119.

20 Søren Kierkegaard, *Works of Love: Some Christian Reflections in the Form of Discourses,* trans. Howard and Edna Hong (New York: Harper & Brothers, 1962), 334.

21 See Hong and Hong, *Kierkegaard's Journals and Papers,* 2:122.

22 Søren Kierkegaard, *The Present Age and Two Minor Ethico-Religious Treatises,* trans. Alexander Dru and Walter Lowrie (London: Oxford University Press, 1940), 402.

23 See Kierkegaard, *The Present Age,* 430.

24 Quoted in Lowrie, *Kierkegaard,* 2:426.

25 See Tony Brown, "Over Seventy Thousand Fathoms," in *The Page's Drift,* ed. M. W. Thomas, 165.

26 See chapter 5 for more on the significance of mirrors and mirror images in Thomas's work.

27 See Lowrie, *Kierkegaard,* 2:631.

28 Cf. *Hamlet* II.i.66.

29 "S. K." was originally published in a somewhat different version as "Kierkegaard" [see *Poetry Wales* 29.1 (1993): 7]. This poem should not be confused with an earlier poem, also titled "Kierkegaard" (P 18–19). Thomas's changes to the text of "S. K." in *No Truce with the Furies,* when pertinent, will be mentioned below.

30 James A. Davies ("Participating Readers: Three Poems of R. S. Thomas," *Poetry Wales* 18.4 [1983]: 72–83) makes a somewhat different suggestion. He argues that "Thomas's work assumes no single homogeneous reader" but, "rather, each poem predicates its own unique responder." This seems to suggest, once again, Kierkegaard's notions of "indirect communication" and "double reflection," but it also involves Kierkegaard's use of "repetition," which he calls "a forward-looking recollection" (quoted in Lowrie, *Kierkegaard,* 2:634); it is clear that, for Kierkegaard, "repetition is a religious category," as Lowrie points out. In short, Kierkegaard's philosophical method was a system of oppositions, contrasts, and contradictions which, he felt, were inherent in existence itself—even if in a paradoxical way. He argued that "the eternal and essential truth, the truth which has an essential relationship to an existing individual because it pertains essentially to existence . . . is a paradox." And because existence for Kierkegaard

is contradictory and paradoxical, a "synthesis of the infinite and the finite, of the eternal and the temporal" (see Lowrie, *Kierkegaard,* 2:631), it resists any systematic attempt by the reason to regiment it, and is, therefore, thought by the reason to be "absurd." Dread is the horror realized by the premonition of nothingness; it leads to despair, the "sickness unto death," which, paradoxically, may in turn lead to new life. Thomas seems to have taken much of this, as he took much of Kiergegaard in toto, to heart.

31 For a succinct one paragraph summary of Kierkegaard's relationship with Regina Olsen see Lowrie, *Kierkegaard,* 1:192.

32 Since the word "nettle" is invariably associated with a man reduced to the lowest state of poverty or despair in the Bible, it is a word that, for Kierkegaard, might well have suggested "the sickness unto death," the phrase that he used as the title of his classic study of despair. And it is no doubt also inevitable to see in Thomas's reference to "a shirt of nettles" an allusion to the "shirt of Nessus" that drove Heracles to set himself on fire. This reference would be especially relevant in the context of Kierkegaard's tormented relationship with Regina.

33 For more on Thomas and the ekphrastic tradition see chapter 6. Even more to the point in terms of the reference here (even though he does seem to be using the reference generically) Thomas included a poem on Dali's "Drawing" (yet another kind of "draft") in *Ingrowing Thoughts* (IT 37). And, of course, Thomas's first wife, Elsi, was an artist.

34 It is well known that Kierkegaard was obsessed by the fate of Jonathan Swift and that he referred to him in a passage that he revised several times, entitled "The Quiet Despair." Kierkegaard wrote: "The Englishman Swift founded a madhouse in his youth and became an inmate of it in his old age. It is related that here he often regarded himself in a mirror and exclaimed, 'Poor old man!' " Lowrie suggests that "this story preoccupied S. K. because he was fearful of the same fate" (*Kierkegaard,* 1:45). The mirror reference in this passage is also intriguing in terms of Thomas's obsession with mirrors. See below for specific reference to this image, and see chapter 5 for more general references to it.

35 In the original version of this poem these lines read: "Imagining / from his emphasis on the true // self that God is not other. . . ." The word "true" followed by both a line break and a stanza break was perhaps too much, and too insistent—as Thomas must have decided. Keeping "self" and "God" on the same line does, of course, increase the parallels and associations between them.

36 The original version of this line reads "on the mind's lightning flash."

37 See chapter 7 for more on Thomas and the father/son relationship.

38 The original version reads "inscrutable as was its reflection."

39 See R. S. Thomas, "Autobiographical Essay," in *Miraculous Simplicity,* ed. W. V. Davis, 17. Cf. "Pre-Cambrian" (F 23): "I am charmed . . . / by the serenity of the reflections / in the sea's mirror. It is a window / as well." For more on mirrors and mirror imagery in Thomas see chapter 5.

40 See Castay, "The Self and the Other," in *The Page's Drift,* ed. M. W. Thomas, 144.

41 See *The Echoes Return Slow* 72.

42 See *Counterpoint* 12.

43 In his original version of the poem Thomas introduced a stanza break after "to an imagined request," thus breaking this section into two stanzas and joining his two final questions in one stanza.

44 These final two lines of "S. K." are rather different from the final lines of Thomas's first version of the poem. In the original version these final lines read: "the reflection in it of / a countenance other than our own?" This earlier version, although not essentially different in meaning, does seem to be clearer in terms of the theme of the poem.

Chapter 10

1 Paul Valéry, "Letter about Mallarmé," *Leonardo Poe Mallarmé*, trans. Malcolm Cowley and James R. Lawler (London: Routledge & Kegan Paul, 1972), 240–41.

2 Valéry, "Letter about Mallarmé," 241–42. Valéry then goes on to describe how "At the still rather tender age of twenty . . . I suffered the impact of Mallarmé's work. . . . I felt myself becoming a sort of fanatic; I had to undergo the overwhelming progress of a decisive spiritual conquest. . . . The heinous train of thought—and a dangerous one for literature . . . was combined in a contradictory fashion with my admiration for a man who, by following his own, had reached a point nothing short of deifying the written word" (244, 249). Valéry concludes, ". . . it might have been of some interest to pursue the analysis of a particular case of *influence* in depth and detail, to show the direct and contradictory effects of a certain work on a certain mind, and to explain how a tendency towards one extreme is answered by another. . . . I concluded that Mallarmé must have an inner system to be distinguished from that of the philosopher and, in a different fashion, from that of the mystics, yet revealing some analogies with both" (253, 248).

3 See Harold Bloom, *The Anxiety of Influence* (Oxford University Press, 1973), 30. In *Kabbalah and Criticism* (New York: The Seaburg Press, 1975) Bloom extends this notion to readers or critics by arguing that "The reader is to the poem what the poet is to his precursor—every reader is therefore an ephebe, every poem a forerunner, and every reading an act of 'influencing,' that is, of being influenced *by* the poem and of influencing any other reader to whom your reading is communicated. Reading is therefore misprision—or misreading—just as writing is . . ." (97).

4 *The Anxiety of Influence*, 15–16. Bloom continues: "British and American poetry, at least since Milton, has been a severely displaced Protestantism, and the overtly devotional poetry of the last three hundred years has been therefore mostly a failure. The Protestant God, insofar as He was a Person, yielded His paternal role for poets to the blocking figure of the Precursor. God the Father, for Collins, is John Milton, and Blake's early rebellion against Nobodaddy is

made complete by the satiric attack upon *Paradise Lost* that is at the center of *The Book of Urizen* and that hovers, much more uneasily, all through the cosmology of *The Four Zoas*. Poetry whose hidden subject is the anxiety of influence is naturally of a Protestant temper, for the Protestant God always seems to isolate His children in the terrible double bind of two great injunctions: 'Be like Me' and 'Do not presume to be too like Me.' The fear of godhood is pragmatically a fear of poetic strength, for what the ephebe enters upon, when he begins his life cycle as a poet, is in every sense a process of divination" (152). Bloom concludes his argument rather ingeniously by arguing that examples of such anxieties of influence "abound": ". . . the hugely idiosyncratic Milton shows the influence, in places, of Wordsworth; Wordsworth and Keats both have a tinge of Stevens; the Shelley of *The Cenci* derives from Browning; Whitman appears at times too enraptured by Hart Crane. . . . The precursors flood us, and our imaginations can die by drowning in them, but no imaginative life is possible if such inundation is wholly evaded" (154).

5   Stevens, *Collected Poetry and Prose*, 683.

6   In "A Collect of Philosophy" Stevens argued that "the idea of God is the ultimate poetic idea" (*Collected Poetry and Prose*, 859) (Stevens would surely have been remembering here that one of the definitions of "collect" is "a short prayer"); in his essay "The Figure of the Youth as Virile Poet," Stevens describes poets as "the peers of saints" (*Collected Poetry and Prose*, 674); in a letter to Hi Simons he said, "I write poetry because it is part of my piety" (see *Letters of Wallace Stevens*, ed. Holly Stevens [New York: Alfred A. Knopf 1981], 473); and in a letter to Henry Church he wrote that his "own way out toward the future involv[ed] a confidence in the spiritual role of the poet" (340). Elsewhere, I have attempted to describe Stevens's "philosophical search" throughout the course of has career and to document its climax in his late poem, "Not Ideas about the Thing but the Thing Itself" (see " 'This Refuge that the End Creates': Stevens's 'Not Ideas about the Thing but the Thing Itself,'" *Wallace Stevens Journal* 11.2 [1987]: 103–10).

7   See Thomas's interview with J. B. Lethbridge," *Anglo-Welsh Review* 74 (1983): 56.

8   Dyson, *Yeats, Eliot and R. S. Thomas*, 306, 323.

9   Ward, *Poetry of R. S. Thomas*, (2001 ed.), 74.

10 Tony Brown, " 'Blessings, Stevens': R. S. Thomas and Wallace Stevens," in *Echoes to the Amen*, ed. Davies, 130. If it is the case that "The Conductor" (T 13) "owes something" to Stevens (and this seems to me a somewhat tenuous suggestion), then I would add "The Musician" (T 19) as another possibility in this mix, since "The Musician" certainly seems related to "The Conductor." M. Wynn Thomas' suggestion that Thomas's poem beginning "It was winter" in *The Echoes Return Slow* (ERS 31) "may . . . be read as Thomas's distinctive response to Wallace Stevens's famous observation that 'one must have a mind of winter' [i.e., Stevens's "The Snow Man," *Collected Poetry and Prose* 8 (see M. Wynn Thomas, " 'Time's Changeling': Autobiography in *The Echoes Reteurn Slow*," in *Echoes to*

the Amen, ed. Davies, 197)] seems even less plausible—unless Thomas means the word "distinctive" to mean "having or giving style or distinction" as opposed to "capable of making a segment of utterance different in meaning as well as in sound from an otherwise identical utterance" (Webster's), as I would tend to take it. Finally, it is intriguing that "The Idea of Order at Key West" has also been cited by Geoffrey Hill in terms of Thomas. In discussing the necessity that the poet "imagine the making of his own language in the immediate process of making it," Hill compares Stevens's theme in "The Idea of Order at Key West" to Thomas's "Wallace Stevens" and says that Thomas's poem "regards Stevens only in the aspect of thought or opinion; and therefore cannot move beyond the impression of 'cold' ascribed to a despairing hedonist. One could as well call Thomas a despairing hedonist" ("R. S. Thomas's Welsh Pastoral," in *Echoes to the Amen*, ed. Davies, 45, 57).

11 "Probings: An Interview with R. S. Thomas," in *Miraculous Simplicity*, ed. W. V. Davis, 34.

12 "Probings: An Interview with R. S. Thomas," 4.

13 Interview with Graham Turner, *The Daily Telegraph*, 4 December 1999: 7.

14 "With Great Pleasure" (2000).

15 Brown, "'Blessings Stevens,'" 112.

16 Stevens, *Letters*, 251.

17 M. H. Abrams, *Natural Supernaturalism: Tradition and Revolution in Romantic Literature* (New York: W. W. Norton, 1971), 334. This seems startlingly similar to Emerson's comment in *Nature*: "Whether nature enjoy a substantial existence without, or is only in the apocalypse of the mind, it is alike useful and alike venerable to me" (*Selections from Ralph Waldo Emerson*, ed. Stephen E. Whicher, 42).

18 For my description of the apocalyptic mode as it applies to Thomas, see chapter 4 above. I have considered the apocalyptic mode in Charles Wright's poetry ("'Bruised by God': Charles Wright's Apocalyptic Pilgrimages," in *The Wider Scope of English: Papers in English Language and Literature from the Bamberg Conference of the International Association of University Professors of English*, ed. Herbert Grabes and Wolfgang Viereck [Franfurt am Main: Peter Lang, 2006], 130–53) and in Louise Glück's poetry in "'Talked to by Silence': Apocalyptic Yearnings in Louise Glück's *The Wild Iris*," *Christianity and Literature* 52.1 (2002) and treated the idea of the apocalyptic in other twentieth-century poets elsewhere.

19 Wallace Stevens, *Opus Posthumous* (New York: Alfred A. Knopf 1980), xv.

20 One wonders whether, having gotten into it, with the necessity of the Stevens model demanding thirteen sections, Thomas, notoriously given to short, singly focused poems, might have run into difficulties in the middle of his poem—although there are, of course, similar, sometimes ironic, shifts in other Thomas poems, and there are also other long poems later on in his career (among them "Anybody's Alphabet" [NTF 88–92], already mentioned).

21 Cf. Thomas's poem "Album" (F 36) in which he describes his own father who "went looking for me / in the woman. . . ."

22 I am here quoting Charles Wright's poem "Snow" (*China Trace* [Middletown, Conn.: Wesleyan University Press, 1977], 14). Wright is often thinking of Stevens, and, of course, in many ways Stevens was an autumnal or wintry poet, as Wright is.

23 Andrew Rudd says that this passage "almost quotes Stevens himself: 'That's it. The lover writes, the believer hears. / The poet mumbles'" ("'Not to the Bible but to Wallace Stevens'—What R. S. Thomas Found There," *PN Review* 30.4 [2004]: 49). And Rudd reminds us of Helen Vendler's definition of a poet as one who is always "mumbling to oneself," as well as of Thomas's own lines about his taking "truth / In my mouth and mumbl[ing] it / . . . till my teeth Grew" (quoted in Rudd 49).

24 Tony Brown points out that the phrase, "The deep spaces between stars," "recalls Robert Frost's 'Desert Places'" and those "empty spaces / Between stars . . . where no human race is." This "echo of Frost," which is "surely revealing and far from coincidental," is, according to Brown, indicative of the "sense of spiritual loneliness [that] seems to haunt [Thomas's] poems of this period." Certainly, Brown is right in noting this bow to Frost (although it is well known that Thomas was not a Frost fan) and right in seeing what Thomas here admired in Stevens, since Stevens was, as Brown says, "a poet who placed the highest possible value on the power of the poetic imagination, on individual intellectual creativity, in a world which . . . was otherwise empty of secure meaning" ("'Blessings Stevens'" 114–15, 117).

25 See chapter 9 for more on Thomas and Kierkegaard.

26 Kierkegaard, *Works of Love*, 334. And, in his *Concluding Unscientific Postscript*, trans. David F. Swenson and Walter Lowrie (Princeton: Princeton University Press, 1944) Kierkegaard argued: "Without risk there is no faith. Faith is precisely the contradiction between the infinite passion of the individual's inwardness and the objective uncertainty. If I am capable of grasping God objectively, I do not believe, but precisely because I cannot do this I must believe. If I wish to preserve myself in faith I must constantly be intent upon holding fast the objective uncertainly, so as to remain out upon the deep, over seventy thousand fathoms of water, still preserving my faith" (182). Both Kierkegaard and Thomas, almost obsessively, come back over and over again to this metaphor of the "seventy thousand fathoms."

27 Note that Thomas describes Stevens's world by saying, "His one season was late fall" in the final stanza of this poem. Brown objects to Thomas's limiting Stevens to "one season," and argues that this is a "partial," "ultimately inadequate," and "demonstrably not true" account of "the cycle of the seasons." In addition, Brown castigates Thomas for ignoring "the colour," the "ludic exoticism," and the "sensual gaiety" present in much of Stevens. He concludes that Thomas's poem "tell[s] us rather more about Thomas at this point in his imaginative career than it does about Stevens" ("'Blessings Stevens,'" 114–15). One wonders if it is not often the case that, in poems by one poet on another, the second is not frequently (even perhaps inevitably) self-referential?

28   Certainly "The Snow Man" was an important poem for Thomas, and there are echoes of it in several of his poems.

29   See T. S. Eliot, *Collected Poems 1909–1962* (New York: Harcourt, Brace & World, 1963), 29–31. In "Gerontion" Eliot imagines "an old man in a dry month," "a dry brain in a dry season," in a "decayed house," "waiting for rain" and for a "sign." This man will witness the coming of "Christ the tiger." It would seem certain that Thomas must be remembering all of this.

30   I am thinking here of all of the meanings of the word "cure," including "the of-fice of a curate" (*The American Heritage Dictionary*).

31   Thomas reports that he always "clung to the King James Bible and to the 1662 Book of Common Prayer, considering the language of both to be indescribably superior" to other versions or translations (Thomas's *Autobiographies*, trans. J. W. Davies, 88–89). Justin Wintle reports on an occasion in which Thomas "arrive[d] at a cathedral to read some of his poems at a service, and stomp[ed] off in a huff when he discovered a modern version of the Bible would be used" (*Furious Interiors*, 373).

32   This tripartite description seems initially to allude to T. S. Eliot, a literal bank-clerk in London, who would have been familiar with double-entry bookkeeping.

33   Perhaps the best examples of Thomas's "double-entry poetics" are to be found in *The Echoes Return Slow*, which contains some of his most personal and most autobiographical poems, as I have mentioned above. Throughout this book the prose poems and the poems in lines face each other, antiphonally responding to one another page by page.

34   See Stevens, *Letters,* 831.

35   *Autobiographies,* 131.

36   This "turning," combined with the "turn" at the opening of the poem ("I turn now / not to the Bible / but to Wallace Stevens.") is reminiscent of the "turnings" that open and close Eliot's "Ash Wednesday" ("Because I do not hope to turn again"; "Although I do not hope to turn again" [*Collected Poems, 1909–1962,* 85, 94]), even if Thomas's resolution of his dilemma is rather different from Eliot's. Still, it is possible that Thomas wished to evoke Eliot both in terms of this rather specific allusion and also in terms of his similar theme. "Ash Wednesday" is the first important poem in Eliot's career, a poem in which, according to Eric Thompson (*T. S. Eliot: The Metaphysical Perspective* [Carbondale: Southern Illinois University Press, 1963], 81), he initiates his "recurrent theme" of the use and misuse of poetry—and Thomas may well be thinking along these lines as well. Certainly Eliot's lines are "crabbed lines" that, as F. O. Matthiessen says, "suggest turning in their very denial of its hope"— lines in which the rhythm "suggests the movement of the mind of the poet back and forth from doubt to acceptance" (*The Achievement of T. S. Eliot: An Essay on the Nature of Poetry* [New York: Oxford University Press, 1959], 119).

Bibliography

Books by R. S. Thomas

Poetry

The Stones of the Field. Carmarthen: The Druid Press, 1946.
An Acre of Land. Newtown: Montgomeryshire Printing Co., 1952.
The Minister. Newtown: Montgomeryshire Printing Co., 1953.
Song at the Year's Turning: Poems 1942–1954. London: Rupert Hart-Davis, 1955.
Poetry for Supper. London: Rupert Hart-Davis, 1958.
Tares. London: Rupert Hart-Davis, 1961.
The Bread of Truth. London: Rupert Hart-Davis, 1963.
Pietà. London: Rupert Hart-Davis, 1966.
Not That He Brought Flowers. London: Rupert Hart-Davis, 1968.
H'm. London: Macmillan, 1972.
Young and Old. London: Chatto & Windus, 1972.
Selected Poems 1946-1968. London: Rupert Hart-Davis, 1973.
What is a Welshman? Llandybie: Christopher Davies, 1974.
Laboratories of the Spirit. London: Macmillan, 1975.
The Way of It. Sunderland: Coelfrith Press, 1977.
Frequencies. London: Macmillan, 1978.
Between Here and Now. London: Macmillan, 1981.

Later Poems 1972–1982. London: Macmillan, 1983.
Destinations. Halford: Celandine Press, 1985.
Ingrowing Thoughts. Bridgend: Poetry Wales Press, 1985.
Experimenting with an Amen. London: Macmillan, 1986.
Welsh Airs. Bridgend: Poetry Wales Press, 1987.
The Echoes Return Slow. London: Macmillan, 1988.
Counterpoint. Newcastle upon Tyne: Bloodaxe Books, 1990.
Frieze. Schondorf am Ammersee: Bable, 1992.
Mass for Hard Times. Newcastle upon Tyne: Bloodaxe Books, 1992.
Collected Poems 1945–1990. London: J. M. Dent, 1993.
No Truce with the Furies. Newcastle upon Tyne: Bloodaxe Books, 1995.
Residues. Ed. M. Wynn Thomas. Northumberland: Bloodaxe Books, 2002.
Selected Poems. London: Penguin, 2004.
Collected Later Poems 1988–2000. Northumberland: Bloodaxe Books, 2004.

Prose

Abercuawg. Gwasg Gower: Llandysul, 1976. Translated into English in Anstey,
    R. S. Thomas: Selected Prose.
Neb. Caernarfon: Gwasg Gwynedd, 1985.
Cymru or Wales? Llandysul: Gomer Press, 1992.
Selected Prose. Edited by Sandra Anstey. Bridgend: Seren, 1983, 1986, 1995.
ABC Neb. Edited by Jason Walford Davies. Caernarfon: Gwasg Gwynedd,
    1995.
Autobiographies. Trans. Jason Walford Davies. London: J. M. Dent, 1997.

Books Edited by Thomas

The Batsford Book of Country Verse. London: Batsford, 1961.
The Penguin Book of Religious Verse. Harmondsworth: Penguin, 1963.
Selected Poems of Edward Thomas. London: Faber & Faber, 1964.
A Choice of George Herbert's Verse. London: Faber & Faber, 1967.
A Choice of Wordsworth's Verse. London: Faber & Faber, 1971.

Works Cited

Abrams, M. H. *Natural Supernaturalism: Tradition and Revolution in Romantic Literature*. New York: W. W. Norton, 1971.

Allchin, A. M. "The Poetry of R. S. Thomas: An Introduction." *Theology* (November 1970): 488–95.

Altizer, Thomas J. J. "Imagination and Apocalypse." *Soundings: An Interdisciplinary Journal* 53.4 (1970): 398–412.

Anstey, Sandra, ed. *Critical Writings on R. S. Thomas*. Bridgend: Poetry Wales Press, 1983; revised 1992.

Arnold, Matthew. *The Complete Prose Works of Matthew Arnold*. Edited by R. H. Super. 11 vols. Ann Arbor: University of Michigan Press, 1960–1977.

———. *Matthew Arnold: Selected Prose*. Edited by P. J. Keating. New York: Penguin, 1987.

Astley, Ben. "Iago Prytherch and the Rejection of Western Metaphysics." *Welsh Writing in English: A Yearbook of Critical Essays* 5 (1999): 101–14.

apRoberts, Ruth. *Arnold and God*. Berkeley: University of California Press, 1983.

Barnie, John. Rev. of *Later Poems 1972–1982*. *Poetry Wales* 18 (1983): 87–95.

Baum, Julius, ed. *Romanesque Architecture in France*. London: Country Life, 1910.

Bazin, Germain. *Impressionist Paintings in the Louvre*. London: Thames & Hudson, 1958.

Beckett, Samuel. *Waiting for Godot*. New York: Grove Press, 1954.

Bedient, Calvin. *Eight Contemporary Poets*. London: Oxford University Press, 1974.

Bernasconi, Robert. "The Trace of Levinas in Derrida." In *Derrida and Différence*. Edited by David Wood and Robert Bernasconi. Evanston, Ill.: Northwestern University Press, 1988.

Bernasconi, Robert, and Simon Critchley, eds. *Re-Reading Levinas*. Bloomington: Indiana University Press, 1991.

Bloom, Harold. *The Anxiety of Influence*. New York: Oxford University Press, 1973.

———. *Kabbalah and Criticism*. New York: The Seabury Press, 1975.

———. *A Map of Misreading*. New York: Oxford University Press, 1975.

Brown, Clare, and Don Paterson, eds. *Don't Ask Me What I Mean: Poets in Their Own Words*. London: Picador, 2003.

Brown, George Mackay. *Selected Poems 1954–1983*. London: John Murray, 1991.

Brown, Tony. "'Blessings, Stevens': R. S. Thomas and Wallace Stevens." In *Echoes to the Amen: Essays after R. S. Thomas*. Edited by Damian Walford Davies. Cardiff: University of Wales Press, 2003: 112–31.

———. "'Over Seventy Thousand Fathoms': The Sea and Self-definition in the Poetry of R. S. Thomas." In *The Page's Drift: R. S. Thomas at Eighty*. Edited by M. Wynn Thomas. Bridgend: Seren, 1993.

Buber, Martin. *Ich und Du (I and Thou)*. Trans. Ronald Gregor Smith. Edinburgh: T&T Clark, 1937.

———. "Prophecy, Apocalyptic and the Historical Hour." In *Pointing the Way*. New York: Harper & Brothers, 1957.

Bunyan, John. *The Pilgrim's Progress*. Edited by Roger Sharrock. New York: Penguin, 1965.

Cadbury, William. "Coming to Terms with 'Dover Beach.'" *Criticism* 8 (1966): 126–38.

Castay, Marie-Thérèse. "The Self and the Other: The Autobiographical Element in the Poetry of R. S. Thomas." In *The Page's Drift: R. S. Thomas at Eighty*. Edited by M. Wynn Thomas. Bridgend: Seren, 1993.

Critchley, Simon. *The Ethics of Deconstruction: Derrida and Levinas*. Oxford: Blackwell, 1992.

Davies, Damian Walford, ed. *Echoes to the Amen: Essays after R. S. Thomas*. Cardiff: University of Wales Press, 2003.

Davies, James A. "Participating Readers: Three Poems of R. S. Thomas." *Poetry Wales* 18.4 (1983): 72–83.

Davis, Colin. *Levinas: An Introduction*. Notre Dame, Ind.: University of Notre Dame Press, 1996.

Davis, William V. "'An Abstraction Blooded': Wallace Stevens and R. S. Thomas on Blackbirds and Men." *The Wallace Stevens Journal* 8.2 (1984): 79–82.

———. "'At the Foot of the Precipice of Water . . . Sea Shapes Coming to Celebration': R. S. Thomas and Kierkegaard." *Welsh Writing in English: A Yearbook of Critical Essays* 4 (1998): 94–117.

———. "'Bruised by God': Charles Wright's Apocalyptic Pilgrimages." In *The Wider Scope of English: Papers in English Language and Literature from the Bamberg Conference of the International Association of University Professors of English*. Edited by Herbert Grabes and Wolfgang Viereck. Frankfurt am Main: Peter Lang, 2006.

———. "The Escape into Time: Theodore Roethke's 'The Waking.'" *Notes on Contemporary Literature* 5.2 (1975): 2–10.

———. "Evidence of Things Not Seen: R. S. Thomas's Agnostic Faith." *Welsh Writing in English: A Yearbook of Critical Essays* 11 (2006–2007): 122–46.

———. "'Going Forward to Meet the Machine': R. S. Thomas's Quarrel with Technology." In *Poetry Now: Contemporary British and Irish Poetry in the Making.* Edited by Holger Klein, Sabine Coelsch-Foisner, and Wolfgang Görtschacher. Tübingen: Stauffenburg Verlag, 1999.

———. "'Like the Beam of a Lightless Star': The Poetry of W. S. Merwin." *Poet and Critic* 14.1 (1982): 45–56.

———, ed. *Miraculous Simplicity: Essays on R. S. Thomas.* Fayetteville: University of Arkansas Press, 1993.

———. "The Presence of Absence: Mirrors and Mirror Imagery in the Poetry of R. S. Thomas." In *Passions of the Earth in Human Existence, Creativity, and Literature.* Analecta Husserliana: The Yearbook of Phenomenology Research 71. Edited by Anna-Teresa Tymieniecka. Dordrecht, The Netherlands: Kluwer Academic Publishers, 2001. Reprinted in *Life—The Play of Life on the Stage of the World.* Annalecta Husserliana: The Yearbook of Phenomenology Research 73. Edited by Anna-Teresa Tymieniecka. Dordrecht, The Netherlands: Kluwer Academic Publishers, 2001.

———. "R. S. Thomas." In *British Writers.* Supplement 12. Edited by Jay Parini. New York: Charles Scribner's Sons and Thomson Gale, 2006.

———. "R. S. Thomas, *The Odyssey*, and Derek Walcott: A Note on the Use of 'No One.'" *Notes on Contemporary Literature* 35.4 (2005): 6–7.

———. "R. S. Thomas: Poet-Priest of the Apocalyptic Mode." *South Central Review* 4.4 (1987): 92–106.

———. "'Talked to by Silence': Apocalyptic Yearnings in Louise Glück's *The Wild Iris.*" *Christianity and Literature* 52.1 (2002): 47–56.

———. "'This Is What Art Could Do': An Exercise in Exegesis—R. S. Thomas's *Souillac: Le Sacrifice d'Abraham.*" *Religion and the Arts* 4.3 (2000).

———. "'This Refuge that the End Creates': Stevens's 'Not Ideas about the Thing but the Thing Itself.'" *The Wallace Stevens Journal* 11.2 (1987): 103–10.

———. "'The Tide's Pendulum Truth': A Reading of the Poetry of Theological Crisis from Matthew Arnold to R. S. Thomas." *Christianity and Literature* 55.3 (2006): 369–91.

———. "'The Verbal Hunger': The Use and Significance of 'Gaps' in the Poetry of R. S. Thomas." In *The Page's Drift: R. S. Thomas at Eighty.* Edited by M. Wynn Thomas. Bridgend: Seren, 1993.

———. "The Waiting in 'Waiting for Godot.'" *The Cresset* 34.4 (1971): 10–11.

Davis, William V. "Wallace Stevens and R. S. Thomas: Influence *sans* Anxiety." *The Wallace Stevens Journal* 30.1 (2006): 86–97.

Deane, Patrick. "The Unmanageable Bone: Language in R. S. Thomas's Poetry." *Renascence: Essays on Values in Literature* 42.4 (1990): 213–36. Reprinted in *Miraculous Simplicity: Essays on R. S. Thomas.* Edited by William V. Davis. Fayetteville: University of Arkansas Press, 1993.

Derrida, Jacques. *Of Grammatology.* Translated by Gayatri Chakravorty Spivak. Baltimore: The Johns Hopkins University Press, 1976.

———. "Violence and Metaphysics: An Essay on the Thought of Emmanuel Levinas." In *Writing and Difference.* Translated by Alan Bass. Chicago: University of Chicago Press, 1978.

Dickinson, Emily. *Final Harvest: Emily Dickinson's Poems.* Edited by Thomas H. Johnson. Boston: Little, Brown, 1961.

Dionysius the Areopagite. *The Divine Names and the Mystical Theology.* Translated by C. E. Rolt. London: SPCK, 1940.

Dyson, A. E. *Yeats, Eliot and R. S. Thomas: Riding the Echo.* London: Macmillan, 1981.

Eliot, T. S. "Arnold and Pater." In *Selected Essays 1917–1932.* New York: Harcourt, Brace, 1932.

———. *Collected Poems 1909–1962.* New York: Harcourt, Brace & World, 1963.

Emerson, Ralph Waldo. *Selections from Ralph Waldo Emerson.* Edited by Stephen E. Whicher. Boston: Houghton Mifflin, 1957.

Feron, Étienne. *De l'idée de transcendence á la question du language: L'Itinéraire philosophique d'Emmanuel Levinas.* Grenoble: Jérôme Millon, 1992.

Ferré, Frederick. *Language, Logic and God.* New York: Harper & Brothers, 1961.

Flew, Antony. *God and Philosophy.* Amherst, N.Y.: Prometheus Books, 2005.

———. "Theology and Falsification." In *New Essays in Philosophical Theology.* Edited by Antony Flew and Alasdair Macintyre. London: SCMP, 1955.

Garff, Joakim. *Søren Kierkegaard: A Biography.* Translated by Bruce H. Kirmmse. Princeton: Princeton University Press, 2005.

Gasché, Rodolphe. *The Tain of the Mirror: Derrida and the Philosophy of Reflection.* Cambridge: Harvard University Press, 1986.

Hagstrum, Jean H. *The Sister Arts: The Tradition of Literary Pictorialism and English Poetry from Dryden to Gray.* Chicago: University of Chicago Press, 1958.

Hardy, Barbara. "Imagining R. S. Thomas's Amen." *Poetry Wales* 29 (1993): 21–22.

Harries, Richard. "The *Via Negativa* in the Poetry of R. S. Thomas." *The David Jones Journal* (2001): 59–73.

Herbert, George. *The Works of George Herbert*. Edited by F. E. Hutchinson. Oxford University Press, 1941.

Hill, Geoffrey. "R. S. Thomas's Welsh Pastoral." In *Echoes to the Amen: Essays after R. S. Thomas*. Edited by Damian Walford Davies. Cardiff: University of Wales Press, 2003.

Hollander, John. *The Gazer's Spirit: Poems Speaking to Silent Works of Art*. Chicago: University of Chicago Press, 1995.

Holloway, John. *The Charted Mirror: Literary and Critical Essays*. London: Routledge & Kegan Paul, 1960.

Homer. *The Odyssey: with an English Translation*. Translated by A. T. Murray. 2 vols. Cambridge: Harvard University Press, 1919.

Hong, Howard V., and Edna H. Hong, eds. and trans. *Søren Kierkegaard's Journals and Papers*. Bloomington: Indiana University Press, 1970–1978.

Hooker, Jeremy. *The Presence of the Past: Essays on Modern British and American Poetry*. Bridgend: Poetry Wales Press, 1987.

Husserl, Edmund. *Cartesian Meditations: An Introduction to Phenomenology*. Translated by Dorion Cairns. The Hague: M. Nijhoff, 1960.

———. *Phenomenological Psychology*. Translated by John Scanlon. The Hague: M. Nijhoff, 1977.

Jaynes, Julian. "Consciousness and the Voices of the Mind." *Canadian Psychology* 27.2 (1986): 1–13.

———. *The Origin of Consciousness in the Breakdown of the Bicameral Mind*. Boston: Houghton Mifflin, 1976.

Kierkegaard, Søren. *Concluding Unscientific Postscript*. Translated by David F. Swenson and Walter Lowrie. Princeton: Princeton University Press, 1944.

———. *Either/Or: A Fragment of Life*. Translated by David F. Swenson. New York: Doubleday, 1959.

———. *Fear and Trembling and The Sickness Unto Death*. Translated by Walter Lowrie. Princeton: Princeton University Press, 1954.

———. *The Present Age*. Translated by Alexander Dru. New York: Harper & Row, 1962.

———. *The Present Age and Two Minor Ethico-Religious Treatises*. Translated by Alexander Dru and Walter Lowrie. London: Oxford University Press, 1940.

———. *Stages on Life's Way*. Translated by Walter Lowrie. Princeton: Princeton University Press, 1940.

Kierkegaard, Søren. *Works of Love: Some Christian Reflections in the Form of Discourses*. Translated by Howard and Edna Hong. New York: Harper, 1962.

Krieger, Murray. "*Ekphrasis* and the Still Movement of Poetry: or *Laokoön* Revisited." In *The Poet as Critic*. Edited by Frederick P. W. McDowell. Evanston, Ill.: Northwestern University Press, 1967.

———. *Ekphrasis: The Illusion of the Natural Sign*. Baltimore: The Johns Hopkins University Press, 1992.

———. "Literature vs. Écriture: Constructions and Deconstructions in Recent Critical Theory." *Studies in the Literary Imagination* 12 (1979): 1–17.

Kronik, John W. "Editor's Column." *PMLA* 107:1 (1992).

de Laborde, A. *La Bible Moralisée* I. 1911.

Lee, Renasselaer W. "*Ut Pictura Poesis*: The Humanistic Theory of Painting." *Art Bulletin* 22 (1940): 197–269.

Levinas, Emmanuel. *A l'heure des nations*. Paris: Minuit, 1988.

———. "A Propos of 'Kierkegaard vivant.'" In *Proper Names*. Translated by Michael B. Smith. Stanford: Stanford University Press, 1996.

———. *De Dieu qui vient á l'idée*. Paris: Vrin, 1992.

———. "Dialogue with Martin Buber." In *Proper Names*. Translated by Michael B. Smith. Stanford: Stanford University Press, 1996.

———. *En découvrant l'existence avec Husserl et Heidegger*. Paris: Vrin, 1974.

———. *Entre Nous: On Thinking-of-the-Other*. Translated by Michael B. Smith and Barbara Harshav. New York: Columbia University Press, 1998.

———. "Jacques Derrida: Wholly Otherwise." In *Proper Names*. Translated by Michael B. Smith. Stanford: Stanford University Press, 1996.

———. "Kierkegaard: Existence and Ethics." In *Proper Names*. Translated by Michael B. Smith. Stanford: Stanford University Press, 1996.

———. "Martin Buber and the Theory of Knowledge." In *Proper Names*. Translated by Michael B. Smith. Stanford: Stanford University Press, 1996.

———. *Of God Who Comes to Mind*. Translated by Bettina Bergo. Stanford: Stanford University Press, 1998.

———. *Otherwise than Being or Beyond Essence*. Translated by Alphonso Lingis. The Hague: Martinus Nijhoff, 1981.

———. "The Trace of the Other." In *Deconstruction in Context: Literature and Philosophy*. Edited by Mark C. Taylor. Chicago: University of Chicago Press, 1986.

————. *Time and the Other.* Translated by Richard A. Cohen. Pittsburgh: Duquesne University Press, 1987.

————. *Totality and Infinity: An Essay on Exteriority.* Translated by Alphonso Lingis. Pittsburgh: Duquesne University Press, 1969.

Lindrop, Grevel. "The Machine Speaks." *TLS* 16 (1983): 1411.

————. "Purity of Intent." *PN Review* 31:6 (2005): 63–64.

Lowrie, Walter. *Kierkegaard.* New York: Harper & Brothers, 1962.

The Mabingion. Tranlated by Gwyn Jones and Thomas Jones. Rutland, Vt.: Charles E. Tuttle, 1989.

Mansel, Henry Longueville. *The Limits of Religious Thought.* Boston: Gould & Lincoln, 1858.

Matthiessen, F. O. *The Achievement of T. S. Eliot: An Essay on the Nature of Poetry.* New York: Oxford University Press, 1959.

McGill, William. *Poet's Meeting: George Herbert, R. S. Thomas, and the Argument with God.* Jefferson, N.C.: McFarland, 2004.

Merchant, W. Moelwyn. *R. S. Thomas.* Fayetteville: University of Arkansas Press, 1990.

Merwin, W. S. "On Open Form." In *Naked Poetry: Recent American Poetry in Open Forms.* Edited by Stephen Berg and Robert Mezey. Indianapolis: Bobbs-Merrill, 1969.

Miller, J. Hillis. *The Disappearance of God: Five Nineteenth-Century Writers.* Urbana: University of Illinois Press, 2000.

————. "Literature and Religion." In *Religion and Modern Literature: Essays in Theory and Criticism.* Edited by B. Tennyson and Edward E. Ericson Jr. Grand Rapids: Eerdmans., 1975.

————. *Poets of Reality: Six Twentieth-Century Writers.* New York: Atheneum, 1969.

Milton, John. *Complete Poems and Major Prose.* Edited by Merritt Y. Hughes. New York: The Odyssey Press, 1957.

Morgan, J. Christopher. *R. S. Thomas: Identity, Environment, and Deity.* Manchester: Manchester University Press, 2003.

Ormond, John. "R. S. Thomas: Priest and Poet." A transcript of the BBC TV broadcast of 2 April 1972. Reprinted in *Poetry Wales* 7.4 (1972): 47–57.

Orwell, George. *Nineteen Eighty-Four.* New York: Harcourt, Brace., 1949.

Phillips, D. Z. *R. S. Thomas: Poet of the Hidden God: Meaning and Mediation in the Poetry of R. S. Thomas.* Basingstoke: Macmillan, 1986.

Pons, Abbé P. *Souillac et ses Environs.* Souillac, 1923.

Porter, A. Kingsley. *Romanesque Sculpture of the Pilgrimage Roads.* 10 vols. New York: Hacker Art Books, 1969.

Richardson, Joan. *Wallace Stevens: A Biography. The Early Years: 1879–1923*. New York: William Morrow, 1986.

———. *Wallace Stevens: A Biography. The Later Years: 1923–1955*. New York: William Morrow, 1988.

Roethke, Theodore. *The Collected Poems of Theodore Roethke*. New York: Doubleday, 1975.

———. "On 'Identity.'" In *On the Poet and His Craft*. Edited by Ralph J. Mills Jr. Seattle: University of Washington Press, 1965.

———. "Open Letter." In *On the Poet and His Craft*. Edited by Ralph J. Mills Jr. Seattle: University of Washington Press, 1965.

Rogers, Byron. "The Enigma of Aberdaron." *London Sunday Telegraph Magazine*. November, 1975: 25–29.

———. *The Man Who Went into the West: The Life of R. S. Thomas*. London: Aurum, 2006.

Rosand, David. "Ekphrasis and the Generation of Images." *Arion* 1.1 (1990): 61–105.

Rudd, Andrew. "'Not to the Bible but to Wallace Stevens'—What R. S. Thomas Found There." *PN Review* 30.4 (2004): 49–51.

Santayana, George. *Interpretations of Poetry and Religion*. Gloucester, Mass.: Peter Smith, 1969.

Sarkissian, Adele, ed. *Contemporary Authors: Autobiographical Series*. Vol. 4. Detroit: Gale Research, 1986.

Schapiro, Meyer. "The Angel with the Ram in Abraham's Sacrifice: A Parallel in Western and Islamic Art." *Ars Islamica* 10 (1943): 134–47.

———. "The Sculptures of Souillac." In *Medieval Studies in Memory of A. Kingsley Porter*. Edited by Wilhelm R. W. Koehler. 2 vols. Cambridge: Harvard University Press, 1939.

———. *Words and Pictures: On the Literal and the Symbolic in the Illustration of a Text*. The Hague: Mouton, 1973.

Scott, Nathan A., Jr. *The Poetics of Belief: Studies in Coleridge, Arnold, Pater, Santayana, Stevens, and Heidegger*. Chapel Hill: University of North Carolina Press, 1985.

Shakespeare, William. *The Complete Works*. Edited by G. B. Harrison. New York: Harcourt, Brace & World, 1952.

Sharpe, Tony. *Wallace Stevens: A Literary Life*. New York: St. Martin's Press, 2000.

Shaw, W. David. "The Agnostic Imagination in Victorian Poetry." *Criticism* 22 (1980): 116–39.

———. *The Lucid Veil: Poetic Truth in the Victorian Age*. Madison: University Wisconsin Press, 1987.

Shepherd, Elaine. *R. S. Thomas: Conceding an Absence.* New York: St. Martin's Press, 1996.

Sloan, Barry. "The Discipline of Watching and Waiting: R. S. Thomas, Poetry and Prayer." *Religion and Literature* 34.2 (2002): 29–49.

Steiner, George. *After Babel: Aspects of Language and Translation.* New York: Oxford University Press, 1975.

———. *Real Presences.* Chicago: University of Chicago Press, 1991.

Stephens, Meic, ed. *The New Companion to the Literature of Wales.* Cardiff: University of Wales Press, 1998.

Stevens, Wallace. *Collected Poetry and Prose.* New York: The Library of America, 1997.

———. *Letters of Wallace Stevens.* Edited by Holly Stevens. New York: Alfred A. Knopf, 1981.

———. *Opus Posthumous.* New York: Alfred A. Knopf, 1980.

Taylor, Mark C., ed. *Deconstruction in Context: Literature and Philosophy.* Chicago: University of Chicago Press, 1986.

Thomas, Gwydion. "Quietly as Snow." An Interview with Walford Davies. *New Welsh Review* 64 (2004): 15–48.

Thomas, M. Wynn. "Irony in the Soul: The Religious Poetry of R. S[ocrates] Thomas." *Agenda* 36.2 (1998): 49–69.

———, ed. *The Page's Drift: R. S. Thomas at Eighty.* Bridgend: Seren, 1993.

———. "'Songs of Ignorance and Praise': R. S. Thomas' Poems about the Four People in his Life," in *Internal Difference: Twentieth-Century Writing in Wales.* Edited by M. Wynn Thomas. Cardiff: University of Wales Press, 1992.

———. "'Time's Changeling': Autobiography in *The Echoes Return Slow.*" In *Echoes to the Amen: Essays after R. S. Thomas.* Edited by Damian Walford Davies. Cardiff: University of Wales Press, 2003.

Thomas, Ned. "R. S. Thomas: The Question about Technology." *Planet* 92 (1992): 54–60.

Thomas, Ned, and John Barnie. "Probings: An Interview with R. S. Thomas." *Planet* 80 [1990]: 28–52. Reprinted in *Miraculous Simplicity.* Edited by William V. Davis.

Thomas, R. S. "Autobiographical Essay." *Contemporary Authors: Autobiographical Series* 4 (1986): 301–13. Reprinted in *Miraculous Simplicity: Essays on R. S. Thomas.* Edited by William V. Davis. Fayetteville: University of Arkansas Press, 1993.

———. "The Creative Writer's Suicide," *Planet* 41 (1978): 30–33. Reprinted in Anstey, *R. S. Thomas: Selected Prose.*

————. "A Frame for Poetry." *The Times Literary Supplement.* 3 March 1966: 169.

Thomas, R. S. Interview with Graham Turner. *The Daily Telegraph.* 4 December 1999: 1, 7.

————. "Introduction." *The Penguin Book of Religious Verse.* Harmondsworth: Penguin, 1963.

————. "Journey." *Poetry Wales* 28 (1992): 3.

————. Letter to William V. Davis. 13 April 1996.

————. "Religion in Its Contemporary Context: The Poetry of R. S. Thomas (The Artist and His Vision)." Interview with R. E. T. Lamb. BBC Radio 4. 1971.

————. "R. S. Thomas." Interview with Naim Attallah. *The Oldie* 79 (1995): 12–15.

————. "R. S. Thomas in Conversation." Interview with Molly Price-Owen. *The David Jones Journal* (2001): 93–102.

————. "R. S. Thomas Talks to J. B. Lethbridge." *Anglo-Welsh Review* 74 (1983): 36–56.

————. "Unity." Translated from the Welsh ["Undod"] by Katie Jones. *Planet* 70 (1988): 29–42.

————. "The Verdict." *Encounter* 50.3 (1978): 3.

————. "With Great Pleasure." BBC Radio Program, 2000.

————. "Words and the Poet." In *R. S. Thomas: Selected Prose.* Edited by Sandra Anstey. Bridgend: Poetry Wales Press, 1986.

Thompson, Eric. *T. S. Eliot: The Metaphysical Perspective.* Carbondale: Southern Illinois University Press, 1963.

Thompson, Francis. *The Collected Works of Francis Thompson.* Westminster, Md.: Newman Bookshop, 1947.

Tillich, Paul. *The Courage To Be.* New Haven: Yale University Press, 1952.

————. *The Shaking of the Foundations.* New York: Charles Scribner's Sons, 1948.

Tinker, C. B., and H. F. Lowry, eds. *The Poetical Works of Matthew Arnold.* London: Oxford University Press, 1950.

Valéry, Paul. "Letter about Mallarmé." In *Leonardo Poe Mallarmé.* Translated by Malcolm Cowley and James R. Lawler. London: Routledge & Kegan Paul, 1972.

van Buuren, M. J. J. *Waiting: The Religious Poetry of Ronald Stuart Thomas, Welsh Priest and Poet.* Dordrecht: ICG Printing, 1993.

Vendler, Helen. *Wallace Stevens: Words Chosen out of Desire.* Cambridge: Harvard University Press, 1986.

Volk, Sabine. *Grenzfähle der Wirklichkeit: Approaches to the Poetry of R. S. Thomas.* Frankfurt am Main: Peter Lang, 1985.

Walcott, Derek. *Collected Poems 1948–1984.* New York: Farrar, Straus & Giroux, 1986.

Ward, John Powell. *The Poetry of R. S. Thomas.* Bridgend: Seren, 1987; 2nd ed., 2001.

Weil, Simone. *Gravity and Grace.* Translated by Arthur Wills. Lincoln: University of Nebraska Press, 1997.

Whicher, Stephen E., ed. *Selections from Ralph Waldo Emerson.* Boston: Houghton Mifflin, 1957.

Wiener, Norbert. *The Human Use of Human Beings: Cybernetics and Society.* New York: Avon, 1967.

Williams, Barbara Prys. "'A Consciousness in Quest of Its Own Truth': Some Aspects of R. S. Thomas's *The Echoes Return Slow* as Autobiography." *Welsh Writing in English: A Yearbook of Critical Essays* 2 (1996): 98–125.

Wintle, Justin. *Furious Interiors: Wales, R. S. Thomas and God.* London: Flamingo, 1996.

Wisdom, John. *Philosophy and Pyscho-Analysis.* New York: Philosophical Library, 1953.

Wright, Charles. *Bloodlines.* Middletown, Conn.: Wesleyan University Press, 1975.

———. *China Trace.* Middletown, Conn.: Wesleyan University Press, 1977.

———. *The Other Side of the River.* New York: Random House, 1984.

———. *The Southern Cross.* New York: Random House, 1981.

———. *Zone Journals.* New York: Farrar/Straus/Giroux, 1988.

Wright, Frank Lloyd. "The Art and Craft of the Machine." In *Collected Writings, Vol. 1: 1894–1930.* Edited by Bruce Brooks Pfeiffer. New York: Rizzoli International Publications, 1992.

excerpts from R. S. Thomas's prose were provided by the following:
 —Orion Publishers: Reprinted from *R.S. Thomas: Autobiographies*, translated by
 Jason Walford Davies (London: J. M. Dent & Sons, a division of The Orion
 Publishing Group, 1997) and used by permission of Orion and Jason Walford
 Davies.
 —Seren Books: Reprinted from *R.S. Thomas Selected Prose*, edited by Sandra
 Anstey (1983, 1995) and used by permission of Seren Books and Gwydion
 Thomas, copyright © Kunjana Thomas 2001.
Souillac illustrations were provided by the following:
 —Jeff Howe: Reprinted by permission of Jeff Howe.
excerpts from Charles Wright's poetry were provided by the following:
 —Wesleyan University Press: Charles Wright, "Skins" from *Country Music:
 Selected Early Poems,* copyright © 1991 by Charles Wright and reprinted by
 permission of Wesleyan University Press.
 —Farrar, Straus & Giroux: Excerpts from "The Southern Cross" and "Three
 Poems of Departure" from *The World of the Ten Thousand Things: Poems 1980–
 1990* by Charles Wright, copyright ©1990 by Charles Wright. Reprinted by
 permission of Farrar, Straus and Giroux, LLC.
excerpts from Wallace Stevens's poetry were provided by the following:
 —Random House/Faber & Faber: Excerpts from *The Collected Poems of Wallace
 Stevens* by Wallace Stevens, copyright © 1954 by Wallace Stevens and renewed
 in 1982 by Holly Stevens. Used by permission of Alfred A. Knopf, a division of
 Random House, Inc., and by Faber and Faber, Ltd.
excerpts from Wallace Stevens's prose were provided by the following:
 —Random House/Faber & Faber: Excerpts from *The Necessary Angel* by Wallace
 Stevens, copyright © 1951 by Wallace Stevens and renewed in 1979 by Holly
 Stevens; and from *Opus Posthumous* by Wallace Stevens, edited by Milton J.
 Bates, copyright © 1957 by Elsie Stevens and Holly Stevens, renewed in 1985
 by Holly Stevens. Reprinted courtesy of Alfred A. Knopf, a division of Random
 House, Inc. and Faber and Faber, Ltd.
excerpts from T. S. Eliot's poetry were provided by the following:
 —Harcourt, Inc./Faber & Faber: Excerpts from "Gerontion" in *Collected Poems
 1909–1962* by T. S. Eliot, reprinted by permission of Harcourt, Inc. and by
 Faber and Faber, Ltd.
excerpts from T. S. Eliot's prose were provided by the following:
 —Harcourt, Inc./Faber & Faber: Excerpts from "Arnold and Pater" in *Selected
 Essays* by T. S. Eliot, copyright © 1950 by Harcourt, Inc. and renewed in 1978
 by Esme Valerie Eliot, reprinted by permission of the publisher and by Faber
 and Faber, Ltd.

Index